"The Other" in Translation

"The Other" in Translation

A Case for Comparative Translation Studies

Alexander Burak

Bloomington, Indiana, 2013

SLAVICA

Front cover cartoon © Phil Watson.

Cover designed by Tracey Theriault.

ISBN 978-0-89357-415-4

Library of Congress Control Number: 2013949239

Slavica Publishers
Indiana University
1430 N. Willis Drive
Bloomington, IN 47404-2146
USA

[Tel.] 1-812-856-4186
[Toll-free] 1-877-SLAVICA
[Fax] 1-812-856-4187
[Email] slavica@indiana.edu
[www] http://www.slavica.com/

For Galya—my Muse and most significant Other

Contents

Acknowledgments

I am indebted to many generous people, all of whom it would be impossible to list here. First and foremost, to those who instilled in me a passion for and fascination with translation—among them my Maurice Thorez teachers Iakov Iosifovich Retsker, Aleksandr Davydovich Shveitser, Iurii Anatol'evich Denisenko, Valentina Ivanovna Yermolovich, Marina Dmitrievna Litvinova, Vilen Naumovich Komissarov, and many others.

I am thankful to the anonymous first two reviewers of my manuscript, who were generous enough to separate the material they were interested in from the rest of the manuscript, leaving me with enough for a couple other books.

I am particularly indebted to my Slavica editors Vicki Polansky and George Fowler for their belief in my project and unswerving support throughout the course of preparing the manuscript for publication.

I am grateful to Michael Gorham, for his advice on how to face the vagaries of the American publishing world and his comments on my research, in general, and parts of the manuscript of this book, in particular;

James (Frank) Goodwin, for his friendship, hair-trigger sense of style, and comments on parts of my manuscript;

the late E. C. Barksdale, who is greatly missed as a source of inspiration and support and an example of resilience;

Timothy Sergay, for being a kindred spirit and a stimulating participant in discussions that helped me work out some important concepts for the book;

Stephen Pearl, for his genuine, deep interest in my work and moral support, which he provided, apparently, without being aware of doing so;

Brian Baer, for our inspiring and truly collegiate interactions at conferences and for his unobtrusive guidance in my presenting some of my research in his TIS journal;

Sofia Lubensky, who was one of my first inspirations for this book, but doesn't know about it;

Galina Rylkova, whose superb instincts as the first reader of the originally voluminous, continually shape-shifting manuscript guided me toward its final version;

and, finally, to the Chairs of the Languages, Literatures and Cultures Department Keith Bullivant, Will Hasty, Ann Wehmeyer, and Mary Watt, for their versatility and creativity in finding funds to enable me to try out many ideas of the book on colleagues at various conferences both in and outside the United States.

Introduction

This book confronts two "double-edged" or "mirror-image" questions. First, what are the specific linguistic means, translation techniques, and cultural assumptions that are involved in the re-expressing or reconstituting in the form of an English translation of those elements of the Russian original text that are alien to English speakers culturally and that are seemingly untranslatable into English linguistically? (The same question is also asked "in reverse"—with reference to English-to-Russian translation.) Second, how does such a reconstituting of complex linguistic and sociocultural meanings conceivably affect the behaviors and cultural perceptions of readers and film viewers in the receiving culture? The answers to these questions are presented in the form of six case studies of different coexisting translations of the same texts carried out with the help of comparative translation discourse analysis (CTDA), which I advocate in opposition to the "aesthetic" approach (Venuti 2011) in translation critiques, consisting of elegantly phrased, scholarly-sounding disquisitions on the quality of translations without sufficient reference to the originals. In the final chapter of the book, I move my discussion to the contemporary Russian translation scene, Russian translation theory, the re-institutionalization of literary and film translation in Russia in the new millennium, and some leading translators' and famous writers' views on the ideal translator.

Comparative Translation Discourse Analysis (CTDA)

One of the founders of discourse analysis, Norman Fairclough, defines discourse as "language as a form of social practice" (1989, 22) and discourse analysis as "a systematic examination and interpretation of the structure and functions of a text (oral and written), the sociocultural circumstances of its production, and its perceived (supposed, expected, or already existing) various readings, depending on the analyst's conceptual framework" (26); "discourse analysis […] is an exploration of how 'texts' at all levels work within sociocultural practices" (1995, viii–ix).

Fairclough confines himself to monolingual and monocultural analysis of discourse. I extend discourse analysis to translation and compare the textual parameters and expected cross-cultural impact of different translations of the same material. Translations of works of verbal art are a very special kind of cross-cultural discourse carried out between pairs of specific languages (in our case Russian and American English) through the medium of a translator who tries to make sense of the sociocultural "other" through the prism of his or her subjectivity. This is a hugely complicated task that affords alternate solutions as different translators have to re-create the multifaceted cross-cultural "other" in local contexts that are alien to and removed from the original in both time and space.

Faced with multiple translations of the same original, a cultural commentator should be capable, if only to a limited degree, of teasing out the differing tightly intertwined strands of the linguostylistic[1] and sociocultural "other" in different translations to make their comparative merits and demerits more transparent to educators, translators, and students of translation. I believe that it is detailed comparative dissections—or "deconstructions"—of the text at different levels of analysis (semantic, syntactic, and pragmatic) that should form the foundation for an informed view of how a translated text works, with reference to its original, in its new sociocultural setting. This is what the present book attempts to do through its case studies. To this end, I offer CTDA in order to counteract what Venuti calls a "belletristic approach" to translation criticism, whereby the critic "assigns [a translation] an aesthetic autonomy from the source text and judges it not according to a concept of equivalence, but according to the 'standards' by which he judges original compositions. [...] this approach [is] belletristic because it emphasizes aesthetic qualities of the translated text itself. It is also impressionistic in the sense that it is vague or ill-defined" (2011).

Aspects of "the Other" in Translation

Today it has become customary to refer to "the foreign" (the alien language, its users and, more generally, its culture) using terms such as "the other," "otherness," or "alterity." The terms cover a wide and varied discursive range in philosophy and cultural studies, where they are employed mainly to describe different kinds of inequalities and power relationships: class, race, ethnicity, national origin, and gender. The amount of literature on the existential difficulty of understanding and accepting representatives of different ethnicities, cultures, the members of the opposite sex, or, for that matter, any human being other than oneself is truly vast, and the list of the thinkers that have been developing the concepts of "otherness" or "the other" in the philosophical, cultural, and psychoanalytical literature of the 20th and 21st centuries includes such celebrated figures as Cassirer, Husserl, Heidegger, Bakhtin, Lévi-Strauss, Habermas, Levinas, Said, Sartre, Buber, and Derrida, to name but a very few. In translation studies, "the other" is also discussed by various trans-

---

[1] "Linguostylistic" means that which displays multiple levels of analysis related to various language domains, i.e., lexical classes, morphology, syntax, semantics, discourse analysis, etc.

lation theorists such as Lawrence Venuti (1995, 1998), Rachel May (1994), Umberto Eco (2001), Maria Tymoczko (2002), Edwin Gentzler (2002), Tim Parks (2007), Theo Hermans (1996, 2006, 2007), Kate Sturge (2007), and Rosemary Arrojo (2005, 2006), to name just a prominent few. These are highly insightful scholarly discussions. But in none of these writings is the concept of "the other" specifically defined and considered as the core of interlingual translation discourse and the object of comparative translation discourse analysis. In other words, many publications consider separate aspects of the "other," "otherness," or "alterity," but these concepts are used in widely disparate contexts, are usually too abstract, or general, and are next to impossible to apply, not least in resolving concrete problems in translating from Russian into English and vice versa. Scholars seem to be more concerned with all-embracing generalities aimed at covering all languages or groups of languages.

In my own present conceptualization of "the other" in Russian-English translation, I take my cue from George Steiner, who, while not defining "the other" nevertheless explicitly uses concepts and expressions that may be subsumed under that category. Thus he talks about "a palimpsest of historical [and] political undertones and overtones" (1998, 180); "a 'chord' of associations" (180); "the irreducible singularity of personal remembrance" (182); "the 'association-net' of personal consciousness and subconsciousness" (182); "a semantic field" (314); "a dialectically enigmatic residue" (316); "formats of significance" (317); "the 'other' language and 'other' culture" (412); "the serious alternity of meaning and expressive form" (413); "a cultural lattice" (413); "the differing idiomatic habits, the distinct associative contexts which generate resistance and affinity between two different languages" (445). These interconnected concepts coalesce in Steiner's definition of the task of the translator, which, compared with Benjamin's (or Derrida's), is much more clearly stated and realizable:

> The translator must actualize the implicit "sense," the denotative, connotative, illative,[2] intentional, associative range of significations which are implicit in the original, but which it leaves undeclared or only partly declared simply because the native auditor or reader has an immediate understanding of them. (291)

Proceeding from Steiner's definition of the task of the translator, I put forward a concept of "the other in translation," which I believe helps elucidate some crucial aspects of any translation process as well as enabling us to form more substantive opinions of translation products. I suggest that the concept of otherness, as the core of translation discourse and the subject of the case studies I consider in this book, should include (1) the linguistically and cul-

---

[2] Of the nature of or stating an inference.

turally alien elements of the original text (in our case, Russian or English); (2) the linguo-socio-cultural personality of its author as imprinted on the text and as perceived by the creator of the text of the translation (the translator); (3) the translator's own linguo-socio-cultural identity as reflected in the created translated text; (4) the translator's adjustments in the translation, made to accommodate the prospective audience's perceived educational background and expectations; and (5) the translator's adjustments in the translation resulting from his/her self-monitoring and self-censoring in a particular sociopolitical and ideological situation.

Two important points need to be emphasized in relation to this definition. First, the most translation-resistant part of "the other" includes the Lecerclean "remainder"[3]—the odd, untidy, awkward, or "verbal-creativity-driven" parts of the text that do not have ready-made correspondences in the translating language and therefore are conspicuously present in or inconspicuously absent from the translation. More specifically, these are the unique elements of authorial style such as diction and text prosody, intertextual allusions, and stretches of language known in translation studies as *"realia."* *Realia* is an earlier specialized term denoting concepts and ways of expression that exist in one language but are conspicuously absent in the other. "The remainder" and *realia* are commonly known as "the untranslatable"—that which has been or is likely to be "lost in translation." Their "omission," or "neutralization," is only discoverable if translation analysts take the trouble to compare original and translation. Alternatively, "the remainder" and *realia* may be quite noticeable due to their conspicuous "otherness," if translated very literally—that is, "foreignized." Second, "the other" includes a sociological dimension—the translator's own education, life experience, cultural outlook, aesthetic preferences, professional competence, and, most importantly, the adopted translation methodology that are reflected in the translation, whether the translator is or is not aware of it. This is the difficult-to-identify translator's imprint on the text of the translation, or "the translator in the text," to quote the phrase in the title of Rachel May's book (1994).[4] The interpenetration and interaction of all the above elements comprise the core of "translation discourse," which I define as a mode of exchanging organized knowledge, ideas, experiences, and

---

[3] "The remainder" is a concept that was originally created by Jacques Lecercle (1990) and further developed and illustrated by Lawrence Venuti (1998), who argued that, although "the remainder" can never be completely formalized, it must be fully recognized as a factor in translation.

[4] In her book *The Translator in the Text* (1994), Rachel May calls the "imprint" left by the individual translator on his or her translation "the translator in the text." "The translator's voice in the translated narrative" has also been discussed by Theo Hermans and other authors. See, for example, Theo Hermans's article of the same title (1996, 27, 42).

aesthetic perceptions through the medium of language as used by translators in concrete contexts.

In performing comparative translation discourse analysis (CTDA), I illustrate the variability of translation by examining and rationalizing different translations of the same texts from the perspectives of semantics, syntax, and pragmatics. I consider the semantic, syntactic, and pragmatic variations in different translations of the same single originals (Russian and English) in relation to five interpenetrating and overlapping modes of cross-cultural appropriation of "the other": neutralization, domestication (naturalization), foreignization, contamination, and stylization.

Given the scope of CTDA, it is easy to get bogged down in its multiple ramifications, therefore, I focus only on those elements in the source texts and their translations which I find problematic. I expect these instances to be interesting to Russian-English translators and students of translation with some knowledge of Russian.

The choice of material for the case studies was determined by two other considerations: first, at the time of writing, the translations I consider were all being actively discussed in different media (I believe, some of them still are), and, second, they contain a lot of translation-resistant elements that constitute the concept I am developing—"the other in translation." The case studies are based on close readings and comparative translation discourse analysis of samples of prose fiction and two film voiceovers. In addition to the popular literary and film texts and their translations that I selected for the case studies, the other sources of data were the latest translation studies literature; translators' prefaces, commentaries, and foot- or endnotes in translated books; conference presentations; face-to-face discussions and interviews with colleagues working in the field of translation; extracts from translations tried out on my students in class; surveys of my students; online discussions; and archival materials.

The Structure of the Book

"The Other" in Translation: A Case for Comparative Translation Studies consists of six chapters, each dealing with a specific case study, a chapter discussing the present-day translation situation in Russia, a concluding section briefly examining the role of translation as an integrating medium in conditions of multiculturalism and globalization, and eight appendices that supply additional material illustrating the issues discussed.

Chapter 1, "The 'Americanization' of Russian Life and Literature through Translations of Hemingway's Works: Establishing a Russian 'Amerikanskii' Substyle in Russian Literature," offers a case study of two "Kashkintsy" translations of Hemingway. This chapter traces the origins of the *"ozhivliazh"* (sexing-up) trend in the literary translations of today back to the "Kashkintsy group" of translators that formed in the Soviet Union in the 1930s and whose influence on the style of literary translation is still felt in Russia today. I argue that it was the "Kashkintsy group" and their followers, such as Rita Rait-Kovaleva, who began to introduce, most likely unintentionally, what I call the "swashbuckling" or "swaggering" style in their literary translations of American prose fiction that came to be generally associated by Russians with the "freewheeling," "devil-may-care," "we're-truly-free individuals" way Americans supposedly talked. The myth persists and the style has been reinforced and gets replicated to this day.

Chapter 2, "Some Like it Hot—'Goblin-Style': *Ozhivliazh*' (Sexing Things Up) in Russian Film Translations," provides a case study of two voiceover translations into Russian of an episode from the American TV series *The Sopranos*—one shown on the Russian NTV television channel and the other on TV-3. I illustrate how the initial tentative "enlivening" of translations initiated by the Kashkintsy and Rita Rait-Kovaleva has escalated today in the medium of Russian voiceover translations of American films. I argue that the widely popular voiceover film translator Dmitrii Puchkov (aka Goblin), whose cachet is to translate English four-letter words with the help of what is generally perceived as publicly unacceptable Russian obscene language (*mat*), misrepresents the sociocultural functions of obscene language in the two cultures by assuming that the set of sociocultural constituencies that use and tolerate *mat* in Russian society is identical to the set or composition of the sociocultural groups that use and tolerate four-letter words in American culture. I also argue that Russian film as a cultural medium has long been resistant to the use of *mat* (unlike contemporary Russian prose, for example), and, therefore, transplanting the seemingly similar language stratum into Russian cinema violates the still relatively restricted standards of decency generally expected of Russian films.

Chapter 3, "Translating *Skaz* as a Whole-Text Realium: Five Modes of Translation (Russian to English)," offers a comparative analysis of two translations of an excerpt from Tolstoy's *War and Peace*. The case study focuses on the two radically different ways in which the translators Richard Pevear and Larissa Volokhonsky (2007) and Anthony Briggs (2006) resolve the problem of translating *skaz* in the parable about two merchants told by one of the characters in the novel, Platon Karataev. I describe five modes of translating that all translators—whether wittingly or unwittingly—resort to in varying degrees. These are textual neutralization, domestication (naturalization), foreignization, contamination, and stylization. While discussing possible rationales behind each of these modes and their combinations, I offer my own translation of part of the passage under consideration.

Chapter 4, "Translating *Skaz* as a Whole-Text Realium: From *Skaz* to Swaggering Pizzazz (English to Russian)," offers a case study of three different translations into Russian of J. D. Salinger's *The Catcher in the Rye*. Compared with the previous chapter, this is a case study "in reverse" because it analyzes three translations from English into Russian. I argue that *The Catcher in the Rye* is a "whole-text" *skaz*, identify the recurring specific language means and devices used by Salinger to produce the effect of *skaz*, and then apply a comparative translation discourse analysis to establish to what extent the *skaz*-like poetics of the Salinger text is replicated in the three existing translations of the short novel in Russian. I argue that, whereas in the first, canonical translation of the novel (1960), its translator, Rita Rait-Kovaleva, was "smuggling in" a vision of an "unattainable," democratic world for the Russian reader to take perverse pleasure in and to contrast with the drab Soviet realities of life, the second and the third translations by Maksim Nemtsov (2008) and Iakov Lotovskii (2010) respectively obfuscate any ideological implications of the Salinger text and replace the somewhat artificial "Amerikanskii" style of narration in Rait-Kovaleva's Russian translation with the harsh Russian youth vernacular of the late 1990s and the 2000s—the kind teenage "rebels without a cause" tend to speak in present-day Russia. The poetics of the Russian translations has thus transmogrified from the starting point of American-style *skaz* in English through a subtly ideologized "Amerikanskii Russian" of Rait-Kovaleva's translation to the non-ideological swagger and pizzazz of Nemtsov's and Lotovskii's translations.

Chapter 5, "Translating Postmodernism: A Translator's Modus Operandi," examines the translator Jamey Gambrell's operations in some translation-resistant passages from the novella *Day of the Oprichnik* (2006; trans. 2011) by the contemporary Russian classic Vladimir Sorokin (b. 1955). The chapter shows how the linguistic and the sociocultural intertwine in creating both an original postmodernist text and its cross-culturally engaging translation.

Chapter 6, "Using Translation as a Political Weapon: Having a Riot Translating 'Pussy Riot,'" examines some radically different ways used in Russia today to translate the name of the Russian punk collective Pussy Riot into Russian following their "punk-prayer" performance at Moscow's Cathedral of Christ the Savior on 21 February 2012. I argue that these different translations are used as means of asserting one's sociopolitical position and cultural identity in the global controversy surrounding Pussy Riot. Among other things, the analyses in this chapter highlight the political and ideological dimensions of translation as a performative activity.

Chapter 7, "Russian Translation Theory: Ongoing Discussions," examines the thinking by three of Russia's foremost translation theorists and practitioners today: Dmitrii Buzadzhi, Viktor Lanchikov, and Dmitrii Ermolovich. In this chapter, I attempt to identify the latest shifts in Russian translation studies and to find its points of engagement with "global" translation theory. This is followed by a brief conclusion, "Negotiating Multiculturalism," examining the role of literary translation as a medium of change in the context of the interacting processes of cultural assimilation, amalgamation (the "melting pot" theory), and multiculturalism (the "salad bowl" theory).

Appendix 1 contains alternative translations into English of a passage from *War and Peace*; Appendix 2 contains the translator Lotovskii's rationale for retranslating *The Catcher in the Rye*; Appendix 3 contains three translations into Russian of the first paragraph of *The Catcher in the Rye*; Appendix 4 lists *skaz*-forming textual elements from *The Catcher in the Rye*; Appendix 5 illustrates the interaction of theory and practice in translating a seemingly untranslatable lexical item—"supercalifragilistiexpialidocious"; Appendix 6 contains Robert Chandler's definition of an ideal translator of Platonov, and I supply some illustrative examples from Chandler's and his collaborators' translations and retranslations of *The Foundation Pit* and *Happy Moscow*; Appendix 7 discusses some translation quality control institutions in Russia; and Appendix 8 is a facetious "instruction manual" for dummies on how to use translators and interpreters.

To sum up, in the chapters and appendices that follow, I try to bring theorists and practitioners together by discussing ways of resolving specific translation problems on the basis of middle-range theories[5] relating to word and sentence semantics and text pragmatics. The middle-range solutions are considered from the perspectives of neutralization, domestication (naturalization), contamination, foreignization, and stylization as modes of negotiating "the other" in translation. The book is research-based: I use six concrete case studies to consider some "accursed" problems ("the untranslatable") of Russian-English translation through the basic method of comparative translation discourse analysis (CTDA). By comparing different translations in specific terms I also show how different translators, in fact, initiate cultural change. Thus comparative translation studies provide us with additional tools to monitor and analyze cultural change.

The book is meant primarily for Russian-to-English and English-to-Russian translators and students of translation with some knowledge of Russian, but it will also be useful to advanced Russian language learners and Russian heritage speakers.

---

[5] Robert K. Merton (1910–2003), best known for developing such universally used concepts as "unintended consequences," "role model," "self-fulfilling prophecy," and "reference group," created the term "middle-range theory" in opposition to the all-embracing word "theory." His problem with the word "theory" was that "like so many words which are bandied about, the word 'theory' threatens to become emptied of meaning. The very diversity of items to which the word is applied leads to the result that it often obscures rather than creates understanding" (Merton 1964, 5). Merton advocated "theories of the middle range," which he defined as "theories intermediate to the minor working hypotheses evolved in abundance during the day-to-day routines of research, and the all-inclusive speculations comprising a master conceptual scheme from which it is hoped to derive a very large number of empirically observed uniformities" (5–6). What Merton said about social theory is, in my view, perfectly applicable to translation theory. To me, trying to create a translation theory that would embrace everything is an illusion—not to say an exercise in futility.

Chapter 1

The "Americanization" of Russian Life and Literature through Translations of Hemingway's Works: Establishing a Russian "Amerikanskii" Substyle in Russian Literature*

The case study that follows is an examination of what I would call the "mysterious ways" in which literary translation works, based on the Russian translations of Hemingway. I consider these translations from three intersecting perspectives. The first takes as its point of departure Antoine Berman's system of textual deformation, according to which twelve deforming tendencies manifest themselves in varying degrees in all literary translations (see Berman 1992). While I use Berman's theory as a general background, I employ my own criteria for analyzing the texts' "artistic distortions," the linguostylistic modifications translators introduce. The second perspective draws on the case studies collected in John Milton and Paul Bandia's *Agents of Translation* (2009). Accordingly, I trace the changes in the behaviors, ideological outlook, and literary tastes of the Soviet people that the agency of translation affected from the 1960s through the early 1980s. And the third perspective consists of my personal observations as an "informed participant" on the Russian translation scene, a perspective that reflects the vagaries and unintended consequences of cross-cultural transfer. More specifically, this case study's focus is the means and results of "engraving" the image of Hemingway as a cultural icon on the collective consciousness of the people of the Soviet Union and, to some extent, post-Soviet Russia through the translations of his works by a group of translators known in the Russian translation world as the "Kashkintsy."

How It All Began

Russia's love affair with America began in 1957 when Muscovites first saw a lot of "real" Americans walking around the Soviet capital during the 1957 International Festival of Youth and Students. The conclusion most Soviet people drew was that Americans were very likeable people, just like Russians; the difference was only that they dressed in a freer and more imaginative way and were more sociable. In 1959 Moscow hosted the first U.S. National Exhibition, showcasing American consumer goods and a model American home,

---

* This chapter was published in the journal *Translation and Interpreting Studies* (TIS) 8: 1 (Spring 2013): 50–72.

complete with all the creature comforts and labor-saving appliances that any American family could allegedly afford. The exhibition opened on 25 July 1959 in Moscow's Sokol'niki Park. On 24 July U.S. Vice President Nixon and Soviet Communist Party leader Khrushchev visited the exhibition. The famous "kitchen debate" between the two leaders on the merits and demerits of capitalism and socialism took place in the model American home's kitchen. Part of the debate was broadcast in the USA and later—in a more abridged version—in the USSR. The six-week exhibition was immensely popular and successful, as evidenced by its more than three million visitors (Richmond 2011).

The festival and the exhibition triggered the beginning of a "moral decomposition" (*moral'noe razlozhenie*) of many so-called "builders of communism" (*stroiteli kommunizma*). The innocuous ingestion of complimentary Pepsi Cola offered at the exhibit initiated this ideological "sickness." Even Khrushchev enjoyed the beverage. The two events also reinvigorated the young Soviet urbanites' *shtatniki* subculture ("*stiliagi*" in official censorious parlance[1]) that in some ways was the Soviet echo and imaginative reinvention of the American 1940s hipsters. Also in 1959, Khrushchev made his triumphant visit to Washington, captivating his American television and radio audiences. American television began to broadcast Russian-language lessons. Following his visit to the U.S., Khrushchev reiterated in nearly all his speeches that "communism was unattainable without overtaking America." Many popular Soviet jokes (*anekdoty*) began to juxtapose Americans with Russians, Germans, and other nationals in awkward situations. The jokes would invariably begin something like, "A Russian, an American, and a German find themselves on a desert island..." Space travel and art facilitated the emblematic friendship between the Soviet people and Americans, represented by the astronaut John Glenn, painters Rockwell Kent[2] and Norman Rockwell, and pianist Van Cliburn, who won the first Tchaikovsky competition in Moscow. But there was one giant that began to tower over the other, "lesser" Americans. That giant was Ernest Hemingway, and it was purely through the

---

[1] *Stilyagi* or *stiliagi* (roughly, "those anxious to be stylish") is the plural of the Russian *stilyaga* (*стиляга*). It was a derogatory appellation for members of a youth subculture in the Soviet Union from the late 1940s until the early 1960s. *Stilyagi* were primarily distinguished by their brightly fashionable clothing, which contrasted with the socialist realities of the time, and their fascination with Western music, especially jazz, the blues, and boogie-woogie.

[2] Rockwell Kent (1882–1971) was an American painter, printmaker, illustrator, and writer. In 1960 Kent donated several hundred of his paintings and drawings to the Soviet Union and became an honorary member of the Soviet Academy of Fine Arts. He was awarded the Lenin Peace Prize in 1967.

medium of translated literature that this "quintessentially American writer" reached the Soviet people from the 1960s and to the early 1980s.[3]

The Kashkintsy

Hemingway's "triumphal march" across one-sixth of the globe's surface, as the Soviet ideologues of the time liked to refer to the Soviet Union, was not entirely accidental. It began in 1959 when the major Soviet publishing house Gosudarstvennoe izdatel'stvo khudozhestvennoi literatury (GIKhL; State Publishing House of Fiction Literature) produced 300,000 copies of a two-volume edition of Hemingway's selected works (*izbrannye proizvedeniia*). The covers of the 1959 edition volumes were black, lending the work its popular name of *chernyi dvukhtomnik* (the "black-cover two-volume edition"). With the exception of *For Whom the Bell Tolls*, which first appeared in a slightly expurgated Russian translation in 1964 (Nesmelova 2006), the two volumes contained all Hemingway's major works up to that time and filled 1,152 pages (Kheminguei 1959). Despite its large print run, the edition immediately sold out and became a highly desired cultural commodity, joining the long list of *defitsitnye tovary* (items in short supply). In comparison, the American magazine *Scribner's* first serialization of *A Farewell to Arms* printed 31,000 copies. When the novel was published in its entirety in 1929, twice as many copies were printed (Salter 2011, 4), but overall the volume of American reprintings of Hemingway's works never drew close to the total massive circulation of his books in the Soviet Union and later in Russia.

The two-volume Russian edition opened with famous translator, literary critic, and translation theorist Ivan Kashkin's (1899–1963) introductory essay, "Ernest Hemingway" (Kashkin 1966). Kashkin was a dedicated Hemingway scholar whose views even Hemingway himself held in high esteem (see Hemingway's letters to Kashkin in Kashkin 1966, 276–87). Kashkin also supplied the text commentaries included as an appendix to the two volumes. This introduction and commentary sealed Kashkin's reputation as the defining Russian authority on Hemingway. Kashkin was a member of the Union of Soviet Writers (USW) and the leader of the Moscow division of USW literary translators. His regular translators' seminars attracted the most ambitious and gifted translators. He provided the very best of them with lucrative state-financed translation projects. These projects, in turn, led to acceptance into the USW. One such project was the translation of the officially approved available works by Hemingway.

---

[3] Ironically, as James Salter pointed out some 60 years later, "none of his novels is set in his own country—they take place in France, Spain, Italy, or in the sea between Cuba and Key West—[and yet] he is a quintessentially American writer and a fiercely moral one" (2011, 4).

The Kashkin circle consisted almost exclusively of the 1959 Hemingway translators, including Vera Maksimovna Toper (1890–1964), Ol'ga Petrovna Kholmskaia (1896–1977), Evgeniia Davydovna Kalashnikova (1906–76), Natal'ia Al'bertovna Volzhina (1903–81), Nina Leonidovna Daruzes (1899–1982), Elena Mikhailovna Golysheva (1906–84), Boris Romanovich Izakov (1903–88), Mariia Fedorovna Lorie (1904–92), and Mariia Pavlovna Bogoslovskaia (1902–74), among others. Following the collection's resounding success, most of these translators began to be referred to as the "Kashkin Group" or simply the "Kashkintsy." The Kashkintsy established a near monopoly on prose fiction translation in the Soviet Union, and today their works are still considered unsurpassed classics of literary translation, often equated with the "Soviet school of translation."

Following in Chukovskii's footsteps (see Chukovskii 1966), the "Kashkintsy" were instrumental in establishing the key principles of the Soviet school of translation, which state (1) that literary translation is a high art; (2) that in translating a literary work, the translator must pursue the spirit and not the letter of the text; and (3) that a translation ought to read as if it originally had been written in the target language. Despite the first principle's epistemological vagueness, the second's subjectivity, and the third's ontological impossibility, these principles and the translators' contributions in their implementation had major implications for Soviet culture.

The 1959 Hemingway edition became emblematic of the "Khrushchev Thaw" that set the stage for subsequent, more "subversive," publications such as Solzhenitsyn's *One Day in the Life of Ivan Denisovich*, published in November 1962 in the Soviet literary journal *Novyi Mir* (New World). The Russians fell in love with the Kashkintsy translations of Hemingway's works and with Hemingway's virile images in Yousuf Karsh's[4] photographs of him in this and subsequent editions. The Russian-American love affair grew hotter in 1968 with the same Khudozhestvennaia literatura publishing house's publication of an expanded four-volume collection of Hemingway's works, *Ernest Kheminguei*, in a print run of 200,000 copies. The subsequent 1981 and 1982 collector's editions were reprints of this expanded collection. During this period, the availability of Hemingway's books in the Soviet Union exceeded that in the USA by several orders of magnitude. Hemingway continued to be published in the *perestroika* and post-Soviet periods. Practically all his works remain widely available today, both individually and as part of a seven-volume compilation of his complete works (Kheminguei 2010a), with print runs of 3,000–4,000 copies. Nowadays the passion may have gone out of the Russians' love affair with Hemingway, but the relationship continues and the resulting blogosphere is very much active.

---

[4] Yousuf Karsh (1908–2002), a Canadian photographer of Armenian heritage, was one of the most famous and accomplished portrait photographers of all time.

Obviously, Hemingway's lasting influence deserves closer examination. I will first discuss what it was that Hemingway seemed to offer to Soviet people and, second, how this image of Hemingway was shaped by his Soviet translators.

Why Hemingway?

At least six semi-related elements conspired to create the Hemingway cult in the Soviet Union: (1) Kashkin's literary preferences and influential position with editorial and publishing spheres and the subsequent 1959 two-volume edition of Hemingway's selected works; (2) the Soviet ideological establishment's upgrading of the previously questionable Hemingway from the status of "a fellow traveler" to that of a mostly "progressive writer" promoting anti-war and humanistic themes; (3) the logocentric (literature-centered) nature of Russian culture with its penchant for uncovering subtexts, both existent and non-existent, in literary works; (4) the stringently supervised and restricted number of foreign literary works translated and published in the Soviet Union; (5) Hemingway's virile, manly appearance, widely replicated and recognized thanks to Yousuf Karsh's photographs; and, last but not least, (6) the "artistic" contributions of the translators to the texts they created.

In her late 1930s diary entry, the famous Russian literary scholar and writer Lidiia Ginzburg (1902–90) described the Soviet reaction to the translation of Hemingway's *A Farewell to Arms* as follows:[5]

> The people of my generation are reacting to Hemingway in a very personal and passionate way. Or, rather, this emotional involvement is not so much with Hemingway himself as with [the novel] *A Farewell to Arms*—a work that happens to epitomize essentially everything that the writer Hemingway has to say. […] he certainly reveals some [important] aspects of reality, and this has given him power over people's minds. In particular, he brings out into the open the way people talk with each other in bed. It turns out that they talk about everything under the sun. These lovers' conversations are the strongest part in *A Farewell to Arms*, and they are the only strong part in *To Have and Have Not*. These conversations contain Hemingway's conception of the quintessential contemporary Western person. (2002, 143)

Elaborating on Hemingway's contribution to literature—or, rather, to the Soviet idea of what was permissible in literature—Ginzburg goes on to say that Hemingway's novels made a bold and strong case for physical love, which until then had been regarded as something needing justification:

---

[5] In this book all translations from Russian into English and from English into Russian are mine unless otherwise indicated.

Hemingway [...] asserts physical love as something that does not need any justification. At the same time, this assertion is inseparable from the tragic essence of love that Hemingway has discovered in 20th-century society. (143)

In a 1977 diary entry, Ginzburg recalls Akhmatova's advice that she read Hemingway: "In the mid-1930s Anna Andreevna showed me a little book and said, 'Read this by all means. It's very interesting.' It was *A Farewell to Arms* by Hemingway, who was still unknown to us at the time. The novel had just been translated" (470).

The Hemingway works to which Ginzburg refers were translated by Vera Maksimovna Toper and Evgeniia Davydovna Kalashnikova, two staunch members of the Kashkintsy Group. In 1935 Vera Maksimovna Toper's Russian translation of *The Sun Also Rises* (1925) became available in the Soviet Union under the title *Fiesta*. Evgeniia Davydovna Kalashnikova's translation of *A Farewell to Arms* (1929) first appeared in Russian under the title *Proshchai, oruzhie!* in 1936. Evgeniia Davydovna Kalashnikova also produced the 1938 Russian translation of *To Have and Have Not* (1937). Thus Ginzburg's comments can more precisely be attributed to the very end of the 1930s. It should also be pointed out, as Ginzburg's diary entries imply, that in the 1930s Hemingway's works were "in limited release" and accessible only to some select circles of the Soviet intelligentsia.

In her book *Slovo zhivoe i mertvoe* (The Word Living and Dead), famous translator and member of the Kashkintsy circle Nora Gal' (1912–91) writes that

the most vivid and memorable event—a priceless gift to all of us from the Kashkintsy—occurred in the mid-1930s when Ernest Hemingway first began to speak in Russian. Indeed, for the reading and writing public—to say nothing of us, students—this was an epochal discovery; we were profoundly shaken, in fact. He was a writer of incredible power, possessed of a unique writing style. His terse, seemingly ordinary texts, with their seemingly overly simple, often slangy, two-or three-word dialogues, imbued with between-the-lines messages, concealed an enormous tension of feeling, meaning, and pain—his proverbial subtext and trademark aesthetic reserve. The intonation of *Fiesta*, his famous stories, and the novel *A Farewell to Arms*, whether consciously or unconsciously, were later imitated by some of our writers; some of Hemingway's mastery became part of our heritage, and there is nothing shameful about it. Hemingway's influence on his contemporaries can hardly be denied. (2003, 252–53)

One should keep in mind, of course, that the accolades refer, first and foremost, to the translated texts rather than to the English originals.

To reiterate, the circle of people with access to the 1930s Hemingway translations was restricted to the Soviet literati and some other members of the *intelligentsia*. During the 1930s purges under Stalin and the Great Patriotic War of 1941–45 against Nazi Germany and its allies, the majority of Soviet people were more preoccupied with physical survival than with the enlargement of their range of reading. They were also more likely to seek guidance in life from such classics as Dante, Shakespeare, and Goethe, if only because their print runs were larger and more readily available. Besides, Hemingway's position on the Soviet cultural scene of the 1930s and 1940s was still ambiguous and criticisms of his works were not uncommon. Even the ideologically innocuous *A Farewell to Arms* received its share of criticism, like the malicious comment that all that the novel portrays comes down to "hasty and coarse soldier's love" (Ginzburg 143). In short, Hemingway's time had not yet come. It was later, in the 1960s and 1970s, that Hemingway would enjoy widespread popularity in the Soviet Union and exert a distinct influence over Soviet life and literature.

"Hemingwayesque" Attitudes and Behaviors in the Soviet Union

Beginning in the latter half of the 1950s, with Khrushchev's mild de-Stalinization and general relaxation of political control, the country's political and economic improvements influenced people's attitudes towards and expectations of life. The novel conditions of the Khrushchev Thaw reinvigorated the traditional Russian cultural "logocentricity." Many Soviet people began to search for or create new literary icons, such as the "village prose writers" (*derevenshchiki*) Valentin Rasputin, Vasilii Shukshin, and Viktor Astaf'ev; the "urbanite writers" (authors of *gorodskaia proza*) Iurii Trifonov and Vladimir Makanin; and young, bold poets like Evgenii Evtushenko and Andrei Voznesenskii. The "progressive American writer" Ernest Hemingway became one such icon. The authors' identities were often fused with those of their literary characters to create inseparable mythologized wholes. Such a fusion was especially true of Hemingway.

The cult of Hemingway swept the Soviet Union due to the efficiency of the planned distribution of Hemingway's books to bookstores, public libraries, and the Communist Party *nomenklatura* (the elite party and government bureaucracy).[6] This resulted in very specific changes in the Soviet people's appearance, lifestyle, worldview, manner of speaking, and ways of interacting with others, as well as in interior decorations and furnishings. In the flush of their new infatuation with the cultural "other" embodied in the person and

---

[6] Book distribution was part of the centrally planned economy of the Soviet Union. Once a writer was approved by the system—and Khudozhestvennaia literatura was part of the system—his or her books were distributed throughout the Soviet Union. In that system, small print runs were not an option.

narratives of Hemingway, the Russian people acted in an expansive way. In his super-popular television and print series *Namedni* (Our Recent Past), the famous Russian television journalist, documentary-maker, and cultural commentator Leonid Parfenov describes the impact of the four-volume edition of Hemingway's works in 1968 as follows:

> In the course of the year [1968], the publishing house Khudozhestvennaia literatura brings out the *Collected Works of Ernest Hemingway*: four volumes with four portrait-style photos. The grizzled, bearded deity has been elevated to the rank of an official classic. In addition to the cult of male strength, female submissiveness, the salty ocean, and the truth that "war is war," verbalized in a laconic style, Hemingway captivates by his own personal example. He doesn't really have to be read at all; and those who have opened his books are far fewer than those who have seen his portraits. The one in which he is wearing a white shirt is a photo on a rough fabric to be hung on a wall; the one in which he is wearing a rough-woven sweater has a glossy surface and is to be put on a desk. The circulation of the photos is mind-boggling. Their impact is both wider and stronger than that of his texts. Whereas twenty years ago you would have been accused of "rootless cosmopolitanism" [*bezrodnyi kosmopolitizm*] just for having the photos, today they are being printed as icons of the no-longer forbidden Westernism [appreciation of the West]. (2009a, 211)

It was a rare Soviet urban home that did not have one of the emblematic portraits of Hemingway on a wall or a desk. You can still see them in some homes today.

In their highly popular book *The 60s: The World of the Soviet Person*, the Russian émigré writers, "Radio Freedom" hosts, and cultural commentators Petr Vail and Aleksandr Genis devote about ten pages to the pervasive influence of translated Hemingway texts and the characters' philosophy of life on the Soviet people's behavior in the 1960s and 1970s (1998, 64–74). Vail and Genis begin their section on Hemingway by saying, in part, that "in reading prose fiction, the Russian readership had long been used to going way beyond particular plots. For the Russian reader, the writer is the creator of a certain way of life—not of a certain literary work. […] Hemingway did not exist for reading. What mattered were the forms of perceiving life created by the writer. These forms could be imitated. They could be filled with one's own context" (64–65).

Soviet men began modeling themselves on Hemingway by growing beards and by imitating his casual style of dressing. Rough-woven sweaters,[7]

---

[7] It is worth noting that in some of the scenes in the 2005 Russian television series *Brezhnev*, the character Brezhnev wears the exact same kind of rough-woven sweater

semi-casual jackets, and flat caps gradually replaced the previously ubiquitous suit, shirt, tie, and hat. This change was not so much a rejection of formal
dress per se as a way of projecting studied indifference towards any outward
luster and intimating the existence of a deep and rich inner world. With more
than a touch of sarcasm, Vail and Genis comment, "It was easier to muddle
through life in a sweater than a suit" (65).

The influence of Hemingway's stories and novels, which circulated
widely throughout the Soviet Union, penetrated deeper than outward ap-
pearances. The narratives reinforced the traditional Russian traits of authenticity, sincerity, simplicity, natural spontaneity, and love of truth (*pravda*), the
latter of which has traditionally combined the ideas of truthfulness, justice,
fairness, and personal integrity. In Hemingway's fictional world, truth—in all
of the above senses—was everything, even if it was not expressed directly
and had to be found in the subtext of the characters' dialogues. And "subtext"
was familiar ground for many Soviet people who were long used to ideological subterfuge as a means of staying out of trouble with the authorities. What
is convenient about a subtext is that, by definition, it is subject to different
interpretations. It is something implied, and, therefore, vague. In other words,
vaguely articulated authenticity as a distinctive feature of Hemingway's
prose was particularly harmonious with and provided authoritative justification for the Russian mentality of the time.

Although by default many Soviet people in the 1960s and 1970s strove to
be quietly critical of the Soviet state while keeping a low profile (*ne vysovy-
vat'sia*), their suppressed views needed an outlet. Close friendships and mutual trust in personal integrity provided this outlet and increasingly became
elevated above productive work for the country's benefit and other "socially
significant" activities (see Shlapentokh 1984; 2004). Leisure time with close
friends became the essence of a meaningful life and was often considered
more important than even love. Leisure often involved hiking, boating, culti-
vating a little plot of land around one's country shed (in most cases grandly
misnamed as *dacha*), hosting *shashlik* (barbecue) parties, or just celebrating significant and not so significant dates and weekends together with friends. The
resulting civic passivity became a means of personal quiet protest against the
futility of any state-encouraged activity ostensibly aimed at "building a radi-
ant communist society" (*postroenie svetlogo kommunisticheskogo obshchestva*),
which was a common cliché of the time.

This valued camaraderie involved a lot of heavy drinking. Drinking was
not considered a vice, weakness, or shortcoming, rather it was a mode of
negotiating the harsh realities of everyday life. Drinking with one's friends
began to overshadow everything else. Soviet life resembled the never-ending

---

that Hemingway wears in some of his iconic Karsh photographs. The series is set in
October–November 1982, just before Brezhnev's death on 10 November.

drinking spree in Hemingway's *Fiesta* (*The Sun Also Rises*). The Soviet alcoholic became the Holy Fool of the Brezhnev era (1964–82).[8]

What Translators Do to Texts

What did this Hemingway-mania have to do with translators? In fact, quite a lot. The Russian Hemingway spoke his translators' language, and his characters moved, drank, and made love under the supervision of his translators. What most Russians fell in love with was the joint effect of the translators' depiction and the widely-circulated virile images of Hemingway. In preparing a text for a different culture, a translator's mediation is inevitably subjective; the translator cannot avoid certain mental and linguistic operations that inevitably leave what might be called his "translator's imprint" on the text. This imprint is manifested in the translator's choices of language and style. At the level of words and phrases, the translator's mediation ("imprint') may involve (1) identifying or misidentifying the presence of a certain emotive charge in a word sense; (2) matching, neutralizing, intensifying, or toning down the level and sometimes the nature of the emotion expressed by a word sense; (3) matching, neutralizing, enhancing, or diminishing the evaluative force of a word sense; (4) matching or changing the functional register of a word sense—sometimes by substituting slang or more elevated vocabulary for neutral language or neutralizing stylistically colored stretches of language; (5) changing the dialectal—that is, regional, temporal, or social—reference of a word sense (more often than not, by substituting neutral language for culturally marked elements); (6) matching or misrepresenting the relative frequency of occurrence of a word sense in the original, source style; and (7) meeting or pandering to the perceived expectations of the audience by radicalizing, subduing, or completely neutralizing the imagery and metaphors evoked by a word sense or phrase in the original language (see Burak 2010). At the sentence level, a translator's mediation may manifest itself in (1) the use of more or less emphatic sentence structures; (2) the division or combination of sentences, thereby creating a different rhythmic flow in the translated text; and (3) a shift in the theme-rheme (topic-message) balance in clauses, sentences, and paragraphs (see Burak [2006] 2013). Collectively these syntactic transformations form another part of the translator's imprint on the text—the translator's own cohesiveness and coherence of the translated text.

For better or worse, such lexical and syntactic transformations are inevitable as the translator strives to authentically represent the text in spite of the "shape-shifting" nature of translation. I submit that, on the whole, the Kashkintsy Group, which tends to be associated with the entire Soviet school of translation, laid the groundwork for the persistent tendency of Soviet and post-Soviet translators to enhance the stylistics of the texts they translated.

---

[8] See Venedikt Erofeev's *Moscow–Petushki* (1973).

This tendency was at first tentative but nonetheless noticeable in the legendary two- and four-volume Hemingway translations. The Kashkintsy and other subsequent translators, most notably Rita Rait-Kovaleva, challenged the ordinariness and the equality-in-adversity spirit Soviet literature promoted by producing in translation an enlivened and retouched American cultural identity that corresponded to their perception of democracy, freedom of choice, and material abundance. This enticing "Americanism," stylistically more striking in the translations than in the English originals, contrasted starkly with everyday Soviet reality. I will later give some examples from Hemingway's two major novels to briefly demonstrate that, in varying degrees, the translations are more vivid texts than the originals.

I further propose that by creating this "Americanism" in their translations the Kashkintsy and their followers maintained the Russian tradition of "Aesopian language."[9] They smuggled the cultural "other" into Russia under the guise of "unacceptability" by ostensibly reflecting in their translations how supposedly anti-capitalistic and decadent literatures depicted "their" (*ikh*) Western and capitalistic individuals and society. In turn, Soviet readers, sick of ideological Soviet pedagogy and starving for lively and relevant narratives, eagerly embraced the American characters and their settings, even in the carefully vetted selections of fiction that influential editors and the political-ideological establishment approved for translation. In other words, the Soviet editors and translators smuggled into Russia stylistically-enhanced portraits of exciting fictional worlds that the readers were eager to visit and with whose characters they were ready to identify. The characters in Hemingway's fiction fit the mindset of the Soviet post-WWII generation perfectly. The verbally-enhanced Americanism Hemingway's translators highlighted in this fictional world captivated Russian readers through the late Soviet and early post-Soviet period.

Finally, I maintain that Soviet translators collectively invented Hemingway's, Salinger's, and Vonnegut's styles in Russian, thereby establishing what I call the "Russian Amerikanskii substyle" within Soviet Russian literature. It was a kind of "Russian American language" (*russkii-amerikanskii iazyk*) marked by slight but engaging linguistic distortions that, to Soviets, sounded "cooler" and *firmenno* (un-Soviet), compared to mainstream Soviet literature, making the translations arguably more interesting than any Russian texts they had encountered before. Thanks to the translators' ingeniously subtle

---

[9] Aesop (620?–560? BCE) was a Greek fabulist who is considered to be the genre's creator. In Soviet times (and, to a certain extent, today) "an Aesopian language" or "the language of Aesop" (*ezopov iazyk* or *iazyk Ezopa*) was any narrative that had a concealed, suggested meaning or a critical subtext that could not be expressed openly for fear of persecution or victimization. The "Aesopian language" relies on the longstanding ability and readiness of Russians always to read between the lines.

"tweaking" of the originals, Hemingway's spare, earthy English prose began to sparkle in Russian translations.

A far-reaching consequence of this translator-made "American style" of expression was that phrases from the translations began to serve as passwords for entry into the company of the like-minded—those "culturally advanced" Soviets who were familiar with un-Soviet literatures. Thus if you said, "Ia liubliu, chtoby v kokteile byla maslina" (Kheminguei 2010b, 252; I like an olive in a cocktail),[10] you were either recognized and accepted into the circle of the initiated or met with uncomprehending silence by those who were "culturally backward"—unfamiliar with Hemingway.

How Hemingway's Diction Was Transformed into the "Amerikanskii Substyle" in Russian Literature

The abovementioned translators' modus operandi can be illustrated with examples from two Hemingway novels that captured the Russians' imagination in the 1960s and 1970s: *The Sun Also Rises*, translated by Vera Toper, and *A Farewell to Arms*, translated by Evgeniia Kalashnikova. The Hemingway texts are paragons of linguistic sparseness and terseness, but the two translators each managed to avoid monotony and detached simplicity in their translations by enlivening the texts. To varying degrees, the translations are stylistically more vivid texts than the originals.

Many factors converged to produce the distinctive "Russian American style" of the translations. The first group of factors includes the translators' choice and stylistic mix of vocabulary. Both Toper and Kalashnikova employed a vocabulary that was uncharacteristic of mainstream Soviet literature. In their translations, the two translators (1) consistently preferred to use more emotionally-charged and stylistically-marked verbs, nouns, and adjectives than those that were used in the English originals; (2) created unusual, vaguely "un-Russian" collocations; (3) favored unusual adverbs; (4) used diminutive suffixes at their discretion; and (5) employed quaint forms of address. A small sample of exemplary verbs, nouns, adjectives, collocations, adverbs, diminutive suffixes, and forms of address creatively used by Toper and Kalashnikova follows.

Verbs:

You wouldn't want to go in the line all the time, would you? (Hemingway 1932, 37)	Khoteli by vy vse vremia torchat' na peredovoi? (Kheminguei 2010c, 41)
I've vomited into a gas mask. (1932, 82)	Ia raz nableval v protivogaz. (2010c, 89)

---

[10] In fact, the original reads, "I like an olive in a Martini" (Hemingway 2006, 248).

I could see the beams of the search-lights <u>moving</u> in the sky. (1932, 94–95)	I mne vidno bylo, kak po nebu <u>snovali</u> luchi prozhektorov. (2010c, 99–100)

In the three examples above, *torchat'* is more like "to be stuck somewhere," *nableval* is the past tense of "to puke" or "to barf," and *snovali* is the past tense of "to scurry" or "to flit." These are obvious enhancements of the neutral English "to go," "vomited," and "moving."

Nouns:

It's a <u>shame</u> you're sick. (2006, 24)	<u>Svinstvo</u>, chto ty bolen. [Back-translation: It's "<u>swinishness</u>" that you're sick.] (2010b, 18)
There are <u>lots</u> of those on this side of the river. (2006, 28)	Ikh <u>propast'</u> v etom raione. [Back-translation: There are <u>scads/a slew</u> of them in this district.] (2010b, 19)
Be <u>good</u> while I'm gone. (1932, 71)	Nu, bud'te <u>pain'koi</u>, poka menia net. (2010c, 77)

In the above examples, "shame" is not really "swinishness," "lots" is not quite "scads" or "a slew," and "being good" is not being a "goody two-shoes" (*pain'ka*) either.

Adjectives:

I think writing is <u>lousy</u>. (2006, 179)	[...] po-moemu, pisat' zaniatie <u>gnusnoe</u>. (2010b, 180)
We have plenty of girls. It's just <u>bad</u> administration. (1932, 70)	Devochek skol'ko ugodno. Prosto <u>skvernaia</u> organizatsiia. (2010c, 76)

In the first example, *gnusnoe* is far more emotionally charged and literary than "lousy" and connotes "vile" or "obnoxious." In the second example, "bad" is stylistically neutral, whereas *skvernaia* is a bookish adjective close to the English "vile" or "abominable." The adjective *slavnyi*, which is arguably a little more formal than the neutral English "good" or "nice," is one of the translators' favorites, alongside *skvernyi* and *gnusnyi*. For example,

He had a <u>nice</u> face. (1932, 89)	U nego bylo <u>slavnoe</u> litso. [Back-translation: He had a *dear/sweet/lovely face.] (2010c, 94)

Similarly, the following example illustrates the enhancement of the English adjective "funny" and the noun "throat":

"Ho, ho, ho," I said bitterly. "How <u>funny</u> if he would cut my <u>throat</u>." (1932, 98)	"Ha-ha-ha," skazal ia serdito. "Vot byla by <u>potekha</u>, esli b on pererezal mne <u>glotku</u>." (2010c, 102)

Back-translated, the second sentence would go something like this: "What a lark it would be if he slit my gullet," because *potekha* is more like "lark," or even "scream," and *glotka* would be "gullet."

The translations also offer some unusual collocations that sound vaguely un-Russian. For example:

[...] to shatter that superior simpering composure. (2006, 28)	[...] lish by pokolebat' ikh zhemannoe nakhal'stvo. [Back-translation: (...) if only to sway/roil their affected impudence/insolence/brazenness.] (2010b, 22)

It is as if the translator had been anxious to turn a catchy phrase, although Toper may be justified here as trying to convey one of Hemingway's uncharacteristic verbal flourishes. One more example of an unusual collocation in the translation:

But there in my country it is understood that a man may love God. It is not <u>a dirty joke.</u> (1932, 76)	Tam, na moei rodine, schitaetsia estestvennym, chto chelovek mozhet liubit' Boga. <u>Eto ne gnusnaia komediia.</u> (2010c, 83)

"Eto ne <u>gnusnaia komediia</u>" would back-translate as "It's not a <u>vile comedy/farce</u>," which shows Kalashnikova's enhancement of the original.

Another enlivening device is the translators' use of grammatically unusual adverbs. For example:

I went inside. It was <u>dim</u> and dark... (2006, 102)	Ia voshel. Vnutri bylo <u>mglisto</u> i temno... (2010b, 98)

Mglisto is, of course, possible in theory, but it sounds very unusual. The same goes for "piano" in the following example:

It [the restaurant] was <u>full of</u> smoke and <u>drinking</u> and singing. (2006, 215).	<u>Bylo</u> dymno, <u>p'iano</u> i shumno. (2010b, 217)

The Russian adverb *p'iano* (in a drunken manner) is not normally, if ever, used as a predicate adjective after the linking verb "to be." It has to modify a "substantive" verb to indicate the manner of an action. It can probably be argued that Toper resorts to a bit of foreignizing literalism here in order to convey the unusualness of the English collocation "it was full of drinking."

The translators also have their favorite adverbs. Two notable examples are the adverbs derived from the translators' above-mentioned favorite adjectives *skvernyi* and *slavnyi*:

It was a <u>bad</u> trip. (1932, 82)	Ekhat' bylo <u>skverno</u>. (2010c, 89)
You are very <u>comfortable</u> here. (1932, 107)	A u vas zdes' ochen' <u>slavno</u>. (2010c, 112)

The two adverbs in question, *skverno* and *slavno*, seem to be the translators' default translations of Hemingway's "badly" and "nicely."

Toper and Kalashnikova use diminutive suffixes sparingly—but again as a means of enlivening the text. For example:

You have <u>nice</u> friends. (2006, 27)	<u>Milen'kie</u> u tebia druz'ia. [Back-translation: You sure have <u>cute little friends</u>.] (2010b, 21)
Have another <u>port</u>? (2006, 50)	Eshchë <u>stakanchik</u>? (Back-translation: Another <u>little glass/drink</u>?) (2010b, 45)
One <u>drink</u> a day with my mother at tea. (2006, 84)	I tol'ko odnu <u>riumochku</u> s mater'iu za chaem. [Back-translation: And just <u>one small drink</u> with my mother at tea.] (2010b, 80)
How's your <u>boyfriend</u>? (2006, 210)	Kak pozhivaet tvoi <u>druzhok</u>? [Back-translation: How's your <u>young little friend</u> doing?] (2010b, 212)
I like to drink <u>wine</u>. (2006, 250)	Ia liubliu vypit' <u>vintsa</u>. [Back-translation: I <u>do</u> like <u>my</u> wine.] (2010b, 254)

Finally, Toper's and Kalashnikova's favorite form of direct and indirect address to males, which subsequently became widely popular in everyday Russian, is *slavnyi/chudesnyi/zamechatel'nyi malyi* (something like "cool dude" *avant la lettre*). For example, in Hemingway's *A Farewell to Arms*, Frederic Henry says to his friend Rinaldi, "You're <u>a good old boy</u>" (1932, 72). This becomes "Vy vse-taki <u>slavnyi malyi</u>" (2010c, 78) in translation, where Kalashnikova arguably over-translates, making her translation sound more like the *avant la letter* "You sure are a cool dude" than Hemingway's more subdued original "You're a good old boy." Two more examples of a similar nature:

He's a <u>fine</u> boy. (2006, 167)   Chudesnyi malyi. [Back-translation:
                                             <u>Wonderful little</u> fellow.] (2010b, 168)

Mike is a <u>swell</u> fellow. (2006, 192)   Maik – <u>zamechatel'nyi</u> malyi. [Back-
                                                    translation: Mike is a <u>remarkable little</u>
                                                    fellow.] (2010b, 194)

The second factor involved in the production of the "Russian American style" is sentence syntax. Hemingway's syntax has a constantly recurring pattern: Subject-Predicate *and* Subject-Predicate *and/but* Subject-Predicate—and sometimes one more *and* Subject-Predicate. In other words, the conjunction "and" may be repeated in a sentence two, three, or even four times. For example: "It had rained a little in the night <u>and</u> it was fresh <u>and</u> cool on the plateau, <u>and</u> there was a wonderful view" (2006, 155). Or: "Now they [wounds] were crusted <u>and</u> the knee was swollen <u>and</u> discolored <u>and</u> the calf sunken <u>but</u> there was no puss" (1932, 102). Such an overuse of "and" is considered poor style in modern Russian and is routinely corrected by school teachers.[11] Toper and Kalashnikova faithfully reproduced Hemingway's innumerable "ands" such that they have become a trademark syntactic feature of Hemingway's style in "Amerikanskii Russkii." The translations of the above two sentences are as follows: "Noch'iu proshel nebol'shoi dozhd', <u>i</u> na plato pakhlo svezhest'iu <u>i</u> prokhladoi, <u>i</u> ottuda otkryvalsia chudesnyi vid" (2010b, 155); "Teper' ikh pokryvala korka, <u>i</u> koleno raspukhlo <u>i</u> pobelelo, <u>a</u> ikra obmiakla, <u>no</u> gnoia ne bylo" (2010c, 107).[12]

Toper repeatedly uses the construction "ia liubliu, chtoby/kogda…." As a consequence, readers began to view Toper's phrase as a distinctive Hemingway turn of phrase, although it is not: Hemingway uses the verb "to like" in an "unmarked" way. For example, Toper writes, "<u>Ia liubliu, kogda</u> sigara kak sleduet tianetsia" (2010b, 61) for Hemingway's "<u>I like a cigar to really draw</u> (2006, 64); and "<u>Ia liubliu, chtoby</u> v dome bylo pivo" (2010b, 88) for "I like a little beer in the house" (2006, 92).

---

[11] This is not to say that this feature is not to be found in classical or canonical Russian literature but that a Soviet high school student's essay with a repetitive use of "and" would be corrected, regardless of Pushkin's and Gogol's influence.

[12] Curiously, the gauntness of syntactic structure and the repetitive use of the conjunction "and" in the same sentence or clause seem to have been channeled by the famous Russian telejournalist Leonid Parfenov in his immensely popular series *Namedni* and *The Russian Empire*. Open any of the *Namedni* books or listen to any episode of the documentary and you cannot but be struck by the similarity between Hemingway's and Parfenov's syntaxes. I have a strong sense that Parfenov, who was born in 1960 and most likely read the Hemingway translations then available in the Soviet Union, is a living example of the abiding influence of Hemingway's narrative style (to a great extent affected by his work as a journalist) on the people who were brought up on the Russian translations of Hemingway.

Given the wide circulation of Hemingway's works in Russian, it is not surprising that some turns of phrase introduced by the Hemingway translators became extremely popular following the publication of the translations. Just a few of the voguish expressions that could be frequently heard in Soviet urban areas beginning in the 1960s are *slavnyi malyi* (great guy, cool dude) as a form of positive characterization; *skvernyi* (rotten, lousy, or nasty) as in *skvernoe nastroenie* (lousy mood) or *skvernoe delo* (vile business); *svinstvo* (swinishness, or something acutely unpleasant); *gadkii* (disgusting, loathsome, or vile); *milyi* (darling, dear, or sweetie); and, of course, the emblematic "Ia liubliu, chtoby v kokteile byla maslina" (2010b, 252)—the translation of "I like an olive in a Martini" (2006, 248). This phrase was used even when the situation did not involve drinking or eating; it acquired the meaning, "I'm too subtle or refined for this kind of business—I have my special preferences."

To complete the discussion of the "Hemingway style in Russian," here is one final sample of Toper's "Hemingwayese" in *Fiesta*: "Svinstvo bylo naslazhdat'sia etim, no ia i chuvstvoval sebia svin'ei. Kon obladal udivitel'noi sposobnost'iu probuzhdat' v cheloveke vse samoe skvernoe" (2010b, 100). Back-translation: "It was swinish [meaning, 'I felt extremely bad about it'] to enjoy it, but I felt like acting in a swinish way. Cohn possessed the wonderful ability to incite people's vilest instincts." In the original, the sentence goes, "It was lousy to enjoy it, but I felt lousy. Cohn had a wonderful quality of bringing out the worst in anybody" (2006, 104).

Although the isolated lexical and syntactic choices in the majority of the above examples foreignized and enlivened the target texts ever so slightly, the overall effect on the literary works was global and readers could not fail to notice them. The Kashkintsy began and their followers, most notably Rita Rait-Kovaleva, continued to create a recognizable "Amerikanskii substyle" within Soviet mainstream literature that in the new millennium evolved into a kind of "swashbuckling," swaggering "Russian Americanese" that more radical "style-enhancing" translators propagate today.

How do Toper's and Kalashnikova's text modifications square with prevalent translation theory? According to what I would call a middle-range perspective on translation developed by the French translator, historian, and translation theorist Antoine Berman, any act of translation involves, to varying degrees, twelve "deforming tendencies,"[13] which generally comprise lev-

---

[13] Berman's "twelve deforming tendencies" in translation are rationalization, clarification, expansion, ennoblement, qualitative impoverishment, quantitative impoverishment, the destruction of rhythms, the destruction of underlying networks of signification, the destruction of linguistic patternings, the destruction of vernacular networks or their exoticization, the destruction of expressions and idioms, and the effacement of the superimposition of languages. For details, see *L'épreuve de l'étranger: Culture et traduction dans l'Allemagne romantique. Herder, Goethe, Schlegel, Novalis, Humboldt, Schleiermacher, Hölderlin* (Paris: Gallimard, 1984), or its translation by S. Heyvaert, *The Expe-*

eling out, subduing, or impoverishing the diction and style of the original. While Berman's assertion is frequently true, the Kashkintsy cautiously started a new trend—the consistent enlivenment of translations through lexical-morphological and syntactic enhancements—that became their signature mediating impact or "imprint."

"The Quiet Heroism of Translators"

John Milton and Paul Bandia's collection of case studies (2009) is a fascinating multicultural historical study of the transformative power of translation that reviews the activities of different courageous and assertive individuals who introduced translations they considered important to the instigation of cultural innovation and political change. The case studies cover several countries in the 19th and 20th centuries. In the majority of the cases, these "agents of translation" knew exactly what they wanted and what they were doing. The Soviet-Russian case is different in that the Kashkintsy did not consciously aim to undermine the Soviet regime or to create a distinctive "American style" in Soviet literature. The Americanization of Soviet life and literature proceeded quietly[14] and gradually, owing to a curious combination of accidental, objective, and subjective factors. Hemingway's success was, in large part, ensured by Kashkin's literary predilections, his relatively influential position in literary and translation circles, the large print runs typical of a totalitarian approach to publishing approved works, the Soviet people's postwar mindset, and the translators' distinctive style of expression. If Hemingway's works had been translated more literally, the zest might have gone out of them and the readers may not have been attracted to them in such large numbers. Other translators quickly picked up the Kashkintsy trend. To quote Parfenov, writing in *Namedni*:

> The rich Russian tradition of translation was reinforced in the Soviet period as books were practically the only window onto the outside world. The translations by Rita Rait-Kovaleva, Viktor Golyshev, and Elena Surits are often written better than the originals. (2009b, 195)

---

rience of the Foreign: Culture and Translation in Romantic Germany (Albany: State University of New York Press, 1992).

[14] Somewhat perversely, I suppose, I associate the unobtrusively subversive "Americanization" of Soviet literature and discourse with Graham Greene's character Alden Pyle in *The Quiet American*. Alden Pyle is an idealistic American who, in his deep naiveté, causes loss of innocent lives during the French war in Vietnam (1951–54). Pyle illustrates the assertion that seemingly insignificant elements may lead to serious consequences. I don't think that Soviet translators consciously encoded subversive content into their translations, but I do think that they wanted to create texts that were different from the standard literary texts of Soviet literature.

The translator and cultural commentator Vadim Mikhailin says that in the 1960s and 1970s "the translators were the quiet heroes of revolution." I believe that they still are, even today, and the tendency to create more vivid and interesting texts in translation is still very evident. As for Hemingway's translators, in matters of style, they have out-Hemingwayed Hemingway.

From Soviet Times into the New Millennium

The *perestroika* period of the mid-1980s and the "wild" 1990s, to paraphrase Samuel Johnson, emphasized physical and social survival in the collective Russian mind. As numerous Russian literary works flooded Russia, after having been suppressed for decades, Hemingway lost his center-stage position and his impact on Soviet mores began to be reevaluated. As early as 1988, Vail and Genis branded the "Hemingway ideal" as negative because "it only negates—it does not create" (74). In 2002 Vadim Mikhailin further developed this theme when he wrote:

> It was symptomatic that the Soviet intelligentsia of the Khrushchev Thaw […] eagerly embraced the literature of the so-called "lost generation." Hemingway's and Remarque's permanently immature—never mind the biological age—characters marched triumphantly across the whole of Great Russia […]. Poignancy, terseness, and a painful yearning for the simple but ineluctable feeling of friendship […] became the hallmarks of the new Soviet literature […]. All of the main character traits of a "lost person"—restlessness, inability to have "productive or status-driven" sex, adherence to simplistic rituals and "battlefield camaraderie," constant readiness for aggression, being "tuned out" of normal social (work, family, etc.) relationships, and a penchant for borderline states of mind and "adrenalin-fueled" pastimes—are indications of such a person's being permanently locked in a marginal, teenage status. By choosing Remarque and Hemingway as their life models the new generation of the Russian (Soviet) intelligentsia had signed off on a death sentence—and not for the first time—for themselves and for the system within whose limits they were shaping their life scenarios. (2002)

Another translator and cultural commentator, Anton Nesterov, also writing in 2002, talks about the formative and transformative agency of translation more directly. He states, "Our 'basic ideas' about verbal art as well as good and evil and what is acceptable and not acceptable are first inculcated by translators. It is what children and young people read that shapes the 'consensus of a generation,' i.e., common tastes, reactions, and 'mutual identification passwords'" (2002, 1). As for Hemingway's influence on the Soviet fashions and mores, he is no less harsh than Mikhailin:

Another quality of translated literature in the Soviet period was its primarily metaphysical status: it was *a priori* something more than just text—it was a vaccine against the impenetrable darkness of the hated reality, a door leading to a different existence, a model to emulate and to adopt as one's own. Recall the role that Hemingway played for Russian readers and his imitators in the late 1950s. The sweaters and the beards—those were trifles. But was it not Papa who was responsible for the national craze of backpack-and-tent hiking all over Russia in those days? Was it not his magic touch that transformed alcoholism into the "professional disease" of the intelligentsia of the 1960s? Just for the record, before Hemingway, engineers, college professors, and research assistants were rather more restrained in their imbibing habits. In those years, books and—it must be emphasized—translated books became for large numbers of people the cornerstone of the structure of their life. (2002)

Concluding Remarks

Since Peter the Great's time, Russia's method of choice of resolving internal cultural problems has been to turn to the West, be it introducing coffee and tobacco, shaving beards and wearing Western clothes, or building ships and cities. Translation was the primary medium through which access to Western experience was obtained. In a very general sense, translation may be defined as portrayal of a cultural "other" that must be fitted into the receiving culture. The fit is never perfect. In fact, translation is always a rationalized distortion. It presents a distorted image of the foreign reality. This distortion may be the result of high professionalism, mastery, and artistry—as is the case with the Kashkintsy—or of the translator's ineptitude.

According to Mikhailin, translation also involves a mythologization of its subject (2002). This mythologization is the result not of looking for genuine foreign experience but of choosing the kinds of experience and their literary expressions that are an approximation to something incipient or already existing in the translator's own culture. It is an attempt to obtain approval of oneself from a recognized authority. In the case of Russia, the sources of mythologized experiences had usually been mostly in Europe, but in the late 1950s through the 1980s, the search for sources of Western experience that could be usefully applied to Russia increasingly spread to the USA as well. Beginning with the Khrushchev Thaw, a number of coincidences collided, and, thanks to translators, the Soviet logocentric readership received a Russian version of Hemingway that perfectly fit and reinforced the mindset of the new Soviet "lost generations" of the 1960s and 1970s, the generations that had become disillusioned with the remnants of Bolshevik values and the idea of "socialism with a human face." The new generations did not choose Kafka and Proust, whose print-runs were negligible. They chose to read authors who were readily available, plain-spoken, and marginally ideologically sub-versive. Their first choice was Hemingway.[15]

By Way of a Coda

It is clear that global connectedness and the absence of literary censorship have created an expansion of the cultural space in which Russian people can exist that is without precedent. But even as Russian literary horizons have expanded, Russian prose fiction itself has lost its erstwhile relevance, attrac-tion, and influence, and Aesopian language, once the lingua franca of refined intellectuals that encoded mildly subversive meaning, has all but fallen by the wayside. Does this diminish the translators' transformative role as mediators of cultural and social change? Hardly, if only because the translators' sphere of activities and medium of influence have expanded to include cinema. It is cinema, in all of its digital manifestations, that has become the dominant venue of mass culture and a prominent means of Americanizing the Russian mentality and speech, as evidenced by the dominant presence of American films in Russian cinemas. In fact, on my frequent trips to Russia, I find it very difficult to see a Russian movie in a movie theatre—they simply are not playing—but I can easily go and see most of the American "blockbusters" that would have been playing in my local multiplex in Gainesville, Florida. As a result of this cultural lopsidedness, alongside the "prison-jargonization" of Russian written and oral speech—from the president and the prime min-ister all the way down to your friendly local plumber—I hear distinct echoes of "Russian Amerikanskii iazyk" or "translationese" that people pick up from the voiceover dubs of the predominantly American films shown in Russia and from the widely published Russian translations of American pulp litera-ture. From conversations in Russia, I get the impression that Russian teen-agers and young adults have a greater familiarity with the plots and language (in its translated form) of the *Batman* movies, the Meyer *Twilight* trilogy, and such American cartoons as *The Simpsons, Beavis and Butt-Head, South Park,* or *Shrek* than with the plots and language of Russian classic and contemporary literature or films. The frequently foreignizing voiceover idiom is modifying the Russian language and modes of interaction. Expressions like "Chto eto bylo?" (What was that?), "Ty v poriadke?" (Are you OK?), "Priiatnogo/ Khoroshego vam dnia" (Have a nice day), "Kakogo khrena?" (WTF?), "My sdelali eto!" (We did it!), "Vau!" (Wow!), and hundreds of others have all

---

[15] Hemingway was closely followed by Erich Maria Remarque, whose most famous novel in the Soviet Union, *Three Comrades* (*Drei Kameraden*) (published in Germany in 1936), became available in Russian translation in 1959. Other officially designated "critics of bourgeois society" such as Antoine de Saint-Exupéry, Richard Aldington, Scott Fitzgerald, and others followed, not in the order of their biological age, but in the order of their being translated into Russian and appropriated by Russian culture.

entered the Russian language from voiceovers of American movies. They are heard all over Russia, just as some translated Hemingway phrases were ubiquitous in the 1960s and 1970s. True enough, such expressions and interjections still sound a little unusual to a native Russian ear of my vintage and that is why some Russian language purists such as Viktor Lanchikov, Dmitrii Buzadzhi, and Dmitrii Ermolovich of the Moscow Linguistic University English Translation Department condemn such usage as distortions of the natural idiomatic language, but, of course, there is no stopping this process. A national language is what the overwhelming majority of its speakers make it.

The bottom line seems to be that we can hardly continue to talk about the translators' quiet, Aesopian-language "resistance" to the oppressive establishment, but we can certainly talk today about the continuing work of translators as "invisible agents" of linguistic change. These once "quiet heroes" of linguistic and cultural change may still be largely invisible, but they have certainly become much more audible than in the 1970s or the early 1980s.

Chapter 2

Some Like it Hot—Goblin-Style: *"Ozhivliazh"* in Russian Film Translations*

This chapter is about English-to-Russian voiceover translating as a translation technique and a medium that responds to and shapes sociocultural identities. It is an illustration of how the incipient "enlivenment" trend in Russian literary translation, discussed in the previous chapter, has spilled over with a vengeance into Russian voiceover film translating. Given the multiple translations of the same cultural products, films included, it is also a case for comparative translations studies as a separate field of research, which may alternatively be called "translation variance studies."[1]

There are several terms for voiceover translation in Russian: *zakadrovyi perevod, perevod-ozvuchka, odnogolosyi perevod, perevod Gavrilova* (after the name of one of the early prominent practitioners of the trade), and *voisover*. In English, in addition to *voiceover translation*, the terms *single-voice translation, single-voice dub* or *dubbing, lectoring*, and *Gavrilov translation* are also used.

Russia is almost exclusively a "voiceover" country as opposed to "subtitling" countries such as Finland, Greece, Portugal, Israel, the United Kingdom, the USA and numerous others. Voiceover translation is relatively cheap (dubbing a movie is prohibitively expensive), technologically uncomplicated, and, in some respects, psychologically and perceptually more authentic and viewer-friendly than subtitling. Voiceovers are done in the same—audio—perception medium as the originals while the background soundtrack preserves the original actors' voice quality and prosody. This allows a more immediate appreciation of the quality of acting, although for some people it may well be a hindrance. The central psycho-physiological convenience and advantage of a voiceover is that the viewer hears and watches the movie as it unfolds in a "seamless" sort of way, that is, without being forced to constantly switch between two media of perception—audio and visual. Voiceovers have another advantage over subtitling: the viewer can hear a fuller text of the translation. With subtitling, it is necessary to squeeze the "translation" into

* A draft of this chapter was presented at the Southern Conference on Slavic Studies (SCSS) in Gainesville, Florida, on 26 March 2010. I am grateful to my co-panelists and especially Galina Rylkova for their comments. It was subsequently published as an article under the same title in the *Russian Language Journal* (*RLJ*) 61 (2011): 5–31.

[1] The term "translation variance studies" emerged in the course of discussions that Timothy Sergay and I had during the SCSS annual meeting in March 2010.

one line of, on average, 35 characters or two lines of about 70 characters at the most for the viewer to have the time to absorb the meaning of the text on-screen. This is dictated by the fact that the speed of oral delivery of a text is generally about one-third higher than the speed of visual perception of a text (Baker 2005, 247). With voiceovers no such constraint exists. As for dubbed films, it can be argued that their authenticity is restricted because they are more independent, somewhat more removed-from-the-original, self-sufficient cultural products. The reason for this is because the originals' entire sound-tracks have been replaced with new ones. That said, it is precisely owing to this nature of dubs that they may provide a more enjoyable overall aesthetic experience for the viewer.

Curiously enough, despite its proliferation, voiceover translation is an under-researched area of translation studies. Of course, there are comments on this translation technique and how to assess its quality scattered in various parts of the Internet, but no substantive research has been done on the subject either in Russia or the USA. Among relatively recent important contributions to the discussion of film translation are the articles by Andrei Gromov, Nikita Bondarev, and Konstantin Egorushkin in the online journal *Russkii Mir* (Gromov 2008; Bondarev 2008; Egorushkin 2008); interesting insights into the workings of voiceover translating are intermittently provided by the leading Russian voiceover translator today—Dmitrii Puchkov—in his online and radio interviews (Puchkov 2009, 2010a; 2010b; 2012); and the leading Russian translation practitioners and theorists, clustered around the *Mosty* translators' journal—I call them the "Mosty Group"—have also begun to take a serious look at this type of translations (Buzadzhi 2011a; 2011b).

Recent Past

Pirate (unlicensed) voiceover translations began to sweep the then Soviet Union—and, later, newly designated Russia—in the late 1980s and the begin-ning of the '90s. The pirate translators were hired privately by the Russian nouveaux riches (*novye russkie*) anxious to watch predominantly the latest American movies. The translators worked out of their homes, or "kitchen studios" equipped very basically with two VCRs and a microphone. The translator recorded his (they were all male) voiceover translations simultane-ously while listening to the original soundtrack. Here is how Leonid Volodar-skii, one of the veterans of the field, describes the technological side of early voiceovers:

> Everything was done using two VCRs, sitting on your knees, basically. One of them had to be stereo. You stuck the original [VHS cassette] into one VCR, a blank VHS cassette into the other VCR, and a mike into this other VCR, too. I translated simultaneously, and my voice was recorded by the second VCR. Then some techie—I'm strictly not

technically-minded—made a master tape of my voiceover. From that point on, it was "Full speed ahead!"—multiple copies were made, and the voiceover hit the popular masses. (Volodarskii 2011b)

Urban legend has it that the first Soviet voiceover translators used clothespins to clip their noses so that the resulting nasal quality of voice would disguise their true voices and prevent discovery and punishment for illicit work. Ironically, it was only Leonid Volodarskii's nasal, somewhat stuttering delivery that was immediately recognizable across the Soviet Union and then Russia, but it was the result of a nose injury in earlier life—no clothespin was involved. The first wave of underground translators churned out translations at incredible speed. The names of these first voiceover "shock workers"—Volodarskii, Mikhalev, Gavrilov, Zhivov, and Gorchakov—are still well known in Russia. These "first-wave" voiceover translations are still available and revered by dedicated fans who consider them to have special cultural value. It is not infrequent that licensed new translations of old movies come out today with bonus additional materials consisting of the previous, unlicensed translations by these "dinosaurs" of voiceovers.

The distinguishing feature of most of these first voiceover translations was that they were done "straight off," generally without watching the movie first, thinking over the difficult parts in it, and making preparatory notes beforehand. As a result such translations contained a lot of *otsebiatina* (something invented and added to the translation by the translator), which camouflaged the obscure stretches of language or idioms and slang unknown to the translator. In a curious way, the remarkable inventiveness and resourcefulness of the translators paid off. They produced highly entertaining texts. Their translations were enjoyed by millions across Russia. When the late 1990s saw the release of the same movies as officially licensed and newly translated products, they were often rejected by buyers as not quite the same thing (*ne to*). People wanted the authentic, pirate versions back.

Present

So what are the latest developments on the Russian voiceover translation scene? These were described—in a nutshell—by the translator and cultural commentator Nikita Bondarev a few years ago, but the description is absolutely applicable today:

In general, translation, by its nature, does not lend itself to any totalitarian control that prescribes one single way of translating to the exclusion of all others. The translation habitat is the wild where various versions of translations of literary works or films should in theory flourish. From this perspective, it can be said that translations of western films are enjoying complete pluralism in Russia today. The latest

Hollywood releases first appear in Russia as imperfect pirated copies, supplied with amateurish translations that oftentimes have little to do with what goes on in the movie. However, they allow desperate devotees of non-Russian cinema to partake of the pop-culture products long before their licensed releases. Then the "official," licensed copy of the movie is released. It is of high visual and sound quality and it is supplied with a translation that lays claim to being an accurate reproduction of the original. The problem is that this "ofitsioz" [officially approved version] quite often turns out to be—to use a phrase from the famous Zakharov/Gorin movie about Baron Munchausen—"too neatly combed, too thickly made-up, and [regrettably] castrated." Eventually, the video retail points are overrun by a translation of the same movie by Dmitrii Puchkov, better known as "Goblin." This man, without a doubt, deserves a separate publication." (2008)

To some extent this chapter fills in this gap.

Goblin

The word "goblin" entered mainstream Russian in the early 1990s after the Russian translator of the American cartoon series *Gummi Bears* (*Mishki Gummi*) translated the word "ogres"—the big, bad guys in the cartoon—as *gobliny* (goblins). The common meanings of the word *goblin* in spoken Russian today are "a despicable, unpleasant person, or someone with a lot of brawn but a lack of brains" (Slovonovo). Recently the word has acquired an additional meaning—"the translator Dmitrii Iur'evich Puchkov" (Slovonovo).

Dmitrii Iur'evich Puchkov (a.k.a. Goblin) is definitely Russia's most famous film translator today.[2] He is widely known for not toning down the "bad language" in the numerous English-language films that he has translated. These include Guy Ritchies's *Snatch*, David Chase's *The Sopranos*, Jody Hill's *Observe and Report*, Quentin Tarantino's *The Inglourious Basterds*, the Coen brothers' *No Country for Old Men*, and very many others. In his interviews (Puchkov 2009a, 2009b, 2010a, 2010b, 2010c, 2011, 2012, and 2013), Puchkov explains the origin of his nickname. In the late 1980s a newspaper article entitled "Goblins in Gray Overcoats" ("Gobliny v serykh shineliakh" in Russian) denounced graft and abuse of authority in the Russian law enforcement agencies. Following the publication of the article, Puchkov—who at the time was working as a chief criminal investigator in St. Petersburg—began to call himself and his coworkers "goblins." The ironic, self-deprecating sobriquet stuck.

---

[2] See Strukov 2011.

Ozhivliazh

One of the central issues that I discuss in this chapter is what I call "*ozhi-vliazh*"—the current trend to liven up (I should really say, "sex up") original English dialogue in Russian film translations, which I will illustrate with an excerpt from Puchkov-Goblin's voiceover of *The Sopranos*. As a backdrop, I will use a translation of the same excerpt executed in the more traditional and familiar "one-size-fits-all" style.

The word *ozhivliazh* (from the Russian *ozhivliat'*—to bring back to life; to liven up) is a professional slang term often used in theater, filmmaking, and fashion modeling. It means "livening up the acting, stage scenery, the actors' lines, the model's body language, the clothes design, etc." I apply it in the sense defined by the Russian poet and translator Ol'ga Sedakova as the prac-tice of "introducing [into the translation] words that are coarser and meta-phors that are more jarring, [...] [thereby] adding to the author's orchestra more percussion and exotic instruments" (Kalashnikova 2008, 437). Speaking less metaphorically, *ozhivliazh* is a conscious, semi-conscious, or unconscious enhancement of any aspects of a translated text as compared to the more neu-tral language used in the original. One hopes that this happens in the course of the perennial search for authenticity but it may equally well happen for reasons of self-promotion, an inflated sense of exceptional professionalism, or misguided idealism.

The *ozhivliazh* trend in film translation may be described as a marginal-izing or—to use Venuti's term—"minoritizing" type of translation (1998, 10–13). By way of contrast, translations that tone down (or neutralize) culturally controversial language of the original film may be designated as a "majori-tizing" type of translation. However, the "*ozhivliazh*-minoritizing" approach has been gaining ground so sweepingly in recent years, with Goblin being its chief proponent and practitioner, that what might be deemed as catering to cultural minorities is currently becoming a "majoritizing" mode of translat-ing. Puchkov-Goblin claims that his translations are uniquely "correct" be-cause they preserve the original content of films in full measure, reproducing the original language "like it really is" (Puchkov 2009a, 2009b, 2010a, 2010b). Puchkov-Goblin's online translation company is suggestively advertised on the "Tupichok Goblina" site as "Studiia Polnyi Pe" (http://oper.ru/trans/?pp), which is a euphemistic rendition of the Russian "Studiia polnyi p***ets" and which—with a certain degree of Goblin-style *ozhivliazh*—could be translated as "F**k Me Studio." In his online blurb, Goblin defines and assesses the distinctiveness of his "correct translations" as follows:

> The translations are distinct in that they reproduce in a maximal possible way the original text of a film. If the original text contains in-decent, unprintable swearing, then it is translated as indecent unprint-able swearing. If there is no swearing in the original (as in cartoons for

kids or old movies), then the translation does not contain any swearing. The translations are single-person [Goblin's] voiceover translations. (http://oper.ru/trans/?pp)

In my analysis of the *ozhivliazh* trend, I am seeking to answer four related questions:

* What are Goblin's—and anybody else's—exact criteria for assessing cross-cultural correspondences ("maximal adequacy," in Goblin's words) between what is somewhat differently perceived by the elusive, so-called general public as indecent, unprintable or marginally acceptable kinds of language in two different cultures—American and Russian?
* How close to the original American culture does Goblin get in his translations from the perspective of the principles of translation pragmatics as defined and accepted by professional translators and translation theorists?
* What kind of and how many different translations of the same film does it seem reasonable to expect film audiences to need? In other words, should there be just one, all-embracing, officially sanctioned (whoever the officials may be) variant or version of a film translation or several translations catering to the tastes of different "cultural constituencies"—to use Venuti's term (1998, 8–30; 67–87)?
* How are we—both translation experts and laypersons—to sort out and assess the concurrent multiple translations of the same cultural product, films included?

Multiple Translations

One of the advocates of multiple translations of the same text was the literary scholar Mikhail Gasparov. He liked to quote a simile used by the famous linguist, translator, and cultural theorist Sergei Averintsev, when the latter talked about getting to know a different culture: "We get to know somebody else's culture the way we get to know a stranger. When we first meet, we look for something that we have in common in order for the acquaintance to take place; but after that we look for something that makes us different in order for the acquaintance to become interesting" (Gasparov 2000, 108). Talking about the translations of *Hamlet*, Gasparov said that "there should be *Hamlet* translations not only for reading but also for every stage production of the play. [The director] Kozintsev didn't film just *Hamlet*—he filmed a movie based on Pasternak's translation. Fitting Lozinskii's text [translation] to the frames of this movie would not work" (Gasparov 2000, 48). Gasparov believed that there should be at least two translation versions of each complex work of verbal art—a simplified (domesticated) one for a "beginning reader" and a special translation for a "prepared [sophisticated] reader," although he never defined in any specific terms what the difference between the two should be (321).

In a somewhat contradictory vein, Gasparov also liked to quote the famous German classical philologist Ulrich von Wilamowitz-Moellendorff, who said, "There is no such thing as a translation from a language into a language—there can only be a translation from a style into a style" (2000, 319). Today most translation theorists and critics go further than that and say that a good professional translation is carried out from culture into culture. For me as a translation theorist, critic, teacher, and practicing translator/interpreter, the central tension that the translator has to resolve is that between the pressure of intralingual (monocultural) pragmatics and the exigencies of interlingual (cross-cultural) pragmatics. Intralingual pragmatics involves communication that takes place in a shared native language inside a shared native culture. Interlingual pragmatics involves communication that takes place via a process of translation across cultures. Since, in my view, the end result of a film translation is determined, in large part, by the kind of communicative pragmatics the translator pursues, a brief overview of the three best-known pragmatics theories is in order.

Theories of Pragmatics: Overview

Paul Grice has developed the concept of pragmatic implicature, which he formulated as a set of rules or "maxims" guiding most "cooperative" conversations. These maxims are "quantity" (do not give too much or too little information); "quality" (say only what you believe to be true); "relevance" (the information that you convey should be directly relevant to the act of communication at hand), and "manner" (the way you convey information should be appropriate to the message you are getting across and conform—as far as possible—with the expectations of the receiver of the information. (For a gist of the Gricean pragmatics, see, for example, Munday [2001, 97–99] and Malmkjær [1998, 25–40]). Geoffrey Leech has enlarged Grice's pragmatics (or the Cooperative Principle as it has come to be known) to include the concepts of politeness, irony, and phatic communion (banter) (1983, 19). Dan Sperber and Deirdre Wilson have developed a relevance theory of communication, according to which the success of any act of communication depends on the pursuit of optimal relevance of the information involved on the part of both the communicator and the addressee (1995). One of the central concepts in Sperber and Wilson's mutual-knowledge perspective is that of context, which they define as follows:

> A context is a psychological construct, a subset of the hearer's assumptions about the world. It is these assumptions, of course, rather than the actual state of the world, that affect the interpretation of an utter-

ance. A context in this sense is not limited to information about the immediate physical environment or the immediate preceding utterances: expectations about the future, scientific hypotheses or religious beliefs, anecdotal memories, general cultural assumptions, beliefs about the mental state of the speaker, may all play a role in interpretation. (15–16)

Substitute "translator" or "interpreter" for the word "hearer" and the whole concept of context—as defined above—could arguably work as a general definition of pragmatics.

The generally accepted, "classic" requirement of pragmatics in translation is for the translator to evoke or achieve the same effect in the mind/s of the receiver/s of the translation (the target audience) as that in the mind/s of the receiver/s of the original text (the source audience). Based on the above theories of communicative pragmatics, I have developed a short, working definition of pragmatics or pragmatic effect: pragmatics is the process and result of using specific linguostylistic means to adjust the language of the translation to the cultural and informational background and expectations of the receivers of the translation as perceived or presumed by the translator. Greater adherence to the perceived expectations of the "internal" cultural audiences (constituencies) involves intralingual pragmatics (greater domestication of the text). Greater adherence to the original text of the film results in "foreign-sounding" stretches of language in the translation ("foreignization" of the text).

The translator's use of combinations of different translation strategies will determine and change the pragmatic effect of the translation, that is to say, it will shape the cultural identity of the cross-cultural "other" in the minds of the target audience in discernibly different ways. Measuring the perceived pragmatic effect is highly problematic, but it is generally agreed that assessments made by the direct participants in the communicative situation, native speakers of both languages, professional translators, and translation experts are good enough indicators of the accuracy of a translation, including its pragmatic impact. Enter the wide masses on the receiving end of a translation of a film. Just what do *they* have to say about the translation in question? And do they have any say at all?

Nizy ne Khotiat Zhit' Po-staromu—A Revolutionary Situation?[3]

As has already been pointed out, the multi-million audience of a mass-culture product would normally consist of multiple sociocultural "constituencies" with widely varying sociocultural experiences and expectations. Aiming for a

---

[3] This is a reference to Lenin's famous definition of a revolutionary situation in society as a state of affairs when the ruling elite (*verkhi*) are no longer capable of ruling in the old way and the subjugated masses (*nizy*) no longer want to live in the old way.

single translation meant for the whole of the audience would a priori reduce the translator's choices to satisfying some kind of a hypothetical median or average consciousness.

In Soviet and much of post-Soviet times, what the general public normally got as a result of such a reductive, "homogenizing" effort was a one-size-fits-all, "blandspeak" version of a translation of a film—to use Chukovskii's term *gladkopis'* in Russian (Chukovskii 1966, 253). The films were practically always dubbed. In such versions the rough edges of vulgar slang and any perceived political (ideological) incorrectness would have been smoothed over or neutralized and the translation would thus have been rendered inoffensive to one and all. This inevitably left some people, constituting different sociocultural groups, feeling vaguely dissatisfied and bemused. To them the way some characters spoke (through the translation) sounded suspect. However, life—as is often the case—is introducing its correctives: regardless of the views of professional and semi-professional translators, translation scholars, critics, or theorists, different versions of translations are hitting the movie theater and video screens, sometimes nearly simultaneously.

The translation versions are predominantly voiceovers that rely on different mixes of intra- and interlingual pragmatics and meet different kinds of sociocultural expectations and levels of ignorance and expertise. On the one hand, a very significant portion of the general public—unaware of the technical intricacies of translation or the fact that it is a high art to most of its theorists and many of its practitioners—prefers the more "populist" kinds of translations. Not to put too fine a point on it, such translations pander to the sensibilities of less linguistically and culturally sophisticated audiences. On the other hand, arguably, a no less populous part of the general public prefers the more nuanced, "scholarly"—more professionally rigorous—translations that attempt to inventively combine both kinds of pragmatics in order to create a distinctive kind of narrative that would be associated with the cross-cultural "other" on a higher level of cultural authenticity. It would seem that—to paraphrase Gasparov's words—in the first case, translators emphasize something that the audience and the film characters have in common in order for the audience's acquaintance with the cultural "other" to take place, while in the second case, translators look for something that makes the audience and the film characters different in order for the acquaintance with the other culture to become interesting (Gasparov 2000, 108).

Two Translations of the Same Episode

The table below contains two transcripts of two different voiceover translations of a short episode from *The Sopranos* TV series that I have chosen for comparative analysis. The translation in the middle column was done for the NTV channel by a translator whose name is unknown. It was shown by NTV shortly before Puchkov-Goblin's translation. No parts of this translation were bleeped out. The translation in the right-hand column was done by Puchkov-Goblin. The words that were "pinged out" in its TV-3 showings are highlighted by italics. The uncensored version of Goblin's translation (with the original language preserved "like it is") is widely available in Russia unofficially.

Transcripts of a Scene at Tony Soprano's Racehorse Stable

The Sopranos. Season 4, episode 8, disk 3 – "Mergers and Acquisitions." First broadcast on HBO in 2003. Brad Grey Television Production, DVD, 2002.	DVD. *The Sopranos. Клан Сопрано.* Сезон 3, 4. Москва: ООО «Мега Видео», 2008 (NTV version).	DVD. Переводы Гоблина. Правильный перевод. *Клан Сопрано.* 3-4 сезон. Коллекционная серия. Москва: ООО "ICE Records," 2009 (Goblin's version for TV-3). The uncensored Goblin translation of this episode can be found at http://www.youtube.com/watch?v=T0wRiNdRB7U.
Tony: You don't feel good, baby girl? You bad girl.	Ты не слишком хорошо чувствуешь себя, малышка? Плохая девочка.	Нехорошо себя чувствуешь, а, девчонка? Плохая девчонка.
Ralph: Fuck this horse-whispering shit.	Эй! Хватит шептать нежности кобыле на ушко.	Ну-ка *на хуй* шептаться с *лошадью.*
Tony: What's this costing us?	Эгх, во что нам это обошлось?	Во сколько нам это встало?
Ralph: Oh, Tony, Valentina. Valentina, Tony Soparano. She works in an art gallery. Helping me to enlarge my collection. And this, my chiquita banana, is Pie-O-My.	О, Тони. Это Валентина. Тони Сопрано. Валентина работает в художественной галерее, помогает приумножить мне художественную коллекцию. А это моя маленькая ягодка, мой сладкий пирожок.	О, Тони, это Валентина. Валентина, это Тони Сопрано. Валентина работает в художественной галерее. Помогает расширить мою коллекцию. А это, моя чикита-банана, мой Пирожочек.
Valentina: She's beautiful.	Она просто красотка.	Красивая какая.

Ralph: There's no stopping this horse. She's gonna go all the way to the Breeders.	Ничто не может остановить эту лошадку. От нее будет роскошное потомство.	Эту лошадь ничто не может остановить. У нее будет роскошное потомство.
Valentina: We'll do the two geldings next. Hon, can you come here a sec? I think I have something in my eye.	Не слишком ты возбуждайся, я ревную. Дорогой, можешь ты подойти на секунду? Мне что-то попало в глаз.	Следующими двух меринов давай. Дорогой, можешь подойти на секунду? Мне что-то в глаз попало.
Ralph: Let Dr. Ralphie have a look. I don't see anything.	Дай-ка доктору Ральфу посмотреть. Я ничего не вижу.	Давай-ка доктор Ральфи посмотрит. Ничего не вижу.
Valentina: Maybe you need more light.	Наверное, тебе нужно больше света.	Может, надо к свету повернуться?
Ralph: What the fuck? I can't believe you did this to me.	А, дерьмо! Я не могу поверить, что ты так со мной поступила.	Ну что за *хуйня*?! Ты чё творишь-то, а?
Valentina: It was a joke, hon.	Это была просто шутка, дорогой.	Это была просто шутка, дорогой.
Ralph: There's nothing funny about it.	Здесь нет ничего смешного.	Ничего смешного не вижу.
Tony: There is from where I'm standing.	А, по-моему, есть.	А я отсюда очень даже вижу.
Valentina: Besides, it's good luck.	Кроме того, это приносит удачу.	Кроме того, это хорошая примета.
Ralph: What?	Что?	Что?
Valentina: It's good luck to step in horseshit. Ask any horseperson.	Наступить в лошадиное дерьмо – это хорошая примета. Спроси кого угодно на конюшне.	Наступить в лошадиное говно – хорошая примета. Спроси кого угодно на конюшне.
Stable attendant: It's true.	Это правда.	Это правда.

Ralph: Then why aren't you, people, walking around all day looking for piles of horseshit to stomp around in?	Тогда почему я не вижу толпы туристов, гуляющих по округе в надежде вляпаться в свежий навоз?!	Ну так чё ж вы тогда целыми днями по говну не топчетесь?
Stable attendant: It only works if it's an accident.	Примета действует, только если это произошло случайно.	Примета действует только если случайно.
Ralph: Fucking sick, all of you. Fucko, where's a hose?	Да пошли вы все! Где здесь кран?	Да вы тут все *йибанутые*. Слышь, *йибанько*, где здесь шланг?

Assessment

If pragmatics means meeting perceived expectations of the target audience, then Goblin's version most likely meets the expectations of a sizeable part of Russian viewers who speak the same kind of language that Goblin uses to translate lower-register lexical items: as the saying goes, some people do not just use *mat* (obscene or profane language)—they routinely speak it. And one does have to admit that *mat* has become a pan-national discretionary sociolect that even refined intellectuals and linguistic aesthetes occasionally resort to.

The absence of censorship (or a very mild censorship of printed and visual matter), the free-wheeling Internet, and the democratization of Russian life in general have led to a very noticeable relaxation of linguistic taboos and time-honored norms. *Mat* has become more visible and audible than before. It is noteworthy that there have appeared some monolingual dictionaries of Russian *mat* (see, for example, *Russkii Mat. Tolkovyi Slovar'*, www.mat.al.ru/).) that delineate vocabulary belonging to the realm of *mat*, with what is missing from the dictionary, by default, belonging to the realm of non-*mat*. To be sure, a sizeable part of the viewers (including those who occasionally use *mat* themselves) would be jarred by Goblin's translation that flouts the traditionally expected standards of decency in the mass media. Until recently the media were only allowed or preferred to use language that, say, members of the whole family could feel comfortable with in one another's presence.

To get a more specific and immediate sense of the intracultural effect of the episode on representatives of present-day American culture I showed the episode to a kind of focus group consisting of 39 of my students aged 18–22. I do not position the results of this mini-survey as sociologically valid—still, this is the reaction of 39 flesh-and-blood respondents at the University of Florida, whose native language is American English and who are steeped in

American culture. Judging from their reactions, the characters' language in this episode produces a less disturbing effect on American viewers than Goblin's arguably harsher linguistic choices in his version of the translation produce on Russian viewers (myself and many of my Russian friends included). Though anecdotal, this evidence confirms my longtime impression that American audiences are generally more tolerant of strong language in movies than their Russian counterparts, no matter what the MPAA ratings may be.

As was already mentioned, what makes Puchkov-Goblin's translations "Goblin translations" is his unabashed choice of vocabulary. Another feature of his translating style is his unique way of reading his carefully prepared in advance voiceover texts. *Mat* aside, the enlivening of the original American soundtrack proceeds along the following lines. At the level of words and non-predicative phrases, "enlivening" involves (1) intensifying the level and sometimes the nature of the emotion expressed by a word sense; (2) enhancing the evaluative force of a word sense; (3) changing the functional register of a word sense—usually by substituting slang or more elevated vocabulary for neutral language; (4) changing the dialectal—that is, regional, temporal, or social—reference of a word sense; (5) misrepresenting the relative frequency of occurrence of a word sense in the original, source style; (6) pandering to the perceived expectations of the audience by radicalizing the imagery and metaphors evoked by a word sense or phrase; and (7) consistently using speech contractions, like "che" for "chto," etc. (see Burak 2010).

At the level of the sentence and paragraph, enlivening is carried out by using more emphatic sentence structures, breaking up sentences, condensing sentences, and using elliptical sentences, thus creating a punchier translation text (see Burak [2006] 2013). All of these elements coalesce into a pragmatics of translating that is essentially domesticating—using the local highly colloquial and profane idiom packaged into truncated, emphatic syntax without any significant foreignization. However, the level of profanity is so harsh that I would expect some viewers to feel alienated, i.e., "defamiliarized" by it. Metaphorically speaking, like an animal beginning to talk out of the blue in a fairy tale, Goblin translations have—especially initially—a defamiliarizing effect.

Goblin's distinct way of reading his translations is that, instead of speaking in the emotionally even-handed monotone traditionally expected from voiceover translators, Goblin differentiates between male and female characters—and sometimes among different characters in general—by changing the prosody of his delivery: 1) the pitch of voice; 2) the movement of the tone of voice (dynamics of pitch); 3) word and sentence stress; 4) loudness; 5) tempo (speed of speech); 6) pauses (their distribution and length); 7) rhythm; 8) timbre; and 9) the general intensity of speech calibrated by varying degrees of muscular effort and resulting in varying degrees of articulatory clarity. (For one of the most recent and comprehensive conceptions of prosody, see Kodzasov 2009.)

In general, Goblin's intensity of speech—its loudness, clarity, and force-fulness of stress—is often more pronounced than that of other translators, and his pleasant and confident speaking voice is widely recognizable. Goblin's lowered style of speech, comprising predominantly highly colloquial syntax and risqué vocabulary, would generally have been considered vulgar and "unprintable" as recently as the late 1980s. To give just one example from the minute illustrative fraction of the whole mammoth *Sopranos* series, it is indic-ative of the greater permissiveness of social norms in the last five–ten years that the word *govno* (shit) is not bleeped in Goblin's version at two points in the dialogue, thus the word is, arguably, being positioned as an acceptable term to the general public, even though it is listed in the dictionary of *mat* referred to earlier (http://www.mat.al.ru/). Significantly, the NTV translation avoids any strong language altogether, substituting the words *der'mo* (a mild version of *govno*) and *navoz* (manure) for Goblin's jarring *govno*.

Judging from Puchkov-Goblin's interviews about his own work, his video reviews of the latest movies on his website, and the aplomb with which he does his voiceover translations, he is very proud of his translations—and rightfully so—given the amount of time and research he puts into the prepa-ration of each of them. Unlike most of the first-wave voiceover translators and present-day underqualified practitioners of the craft, Puchkov first carefully studies the whole movie and writes down his translation of the whole text heard and seen in the movie. Only after that does he get down to recording his voiceover.

Does Goblin's "sexing up" of the original text matter to the majority of different cultural contingents that watch Goblin-translated movies? I think it does, although not to the extent that many professional translators and trans-lation scholars and critics would have one believe. What would fit Venuti's definition of "minoritizing" translations—like the ones provided by Goblin—reach out to multiple cultural constituencies, and especially to the "minori-tized," marginalized cultural groups. A neutralized, "smoothed-over" trans-lation makes it hard for such groups to suspend disbelief when they hear, for example, supposedly hardened criminals talk like university professors. Such a "blandspeak" translation may satisfy a large audience but it loses out on its effect on and fulfillment of expectations of numerous more specific, although intersecting, social groups not particularly averse to using marginalized Russian.

A Goblin translation meets the expectations of such groups by having an emotive effect they can identify with. To them it sounds authentic. At the same time, Goblin's professedly "correct" translations contribute to creating a false or distorted translation canon for the widespread "four-letter" elements in casual, low-register American speech. In place of the "blandspeak" canon that used to be acceptable to one and all in traditional Russian translations of films, Goblin establishes a kind of "y*b-v*shu-mat" (f**k me—or is it you?)

canon in Russian translations of low-register speech, which is still not the kind of Russian one normally hears onscreen.

It should be noted in passing that, despite the fact that the series *The Sopranos* has been shown by two television channels, it has not become popular in Russia. According to the many retail clerks I talked with, the DVD sales have been disappointing. Among the—no doubt—multiple reasons for this lack of popularity of an American blockbuster TV drama in Russia I would single out the following: There is too much vulgar swearing in the Goblin translation that makes people turn away from his version while, simultaneously, people who are unfazed by unabashed swearing are turned off by the interminable bleeps in the officially licensed version; the NTV version is too bland (*intelligentnyi*) to attract the "coarser" social elements; and, in any case, the series is too long and too foreign to make Russian viewers identify with its setting and culture or sustain a prolonged interest in it. Some people bought the DVD because it was advertised as a Goblin translation, and the Goblin fad is very strong these days.

The "Mosty Group" Speaks Out

Goblin's work has triggered a lively discussion within the translators' community in Russia. The famous translator and media personality Leonid Volodarskii has a Web site called "Volodarskii Leonid Veniaminovich," on which he is often asked questions about his views on translation. On 26 January 2011, a college student, who has lived in the USA for the past five years, asked him the following:

> How do you assess the quality of present-day translations of American movies into Russian? I'm writing a college thesis on text adaptation in translating foreign films, and I've watched several contemporary American films with Russian translation. To tell the truth, if I hadn't seen the originals without any translation, I would have had trouble understanding what was going on in the movies. The translations leave a lot to be desired. There are numerous coarse words and expressions in them, and, in general, the Russian used grinds on the ear.[4]

Volodarskii had this to say in response: "At present, literary translation into Russian is going through a difficult time. It's quite obvious. And it is true that many translators quite often overuse slang and profane language when the [original] text doesn't really call for it."[5] Volodarskii does not mention Puchkov specifically, but other professional translators and translation theorists

---

[4] See the rubric "Vashi voprosy" on Volodarskii's site http://volodarskiy.ru/section/questions/?sid, accessed 27 January 2011.

[5] Ibid.

do. They assess Puchkov's creative work in different ways. On the one hand, there are those who praise his talent, sense of humor, and high level of professionalism. On the other hand, there are those who accuse him of overconfidence, lack of professional training as a translator, and pandering to unsophisticated audiences. Here is a very brief sample of views on the Goblin phenomenon of some prominent translation figures in Russia, all of them belonging to the "Mosty Group."[6]

The translator and frequent contributor to the *Mosty* journal Mikhail Zagot gives a generally positive evaluation of Goblin's work by saying that "overall, he's a pretty good translator [...] that does have a feel for his native language." While admitting that Goblin does well in both genres—"funny" and "correct" translations—Pavel Palazhchenko, Gorbachev's longtime translator and also a frequent contributor to *Mosty*, has some reservations about Goblin's penchant for using *mat*. He does not believe that "profanity will entrench itself in Russian culture—in Russian cinema, in particular—the way it has happened in American cinema. First and foremost, because obscenities in American English don't have the same edge as they do in Russian." The Chair of the Translation and Interpreting Department at the Moscow Linguistic University, Professor Dmitrii Buzadzhi, is moderately critical of Goblin's M.O.:

> Goblin is not a "new word in translation," he's not a "trail-blazer," but nor is he a villain or talentless nonentity. [...] He is superficial. His translations have textual unity but at the same time contain a whole array of translator's errors. Swearing in his translations is just a diversion—he shocks the public in order to conceal behind this "slap in the face of public taste" some embarrassing gaps in his translation technique. He proudly declares that he "ain't been to no academies" [...], which, in fact, is nothing to be proud of—a lack of professional training is very noticeable. I think that those who refuse to discuss Goblin's translations seriously are making a mistake because, in the absence of serious critique of his work, he has already begun to be referred to as a "famous translator" and an "expert." People who are incapable of assessing translation quality believe this. (Berdy et al., 2010)

Professor Viktor Lanchikov of the Translation and Interpreting Department at the Moscow Linguistic University dismisses Goblin's claim to "correct" translations out of hand:

> If you throw all the profanities out of Goblin's translations, you will get translations of such quality as to be totally indistinctive. I asked my

---

[6] For the full text of the "Mosty Group"'s discussion of Puchkov/Goblin's work, see Berdy et al. (2010).

students, who were curious about Goblin's translations, what they could remember about his translations besides the profanities. They remembered nothing else. The whole "correctness" of his translations is in the fact that he presents Russian profanity [*mat*] as a full-fledged equivalent of "four-letter" words in English and is surprised that nobody else has made that discovery before him. That's the extent of his translator's achievement. (Berdy et al., 2010)

Dmitrii Ermolovich, the famous lexicographer and a professor in the Department of Translation and Interpreting at the Moscow Linguistic University, is very harsh:

I don't think Goblin has any "correct" translations at all. From the perspective of translation technique, Goblin is not really a very good translator. [...] Either consciously or intuitively, Goblin meets a social need that calls for—to put it mildly—an adaptation of a film text to the tastes of a certain part of the viewing public. The range of such adaptations is rather wide—from a funny parody to downright vulgarization. But what can you do if some folks just need that kind of stuff? [...] His opuses filled with obscenities [...] are what I would call "translation pornography." (Berdy et al., 2010)

Michele Berdy, a famous translator, writer, and former weekly columnist in *The Moscow Times* newspaper, adds to the sociolinguistic dimension in the discussion of the quality of Goblin translations introduced by Ermolovich:

It has to be admitted that beginning translators don't understand that Russian *mat* and "four-letter words" are different things. In English, these words often indicate class affiliation. The fact that we hear Hugh Grant's character say "fuck" fourteen times at the beginning of the film *Four Weddings and a Funeral* and that the Queen of England has seen and approved of the film doesn't at all mean that everybody speaks that way in Britain. In the movie, the use of "fuck" signals a social characteristic of the hero: a British intellectual with a left-wing outlook ("left-wing" in the Western sense of the term). Using this kind of language as a marker of a left-wing worldview became noticeable following the 1960s counter-cultural revolution. Incidentally, if Grant's hero had used milder language—like "shit" or "damn"—the viewers wouldn't have been able to identify him as a typical Oxford "lefty." Substituting—Goblin-style—a Russian *mat* expression for "fuck" here would destroy the implication. Grant's character would sound like some kind of a desperado [*bespredel'shchik*]. (Berdy et al., 2010)

Berdy leaves the question "So how exactly do you translate 'fuck' in the given example?" unanswered. I am afraid, a Goblinesque solution, using the elliptical "Tvoiu mat'!" several times would, in fact, work here, conveying the "liberal" non-aversion to strong language that has become quite widespread in Russian well-educated circles. Having said that, I have to agree with Goblin's critics that, in most cases, Russian *mat* is more emotionally charged and less publicly acceptable, especially onscreen, than obscenities in American movies or prose fiction. I personally would use it in a voiceover only if it were absolutely crucial to the film's plot or esthetic conception. But, of course, the esthetic conception, as the current Russian experience shows, is in the eye and ear of the translator. While being illuminating, the "Mosty Group"'s views on Goblin's work need to be augmented with a more comprehensive and profound examination of its interlinguistic and sociocultural aspects, especially in the context of the work of the other prominent voiceover translators in Russia today.[7] It is hoped that this chapter is a step in that direction.

Interpreting Goblin's Success Story

How can the Goblin phenomenon be accounted for? I will begin with an anecdote told by the translator and cultural commentator Nikita Bondarev in his article "Zakon mozaiki protiv zakona Moiseia" (2008):

> An American with a more or less decent knowledge of Russian arrived in Moscow on a short visit, and his Russian friends decided to give him a surprise by showing him the "Goblin" translation [*smeshnoi perevod*—"funny translation"] of the "Lord of the Rings." The DVD [purportedly in Puchkov's translation] is duly bought from the nearest street vendor but it turns out that this is not a translation by Puchkov himself. It turns out to be a much less witty imitation of his translation style by somebody else posing as Puchkov. They explain the situation to their American friend: "You know, this isn't what we wanted to show you. This is, well, a pirate version of a pirate version of a translation..." All the amazed American can say in response is: "A pirate version of a pirate version?... And you still complain that you have problems with democracy..."

So Goblin has become a cult figure with an unmistakable style and identity. But in order to create a cult following, one first has to do something distinctive and then publicize the distinction widely so it becomes an immediately recognizable cachet. An element of prurience or luridness is very helpful for titillating public sensibilities. The first voiceover translators of the 1980s

---

[7] For the latest information about Russian film translators today, visit the KinozalTV site, accessed 16 August 2013, http://forum.kinozal.tv/showthread.php?t=61079.

and 1990s acquired their cult status by doing something that had not been done on a large scale before: they produced voiceover translations of previously totally inaccessible movies, and the VHS cassettes with the translations became readily available through a rapidly developing network of private video rental shops. An added titillating attraction for the renters and buyers of the translations was the sense of doing something vaguely illegal: the translators plied their trade semi-legally (their work was illicit employment), and the frequently risqué language of the translations was not approved by the cultural establishment. Everybody felt they were partaking of the proverbial forbidden—and exotic—fruit.

Goblin started learning English in about 1985 in a school for law-enforcement workers. At the same time he became very interested in the computer games that were just appearing on the Russian market. He started to translate and sell computer games, gaining a measure of recognition among the computer-savvy segment of the population. Being an avid enthusiast of the English language, he then began to make public fun of the inept first-wave voiceover translations that were flooding Russia. His serendipitous, accidental-masterpiece kind of creative find was what he called *"smeshnye perevody"* (funny translations). These were English-language movies in which Goblin and his team, appropriately and euphemistically called "Studiia polnyi pe," replaced the whole of the original soundtrack with a totally different text that parodied the original material and contained a lot of "unprintable Russian" (*mat*). His funny translations of *The Matrix* and *The Lord of the Rings* became instant hits among large-city movie cognoscenti. This was an ingenious way to attract public attention to the importance of voiceover translations for the appreciation of a film. The next step came logically—Goblin-Puchkov began to offer his own—"correct" translations of the predominantly American cine-fare deluging Russia. Thus he produced a titillating product while commanding a powerful channel of distribution—the newly arrived DVDs that replaced VHS cassettes and the Internet. Puchkov's charisma, talent, resourcefulness, and hard work have paid off. Today he enjoys icon-like recognition in Russia, and his site Tupichok Goblina is extremely popular. The classical conflict between the popular success of a cultural product and its critical expert assessment is very much in place.

Concluding Remarks

While some of the criticisms leveled at Goblin by some leading translation analysts reproduced in this article may seem a little harsh, they come close to formulating—although they do not formulate clearly—the sociolinguistic problem that Goblin's translations often face but fail to resolve entirely satisfactorily, if such a resolution is at all possible. The problem is that Goblin treats swear words more like dictionary items than parts of complex communicative intentions realizable in speech acts (see Grice 1957 and Davis 2013).

In his own words, Goblin translates "what is swearing as swearing" (Puchkov 2009a, 2009b, 2010a, 2010b, 2012), but, in actual fact, from the perspective of different implicatures of speech acts, what has the outward form of swearing may express a wide range of implications—from the phatic function in order to maintain friendly contact to familiar endearments to self-identification, ad hoc or otherwise, as a member of a certain sociocultural group or class. Profanities cannot be transferred from one language into another intact, verbatim. They often need pragmatic modification.

In Gricean terms, Goblin tends to recognize encoded content ("natural" meaning), whereas he should also strive to recognize and represent non-encoded content ("non-natural" meaning)—those meanings and different kinds of implicatures that are understood beyond an analysis of the words themselves, i.e., by looking at the context of speaking, status of the speakers, genre of the story, the speakers' tones of voice, and so on. A "fucker" does not always translate as *eban'ko, pizdiuk,* or *khui morzhovyi;* it can also be *urod, debil, kozel, pidar,* or plain *pridurok.* By translating "fucko"—a pretty exotic, Italian-evoking word in English—as *eban'ko,* Goblin domesticates the original swear word by using a totally natural and commonly used vulgar Russian expression, but there is one catch here: *eban'ko* is what might be called a piece of "Ukrainianized" Russian slang, modeled on a typical ending of Ukrainian surnames and triggering associations with "dumb Ukrainian *khloptsi* [guys]" common in Russian jokes (*anekdoty*). The translation is domesticating and de-familiarizing at the same time because the mobster Ralph is not your typical "dumb Ukrainian *khlopets'.*" It seems that something like "*urod, debil,* or *pridurok* would have worked well enough without creating a deviant cross-cultural web of associations. In my illustrative sample of the voiceovers, the NTV translator avoids the problem by elision while Goblin "sexes up" his translation, causing it to be bleeped in the TV-3 copy, with the bleeped word being easily "guessable."

Goblin does not seem to be sensitive to complex interactions of the two types of translation pragmatics, nor does he seem to be fully aware of the possibility of different implicatures of the same vocabulary within either or both types of pragmatics. Goblin's level of adequacy and accuracy in translating low-register texts from American English into Russian is based on intuitive, vaguely defined criteria—"what is swearing in English is swearing in Russian" (Puchkov 2012). A more nuanced approach would have to integrate the two types of pragmatics: intralingual and interlingual. An intralingual (mono-cultural) pragmatics would cater, within the target culture, either to the whole multiplicity of overlapping cultural identities (that is, variously instituted social groups) or to a specific set of these variously instituted social groups. This intralingual pragmatics would have to be imaginatively, but consciously, intertwined with an interlingual (cross-cultural) pragmatics that would aim to convey a sense of the distinctiveness of the specific foreign cultural identities ("the other") to the same multiplicity of cultural constituencies or a select set of them.

This is, of course, a tall order, but, given these constraints, "hybridization" is inevitable, so that it seems reasonable to expect at least three different types of film translations to emerge: 1) "minoritizing" ones (like those by Goblin), satisfying the theoretical perspectives of Venuti (1998), Bourdieu (1984), Lecercle (1990, 1999), and other authors but projecting somewhat distorted cross-cultural identities; 2) "majoritizing" ones (like those that were routinely released in Soviet and post-Soviet times), glossing over the less "palatable" segments of the original; and 3) some hybrid versions in between (like *The Sopranos* translation commissioned and shown by the Russian NTV channel). The hybrid ones will tentatively test the general audience's sensibilities of decency but will still lean toward generally accepted standards of public decency. Given the complexity of the translation enterprise, attempts at creating cross-cultural identities of the "other" through the medium of distinctive film translations will continue and result in multiple versions of translations of the same films. And that is exactly what is already happening on the Russian film translation scene. Ironically, in Russia, what Venuti termed the "minoritizing" type of translations seems to be morphing into its opposite—the "majoritizing" one. The professional elite of the "high-art" school of translators are scrutinizing the process with jealousy, suspicion, and unease, but are having little effect on or control over the process, which is not to say that they have not been vociferous—although in a disjointed and often contradictory fashion—in expressing their criticism. (One may want to follow, for example, the eight-year-long debate on the accuracy and adequacy of different translations in the Russian professional translators' journal *Mosty* or the abundantly quoted here most recent round-table discussion on the subject by leading translation experts in Russia.) It has to be admitted, though, that there is no getting away from the "violence of language" (Lecercle 1990) and that—to paraphrase Tony Curtis's character Joe in the famous Billy Wilder movie: "Some will still like it hot while some will continue to prefer classical music."[8]

One of the "cursed" Russian questions is, as usual, "What is to be done?" How will or should the multifarious community of translation practitioners, theorists, and critics deal with such a "multi-translational" state of affairs? I would suggest engaging more actively, rigorously, and coherently in the

---

[8] *Some Like it Hot* is a 1959 Billy Wilder comedy in which two unemployed musicians, Joe and Jerry, while on the run from the Mafia that wants to eliminate them as witnesses, disguise themselves as young women and join an all-female jazz band, playing jazz—the hot music at the time—in the company of hot women making up the band. Hence the title of the movie. The film was immediately dubbed into Russian under the title *V dzhaze tol'ko devushki* (Jazz by Women Only). It has been very popular ever since.

assessment of retranslations and multiple translations that represent one and the same foreign source—be they films, prose fiction, or poetry—thereby constituting the raw content for what may be called "translation variance studies," or comparative translation studies.

Chapter 3

Translating *Skaz* as a Whole-Text Realium: Five Modes of Translation (Russian-to-English)*

Tolstoy's world-famous novel *War and Peace* has been translated into English at least twelve times. The three most recent translations are those by Anthony Briggs (2005), Andrew Bromfield (2007),[1] and Richard Pevear and Larissa Volokhonsky (2007). One of the reasons for retranslating the same original is the fact that any text is an open-ended system of signifiers lending itself to multiple subjective interpretations by different translators even in similar cultural and sociopolitical settings. There are also other—more specific— reasons: the need to correct linguistic, stylistic, and cultural errors; bring the language of an existing translation in line with current usage; or bring the expressive means of a translation closer to the individual style of the author.

In this chapter, I will look at an excerpt from two of the three translations of *War and Peace* that I referred to above—one by Anthony Briggs and the other by Richard Pevear and Larissa Volokhonsky. The excerpt is a parable about two merchants as told by Platon Karataev, an important character in the novel (Tolstoy 1963, 176–79). The main reason I have chosen this particular excerpt is because it exemplifies the use of *skaz* as a character-defining literary stylistic device, and *skaz* always presents major textual and cross-cultural difficulties for translation. The main purpose of this chapter is to analyze and evaluate the translation strategies used in the two translations. It should be noted in passing that Tolstoy himself considered the story about the two merchants to be one of his best pieces of writing, so I find the passage under consideration interesting not only from the point of view of the

---

* This chapter was originally published as an article in the *Slavic and East European Journal (SEEJ)* 54: 3 (Fall 2010): 453–75.

[1] The publication of Andrew Bromfield's translation of the allegedly original version of *War and Peace* immediately started a controversy among literary and cultural scholars as regards the status of both the Russian text and its translations, with many scholars maintaining that the Russian presumably preliminary text that A. Bromfield used—if it is indeed a genuine draft by Tolstoy—cannot be accepted, for various reasons, as a legitimate preliminary text of *War and Peace*. One of the first to start the discussion, in October 2007 (the translation was published in September 2007), was National Public Radio (see Neary 2007). I refer to Bromfield's translation in this chapter only to emphasize the interest that Tolstoy's novel is still generating in the translating and publishing communities.

translation difficulties it presents but also from the point of view of how a brief sample of Tolstoy's prose poetics is captured or not by different translators. I should emphasize at this point that I will compare the two translations not from the perspective of their deficiencies or inadequacies but from the perspective of the specific measures or decisions taken by the translators to accommodate the source language meanings and authorial style in the target language versions. I will also try to conceptualize the differences between the two translations in terms of their perceived pragmatic impact on present-day readers. In this particular case, these were my own students in an advanced Russian-to-English translation seminar at the University of Florida and some of my colleagues. For clarity of argument, I will define the pragmatic impact or pragmatics of a translation as the result of using specific linguostylistic means to adjust the language of the translation to the cultural and informational background and expectations of the receivers of the translation as perceived or presumed by the translator. I intend to show how using combinations of different translation strategies will determine and change the pragmatic effect of a translation.

One of the conventional wisdoms in translation circles is that a translation should represent the golden mean between "literalist translation" (*bukvalistkii perevod*) and so-called "free translation" (*vol'nyi perevod*). "But is this [the golden mean] at all possible or necessary?" Mikhail Gasparov famously asked. "Wouldn't it be more useful to clearly define and clearly contrast these two tendencies in order to choose one of the two unequivocally and adhere to it to an extent that the translator defines himself/herself? It is better than rushing from one side to the other because, as is known, the golden mean is unattainable" ([1971] 1988, 7). Judging from this quote, Gasparov seems to advocate a certain degree of consistency in pursuing either a more literalist or a more free translation; however, he does not define any factors or grounds—textual or extratextual—that might influence the translator's choice one way or the other. In this chapter, in not accepting Gasparov's black-or-white approach, I will supply some essential details missing from Gasparov's general thesis. To do so, I will use a deductive procedure on the basis of analyzing the two totally acceptable translations of a seriously translation-resistant *skaz*-like text in order to determine what conscious or unconscious decisions Pevear and Volokhonsky and Briggs made and what results they achieved.

Skaz and Realia

Pierre Bezukhov, a central character in the novel, meets Platon Karataev in French captivity following the devastating fire in French-occupied Moscow in August–September 1812. Karataev is a former peasant and soldier captured as an enemy combatant and Bezukhov is being held as a suspected incendiary. Together with the other prisoners, Bezukhov and Karataev have to endure the harsh realities of being POWs. In the course of their numerous interactions,

Karataev keeps telling Bezukhov a tragic parable-like story about two Russian merchants. In the episode under consideration, Bezukhov listens to Karataev's telling the story of the two merchants to some other prisoners sitting with him around a camp fire. Here is the beginning of paragraph 3 of the excerpt which already provides a foretaste of the kind of translation challenges the translators had to deal with (for the full text of the excerpt and its two translations, see Appendix 1):

Tolstoy's original text (see Tolstoy 1963, 176–79):	R. Pevear and L. Volokhonsky's translation (see Tolstoy 2007, 1062–63):	Anthony Briggs's translation (see Tolstoy 2005, 1181–82):
[3] – И вот, братец ты мой […], проходит тому делу годов десять или больше того. Живет старичок на каторге. Как следует, покоряется, худого не делает. Только у бога смерти просит. – Хорошо. […]	And so, brother mine […], ten years or more go by after this affair. The old man lives at hard labor. Duly submits, does nothing bad. Only asks God for death. Good. […]	So, listen, brother… […] After this a dozen years or more goes by. The old man is still a convict. Resigned to 'is fate, 'e is, as is only right. Never does nothin' wrong. The only thing 'e prays to God for is death… Right then… […]

Karataev's story is a sample of one of the two types of *skaz* narration as defined by Iu. Tynianov, B. Eikhenbaum, and V. Vinogradov (see, for example, Vinogradov 1980, 49, 54). This type of *skaz* represents a literary character's individualized direct speech imitating the style of an epic poem or folkloric discourse that is distinct from the authorial narrative style. *Skaz* has its distinctive lexical, grammatical, and stylistic properties organized by the author/narrator—whether intentionally or unconsciously—in ways to produce a certain intellectual, emotional, or esthetic impact on the reader. Different readers and translators may perceive the effects of *skaz* narration in different ways. Some translators may be oblivious to the often hidden special effects of *skaz* or consciously avoid rendering the culture-specific elements of *skaz* either in order not to disrupt the smooth flow of their translation or in the belief that the elements from which *skaz* is constructed are untranslatable. However, a good translation has to accommodate, if only partially, the style and purport of *skaz*.

 Realia (the plural of *realium*) is a well-established term in translation studies (*realiia, -ii* in Russian) that is usually defined as discrete, culture-specific lexical items (more rarely, sentences—proverbs, popular sayings, etc.) that have no equivalents in the translating language (see Vlakhov and Florin 2006). I am putting forward a new, additional conception of realium involving a whole distinct and autonomous part of a narrative. I submit that Karataev's story—and *skaz* in general—is a special type of realium operating at the level of text (i.e., it is a whole-text realium).

Strategies of Translating *Skaz*

The methods of translating individual lexical realia may be grouped under the following five general headings: (1) neutralization, (2) domestication (naturalization), (3) foreignization, (4) contamination, and (5) stylization. I submit that the same methods can be used in translating *skaz* as a whole-text realium.

(1) Neutralization

There is a general tendency among translators to appropriate the speaking narrator's text and make it more neutral stylistically or more logical. They are driven by a subconscious urge to explain and neutralize in order to turn out a well-ordered product. As Rachel May puts it, "the translator appears not to trust the narrator-reader communication to work. [...] Editors and readers [also] look to the translator [...] for some sense of authority and clarity. [...] Thus, the translator is supposed to convey more authority than the author while possessing far less" (1994, 84–85). This tendency often leads to what Kornei Chukovskii called "blandscript" (*gladkopis'*)—insipid, pale, and trivial translations that obfuscate the original author's individual style and different narrative voices. In other words, neutralization is a reader-oriented strategy generally consisting in substituting neutral-style lexical items and smoothly-flowing syntax for any irregular, unusual, or socioculturally-driven language used by the author. Although translators should do their best to harmonize rather than neutralize different voices in a literary work, resorting to neutralization is often unavoidable.

(2) Domestication/Naturalization

Domestication (or naturalization) is also a reader-oriented approach that may be viewed as a variety of neutralization taken to its limits. Domestication involves pragmatic modifications of the target text caused by the culture-specific elements of the source text in an attempt to make the translation sound natural to the intended readership. Lawrence Venuti defines domestication as a translation strategy involving "an ethnocentric reduction of the foreign text to target-language cultural values" (1995, 20). He believes that domestication dominates Anglo-American translating culture. While accepting domestication as a legitimate translation technique, I believe that it should be used cautiously because it may lead to pragmatic deformations of the original in the target text. For example, the Russian phrase *ekhat' v Tulu so svoim samovarom* (literally, "to bring your own samovar to Tula") can be translated as "to take/carry coals to Newcastle"; or the phrase *stat' zhertvoi chernogo piara* (literally, "to become a victim of black PR") can be translated as "to be swift-boated." These are reader-oriented solutions and they are fine, but they do produce networks of purely British or American cultural references and associations, of which the Russian originators of the two sentences or their readers would be totally unaware.

(3) Foreignization

Foreignization is the opposite of domestication. In Venuti's words, the foreignizing method is "an ethnodeviant pressure on [target-language cultural] values to register the linguistic and cultural differences of the foreign text, sending the reader abroad" (quoted in May 1994, 147). In simpler terms, foreignization involves literal translations, word-for-word translations (calques), transcriptions-cum-transliterations, or insertions into the translated text of words and phrases of the source language without translating them. This is done to evoke local color and thereby bring the receivers of the translation closer to the culture of the original. This is a text-oriented strategy. Extreme cases of foreignization can frequently be heard, for example, on Russian television. I can easily imagine the mental confusion of an old Russian lady living in a village to the east of the Ural Mountains when she hears the punch line of the Wrigley's Spearmint chewing gum commercial on Russian television that goes: "Rigly spirmint dzhusy frut—kul'ny chuing-gum!" That is foreignization gone over the top—even that of the Ural Mountains. Having said that, I agree with Rachel May—especially with reference to translating *skaz*—who says, "If we persist in believing that a reader should not be able to tell that she is reading a translation, then we […] remove one of the main reasons to produce or read translations in the first place: the chance to glimpse another culture. […] Stylistic methods, such as *skaz* […], may […] be as culturally significant as *borshch*, and therefore just as worthy of a certain degree of departure from 'normal' English" (109).

(4) Contamination

Linguistic contamination of the target text involves the use of recognizable so-called substandard modes of expression in the target text in order to signal the presence of substandard language in the source text. Contamination is often a compensatory strategy involving different elements of the source and target languages. This displacement is caused by the lack of parallelism in the perceived deviations from the prevalent conventions in the two languages. Excessive contamination jars on the linguistic and cultural sensibilities of the reader. Numerous instances of linguistic contamination used as a domesticating device can be found in Briggs's translation of the excerpt under discussion (see Appendix 1).

(5) Stylization

Stylization is often used as an umbrella term subsuming different translation techniques or strategies. I define stylization as the naturalization, domestication, foreignization, contamination, modernization, and archaization of a source text—undertaken selectively and in different combinations—with the aim of accommodating the regional, temporal, sociolectal, professional, or authorial modes of speech of the original in the target text. Arguably, the enumerated strategies of translating individual realia and *skaz* narration are extensions and aspects of one another. In some cases, however, it is useful to define the kind of stylization used more specifically. For example, historical stylization—which may be viewed as a type of naturalization—involves archaizing (aging) and modernizing the target text. This usually involves a selective adaptation of contemporary language to signal an outdated style rather than trying to reproduce the original outdated language of a period with all of its cultural-historical implications that are mostly lost on the translator and the target audience.[2] *Skaz* is a type of stylized narrative in the source text, and it is even more so in the target text.

The two translations I am examining show different extents to which the five strategies that I have outlined have been used (see Appendix 1). The first two paragraphs of the excerpt introduce the story, and paragraphs 3 and 5 represent a variety of *skaz* narration, or what may be called in this case a stylized sociolect.

My Analysis and Evaluation of the Two Translations

My impression following a careful study of the two translations—and it may be a purely subjective one—is that little, if any, effort was made to follow a clearly defined methodology of translation: It seems that the translators approached and executed their task intuitively. While admitting that intuition and epiphany are significant factors in the art of literary translation, I firmly believe that translation is also a scientific procedure that is supposed to lead to some predictable or at least generally expected results. I submit that the first stage in the process of translating embedded *skaz* narration is for the translator to develop an informed idea of the intellectual, esthetic, linguistic, and pragmatic effect that the *skaz* segment of the source (original) text may conceivably have on its "indigenous" (source) audience. The translator should then use a variety of linguistic means and translation strategies to produce a translation that would have an effect on the target ("foreign") audience comparable to that of the original. At the best of times, the sought-after effect will necessarily be—to a larger or lesser extent—subjective and elusive. How-

---

[2] See the excellent description of this translation strategy in Lanchikov and Meshalkina (2008).

ever, without conceptualizing or internalizing it in advance, the translator is on a wild goose chase from the word "go."

Let us have a closer look at some specific means that were employed in producing the two translations under discussion. Pevear and Volokhonsky's prevalent approach to translating the excerpt in question is to stylize by foreignizing through literal translation of significant segments of the text. Their translation throws into relief the peculiarities of Russian language usage—as compared to that of English—by reproducing some of the grammar (tenses and syntax) and some of the imagery of the original. As a result the syntax is in places disjointed, the sequence-of-tenses rule (back-shifting tenses in a narrative of past events) is not observed, the way it would not be in standard Russian usage, and the overall impression is somewhat jarring, i.e., the level of neutralization and domestication is not high.

The overriding translation strategy that Briggs uses is stylization through domestication with strong contamination of the target text with elements of substandard grammar and vocabulary. There seem to be no deviations from the suggested imitation of British lower-class sociolect that might have been induced by the peculiarities of Russian usage: namely, the sequence-of-tenses rule is fully observed—in fact, the historic present tense is used throughout; the level of literalism is low; and, finally, most of the stretches of language in the Russian original that, if translated literally, might jar on the native speaker's linguistic sensibilities have been neutralized (or naturalized).

From the perspective of its general pragmatic effect, the strong point of the Briggs translation is that it is cohesive and effective in conveying the social status of the speaker and the general mood of the episode. It also provokes considerable sympathy and compassion on the part of the reader. But the translation is overly contaminated and domesticated, producing a network of cultural references that exist only in the target culture. Tolstoy's individual language style does not come through.

From the same perspective, the strong point of the P/V translation is that it gets across some idea of the earthiness and certain inelegancies and "angularity" of Tolstoy's style and thus brings the reader closer to the Russian original. At the same time, their translation is, in places, too literal and does not always differentiate between natural Russian usage and the features of style typical of Tolstoy. This latter problem was first pointed out by Viktor Lanchikov and Michele Berdy in a large article about P/V's translations in the Russian translators' journal *Mosty* (Berdy and Lanchikov 2006). According to Lanchikov and Berdy, the distinctive feature of P/V's translations in general is that they tend to conflate intentionally or confuse unconsciously linguistic norm and accepted habitual language usage with what the two translators perceive as unique authorial features of style. As a result, standard, run-of-the-mill language usage that goes unnoticed in a Russian text sometimes comes through in the P/V translations as original turns of phrase, borderline grammar, or overt defamiliarization. Such parts of their translations intrude on the reader's consciousness, while their counterparts in the Russian text go unnoticed. The P/V translation of paragraph 3 of the excerpt provides some examples that seem to corroborate Lanchikov and Berdy's thesis (see Appendix 1). Thus, in parts of their translation, the sequence-of-tenses rule is disregarded. True enough, this rule is not always observed in English—and there are usually good reasons for that. By contrast, in Russian, this rule does not exist at all—so jumping from one temporal dimension to another is linguistically normal and does not draw any attention to itself. However, if imported into an English translation wholesale, this feature of Russian becomes salient (see paragraph 3 of the excerpt).

Another point: It is a general requirement of English grammar that a grammatical structure in English has to be complete. Russian is a synthetic language, with syntactic clues given by case and conjugation endings, whereas English is an analytic one, with syntactic structure being established by "formal" sentence elements such as "it," "there," the "impersonal 'they,'" passive constructions, etc. In other words, in English, structural clues are given by adding (or not leaving out) key words. In colloquial Russian, elliptical sentences without subjects are common and do not stand out. In English, ellipsis in a spoken style is also common, but it has to create a sense of structural completeness and unambiguity all the same. Even Mr. Jingle's telegraphic style of speech in Dickens's *Pickwick Papers*—which is Mr. Jingle's distinctive characteristic—adheres to the rule of sufficient structural completeness. In paragraph 3, we have elliptical sentences that immediately leap to the eye, so to speak, which they do not do in the Russian text. This is not Tolstoy's distinctive style, it is normal colloquial usage. P/V's literalism is evident in one more respect. Discourse markers or pragmatic connectors, like the Russian *"khorosho," "tak i tak, govorit," "znachit,"* and others (see paragraph 3), cannot always be translated literally as "good," "thus and so, he says," or "that is." In the Russian text, these are invisible and inaudible lubricants of colloquial narration. In the translation, they stand out. As do the forms of address "brother mine" and "little falcon," which are jarring literalisms (see paragraph 5).

Finally, a few words should be said about the relative lengths of the two translations. It is a well-known empirical fact that a translation from English into Russian tends to be longer than its original in terms of both pages and computer symbols by about 10–15 percent (see, for example, Ubin 2004, 44–45). It is as if the translator were unconsciously anxious not to leave anything out in the translation—not to "undertranslate." I call this phenomenon the "anxiety of undertranslation," to borrow Harold Bloom's phrasal formula. Conversely, a translation from Russian into English tends to be somewhat shorter than its Russian original. But not always. My observation of translation practice has convinced me that the more domesticated or "naturalized" the translation, the higher its word count. The two translations under review confirm this purely formal observation. The length of the Pevear/Volokhonsky translation is 696 words as compared to the 518 of the Russian original, whereas Briggs's translation is 809 words. Briggs's wordier translation is caused, in part, by his domesticating strategy of using repetitions or "echo structures" to imitate a British English non-educated colloquial style.

Survey

I conducted a five-stage semester-long survey in my translation class of twelve undergraduates aged 18–22[3] in which they first had to read Pevear and Volokhonsky's and Briggs's translations without seeing the original or being told that these were translations and assess the quality and style of the language in the two passages by responding to the following questions:

1. How does the passage read? Does it read smoothly or did you "trip over" certain stretches of language, i.e., do any double-takes?
2. Underline and number in the text the words, phrases, or sentences that sound strange to your ear. Specify in what sense you find them strange.

There was a three-week break between the readings of the two translations. At this stage of the survey, I wanted to find out what vocabulary, grammar, and stylistic features of the translations would strike 18- to 22-year-old American students as unusual English. I needed this input to get a sense of the extent of foreignization and the translators' success in conveying the style of the excerpt as felt by young Americans today. In Appendix 1, the stretches of language which the students found problematic are italicized in the English translations, and selected illustrative examples of different translation strategies are underlined and specified by abbreviation.

I should emphasize very strongly at this point that this survey lays no claim whatsoever to sociological validity. Its sample is a relatively random and accidental group of respondents, and, therefore, it is unrepresentative; the questions are open-ended and so the answers to them are difficult to process in a scientific way; and, finally, the fact that the students were asked the same questions about the same two translations at regular intervals was, very likely, a basis for contaminating or interfering with the way they responded in stages 2–5 of the survey. However, if the four-week discussion of the new translation of *War and Peace* by Richard Pevear and Larissa Volokhonsky in the pages of the *New York Times* from 14 October to 9 November 2007[4] is

---

[3] Eight of the students in my translation class of twelve were native speakers of American English (NSA) after four years of studying Russian from scratch and four were Russian heritage students (RHS) who have spent variously from seven to eleven years of their lives in the USA.

[4] See the Web site of *The New York Times*, 14 October 2007, http://www.nytimes.com/2007/10/14/books/review/Pevear-t.html?pagewanted=all&_r=0; and *The New York Times*, "Reading

anything to go by, then my little experiment should not be judged too harshly but looked at for what it is—just an instructional activity set up to teach elements of literary translation and translation analysis. It should also be noted in passing that in the course of the online discussion of the new translation of *War and Peace* in the *New York Times*, more than half of the respondents did not know Russian, and even the limited number of those who did bothered only rarely to compare the translation with its original.

So what did my students think of the "readability" of the two English translations of an excerpt from a world-renowned Russian classic? Interestingly and intriguingly, the students' collective reactions to the styles of the two translations—with minor differences—were practically mirror images of each other: in the first stage of the survey, eight students found the P/V text stilted and not flowing smoothly, while in the second stage of the survey, eight students thought it was the Briggs translation that did not read or flow smoothly. In both cases the wording of the responses was practically identical (and that may well have been the result of the responses in the first stage of the survey contaminating the second stage of the survey). The responses to both passages can be summarized as follows:

1. The text doesn't flow smoothly—it is "choppy," "clunky," "jagged," and "stilted."
2. The text contains some unusual turns of phrase and strange syntax. The sequence-of-tenses rule is broken in some places.

In the third and fourth stages of my survey—also conducted with a three-week break—I aimed to establish the extent of the translators' success in conveying the author's intended positive emotional effect of the parable as a whole-text realium. The students had to answer the following questions:

1. What is your impression of Platon Karataev—the narrator of the parable? What kind of person does he seem to you? How would you define his social status? What attitude have you formed toward him after reading the passage? Can you summarize (very briefly) his philosophy of life? Is it the kind of philosophy you feel you might share or is it alien to you?
2. What associations (with particular people, ideas, moods, emotions, etc.) does the text conjure up in your mind? Does the passage evoke any particular emotion/s in you that you could define?

To be more specific, I wanted to find out if Karataev's delivery of the story and the parable itself would make present-day American readers interested in

Room: Conversations about Great Books," 9 November 2007, http://readingroom.blogs.nytimes.com/tag/Tolstoy/.

and/or moved by Karataev's perceived philosophy of life as expressed through the story about the two merchants. It will be remembered that Karataev accepts the harsh realities and cruel ironies of life calmly and unflinchingly while managing at the same time to preserve infinite humility, piety, compassion, and gentleness toward everyone with whom he comes into contact. Karataev's attitude to life provides Pierre Bezukhov with an ideological and emotional anchor as well as a sense of salvation. It should be noted in passing that in the text of the novel Tolstoy himself clearly describes the overall positive, life-asserting effect of Karataev's story on Bezukhov (see, for example, Tolstoy 1963, 179). Would similar sentiments come through in the translation as read by young Americans today? I wanted to arrive at some kind of "empathy"–"indifference"–"antipathy" curve.

The Survey's Empathy–Indifference–Antipathy Curve

According to the reactions of my students after reading the two translations of the excerpt without seeing the Russian text, the authorial purport of the passage, i.e., an attempt to arouse empathy in the reader, seems to have been somewhat more successfully conveyed by the P/V translation—five students, including two Russian heritage students (RHS), felt empathetic toward P/V's translation as opposed to three students, including two RHS, in regard to the Briggs translation. There was also just one indifferent student (a native speaker of American English—NSA) in regard to P/V's translation, but five students, including one RHS, in regard to Briggs's translation. Six students (including two RHS) were critical of the parable's philosophy as conveyed by P/V's translation and four students (including one RHS) who were critical, based on the Briggs translation. The students' responses to the pragmatics of the two translations can be more graphically represented with the help of the following table:

P/V:		Briggs:	
5 (incl. 2 RHS)	+	3 (incl. 2 RHS)	+
1 (NSA)	– / +	5 (incl. 1 RHS)	– / +
6 (incl. 2 RHS)	–	4 (incl. 1 RHS)	–

The students' prevailing opinion about the Karataev of both passages can be summarized as follows: Karataev comes across as "some kind of religious preacher" or "fanatic," and while the general idea of facing the harsh realities of life stoically is appealing, Karataev's and the old merchant's religious humility is not. The students who felt empathy said that the text was sad, that the philosophy of the parable helped one attain inner peace, and that it made one more aware of the injustices of life. Some of the indifferent students made no comments, others said that Karataev was "a very simple man," still others did not feel emotionally moved in any way and felt that Karataev was just a "seasoned old guy," and somebody said that the text lacked any mystical quality. The critically-minded referred to Karataev as "a country bumpkin," said that he had an ironic and pessimistic view of life, which they could not share, felt alienated toward the philosophy of life encapsulated in the parable, or believed that the merchant's and Karataev's religiosity was excessive—this from a religious student.

There were some amusing, imaginative, and insightful comments in the students' response papers, illustrating the open-endedness of the text and the extent to which the reader's general background knowledge and awareness of a wider context of the text come into play in the course of the reader's inter-action with the text. Here is a sample of such comments (and let's be tolerant of some obviously naïve and immature responses), with the translations com-mented upon indicated by the names of their authors in parentheses:

"It was hard for me to tell who was speaking: the author, the narrator, or characters in the story." (P/V)

"Karataev sounds like he's hiding something, like he doesn't want to tell something to the other prisoners." (P/V)

"We don't know much about Karataev. He may well be the murderer of the rich merchant, who managed to escape justice somehow, and is now seeking redemption by telling the story over and over again and identifying himself with the old merchant in the story." (Briggs)

"Karataev's language and style seem to appeal to the quintessential notion of an old grandfatherly type given to didactic lectures. He comes across as the quintessential old man seeking to educate the lis-teners through moralistic tales, the likes of whom you might meet on a park bench." (P/V)

"Karataev sounds like a low-class redneck. The text makes me feel like I'm in an old wooden shack somewhere out in the mountains." (Briggs)

"It [the text] would be more intelligible if it were not so stylized and were a bit closer to standard English. I found this passage to be drudg-ery." (Briggs)

"The passage is like something out of a Dickens novel." (Briggs)

"Karataev's way of telling the story is similar to southern colloquial speech." (Briggs)

"Karataev sounds like a pirate or an Irishman. I felt like I was reading a pirate's tale. […] His linguistic skills are terrible." (Briggs)

"It reminds me of stories about slaves telling stories about how other slaves ran away or were suffering unfairly." (Briggs).

"Karataev speaks like a Cockney, and this immediately marks the passage as British." (Briggs)

Which Is the "Better" Translation?

At the end of the semester, in stage 5 of the experiment, the students were asked to express their general preference for either of the two translations and substantiate their choice in writing. This time they were given the Russian original alongside the two translations. Nine students out of twelve expressed a clear preference for the translation by Pevear and Volokhonsky; two students—native speakers of American English—for the Briggs translation; and one student—also a native speaker of English, who has a partial British background—was undecided and wrote: "If I were reading for pleasure, I believe I'd like the Briggs version. However, if I were feeling picky about accuracy, I'd choose the Pevear and Volokhonsky version. Honestly, it really just depends on my mood." One of the two students who clearly preferred Briggs's translation wrote in part with regard to P/V's translation: "To be honest, when I first read, 'And what do you think, little falcon?' I really pictured an Indian chief telling a story to another Indian. 'Little Falcon' sounds like the name a Native American would use."

In addition to surveying my students, I have also tested the two translations on some of my colleagues—native speakers of American English. All of them are versed in literary traditions other than Russian, so they did not read the Russian original. On condition of strict anonymity, three of them expressed their immediate impressions of the two translations of the excerpt as follows:

1. "Briggs's translation sounds like a Cockney from the East End of London."
2. "Briggs's translation reads like the soundtrack of the *Pirates of the Caribbean* movies."
3. "The P/V translation puts me in mind of a southern redneck."

What about myself? What kind of general emotional-esthetic effect do the two translations have on me—someone who has been reading *War and Peace* since childhood? I must admit that both translations of the passage make me empathize with both Platon Karataev's and the old merchant's life philosophies to a greater extent than was the case with my students. But, of course, my attitude has been predetermined by my age, my experience of the novel, and my being a product of Russian culture. In this respect, the translators faced the intractable pragmatic problem of negotiating the two different national characters, mentalities, mindsets—or whatever we may call it—as well as the temporal and cultural gap between the source and target texts. The Russian early 19th-century contemplative, fatalistic, and religion-based attitude to life had to be somehow made conceivable to present-day readers. Proceeding solely from the passage itself, without the benefit of the wide context of the whole novel, my informants were somewhat disoriented. In spite of that, their reactions showed that, on the whole, the P/V translation—as regards its general effect—was accepted in a somewhat more favorable way. The main reason for the general preference seems to be that the P/V translation is not overloaded with culture-specific dialectal elements and as a result the Russian peasant-soldier Karataev does not sound in the P/V translation like somebody from the lower classes of English society. In other words, judging from my students' responses, Pevear and Volokhonsky seem to have done a better job of translating the parable as a whole-text realium owing to their more aggressive foreignizing and literalizing of the original. My past experience also suggests that the students' preference may have been influenced, to a significant extent, by the fact that native speakers of the American variety of English had to compare a translation executed in American English with a translation done in British English. I suspect that an audience consisting of native speakers of British English might well prefer Briggs's translation.

A rather tentative conclusion that I personally have arrived at over the years and that seems to have been confirmed by the present casual survey is that if the source text and its translation or translations are compared by someone who knows the two languages but is not a totally or nearly bilingual professional translator, then the preference will, likely, be given to the translation that contains a greater number of more formal textual correspondences to the original. A totally or nearly bilingual professional translator making comparative evaluations of translations would tend to be more discerning, i.e., less prone to endorse literalism and more careful in weighing each instance of possible domestication or foreignization as compared to a semi-professional. A case in point is the preference of my students for the P/V translation, which may well have been determined by the contrast between a somewhat stilted text that is recognizable as a translation seemingly close to the original text and an overly domesticated and contaminated translation that is reminiscent of London's East End Cockneys or 18th-century pirates of the Caribbean.

My Own Translation of Paragraph 3

I think it would be appropriate for me at this point to go for a difficult balancing act myself and offer my own alternative translation of paragraph 3. In my translation below, selected markers of *skaz* are italicized in the Russian original, and selected illustrative examples of translation strategies used to convey a sense of *skaz* are also italicized and indicated by the following abbreviations: neut. (neutralization), dom. (domestication), for. (foreignization), contam. (contamination), and styl. (stylization).

3] И вот, *братец ты мой* (→ neut., styl.) (на этом месте Пьер застал рассказ Каратаева), проходит тому делу годов десять или больше того. Живет старичок на каторге. Как *следовает*, покоряется, худого не делает. Только у бога смерти просит. – *Хорошо* (→ styl., dom.). И соберись они, ночным делом, каторжные-то, так же вот как мы с тобой, и старичок с ними. И зашел разговор, кто за что страдает, в чем богу виноват. Стали сказывать, тот душу загубил, тот две, тот поджег, тот беглый, *так ни за что* (→ contam.). Стали старичка спрашивать: ты за что, мол, дедушка, страдаешь? Я, братцы мои миленькие, говорит, за свои да за людские грехи страдаю. А *я ни душ не губил* (→ contam.), ни чужого не брал, *акромя что* (→ neut.) *нищую братию оделял* (→ neut.). Я, братцы мои миленькие, купец; и богатство большое имел. *Так и так, говорит. И рассказал им, значит, как все дело было, по порядку* (→ neut.). Я, говорит, о себе не тужу. Меня, значит, бог сыскал. Одно, говорит, мне свою старуху и *деток* (→ styl., contam.) жаль. И так-то заплакал старичок. Случись в их компании тот самый человек, значит, что купца убил. Где, говорит, дедушка, было? Когда, в каком месяце? все расспросил. Заболело у него сердце. *Подходит таким манером к старичку – хлоп в ноги* (→ neut.). За меня ты, говорит, старичок, пропадаешь. *Правда истинная* (→ dom., styl.); безвинно напрасно, говорит, *ребятушки* (→ neut.), человек этот мучится. Я, говорит, то самое дело сделал и нож тебе под голова́ сонному положил. Прости, говорит, дедушка, меня ты ради Христа.

"And so, *my dear brother* (neut., styl.)" (at this point Pierre came in on Karataev's story), "ten or more years go by. The poor old man serves his time. He duly submits and does nothing wrong. The only thing he asks God for is death. *Bless his soul* (styl., dom.). And they got together one night—the convicts did, just like you and me here, and the old man with them. And they got to talking about who was in for what and who was guilty of what before the Lord. Each told his story: this one killed one man, another killed two, another was in for arson, and still another was a runaway, so *he hadn't done nothing* (contam.). And they asked the old man: 'What are you suffering for, grandpa?' 'I, my dear brothers,' he says, 'am suffering for my own and other people's sins. I *didn't kill nobody* (contam.) and I didn't take anything that wasn't mine—*on the contrary* (neut.), I *gave to the poor* (neut.). I, my dear brothers, used to be a merchant, and I had great wealth.' *And so he told them how it all happened* (neut.). And then he says, 'I don't grieve over myself.' 'God,' he says, 'has found me.' 'I only pity,' he says, 'my old woman and *the little 'uns'* (styl., contam.). And the old man wept bitterly. And it just so happened that in their company was the very same man that had killed the merchant. 'Where did it happen, grandpa?' he asked. 'When, in what month?'—he asked to know every detail. And his heart ached. *So he went up to the old man and dropped at his feet* (neut.). 'You're perishing because of me, old man. *It's God's own truth* (dom., styl.). This man is suffering, *brothers* (neut.),' he says, guiltlessly and needlessly. I did that deed,' he says, 'and put the knife under your pillow while you slept. Forgive me, grandpa,' he says, 'for the love of God.'"

In my translation, I pursued moderate domestication (naturalization) by avoiding overt regionalisms and literalisms, while having in mind an audience whose native language is American English or a more general English-speaking audience.

Speaking of translating fiction and, in particular, poetry, the poet Vladimir Gandel'sman said that "translation is an art of [justifiable] imprecision" (2008). Rather wrenchingly, he warns against literalism in translating fictional texts by using a somewhat gruesome metaphor in the form of the following quatrain:

Он тем страшнее, чем точней,	The more precise the translation—the more harrowing it is,
Поскольку труп уже ходячий,	Because precision turns it into a walking corpse;
Неточный – все же труп лежачий,	An imprecise translation is like a corpse lying down,
А это несколько родней	And we're somewhat more used to corpses that don't walk.
	(My unrhymed prose translation)

I agree in general that translators should always be on their guard against literalism. However, a certain degree of literalism or foreignization may be—and sometimes unavoidably is—a useful means in translating stretches of language constituting *skaz*. As for my overall approach to translating *skaz*, it can be summed up as follows: I first identify the embedded *skaz*-like segment of the text which in my view constitutes a distinct realium-like semantic, syntactic, stylistic, and pragmatic unit of the whole text subordinated to some authorial purpose, which may range from the definitely positive to the definitely negative evaluation of the situation that is being described; second, I try to self-analyze my emotional and aesthetic reaction to the text and try to decide for myself whether that reaction was the original authorial purport of the text (this is a purely subjective interaction with the text); having established for myself the perceived implicatures of the *skaz*-segment of the text, I analyze the linguistic means that the author used to achieve them; and finally, I decide on a specific combination of the five translation strategies I have outlined in order to convey the author's perceived intent. The choice of the strategies and linguistic means is also determined by my considered assumptions about the prospective readership's general background knowledge and expectations from the text. In other words, it is not at all necessary to try to translate all of the individual realia in the *skaz* section of the narrative so long as the intended overall effect of *skaz* as a whole-text realium supposedly comes through in the target text. The results of this methodology are exemplified in the translation above.

Concluding Remarks

Practice and theory are convincing proof that there will always be as many different translated versions of the same text as there are translators. Translators will constantly be forced to make compromise decisions based on their interpretation of the source text and their determination of its expected reception by the cultural Other. Translation is always interpreting, and, in the words of Umberto Eco, "interpreting means making a bet on the sense of the text [...]. This sense that a translator must find—and preserve, or recreate—is not hidden in any pure language, neither a divine *reiner Sprache* nor any Mentalese. It is just the outcome of an interpretative inference that can or cannot be shared by other readers. In this sense a translator makes a *textual abduction*" (2001, 16). It should be remembered, however, that any such abduction has its consequences. Kornei Chukovskii firmly believed that "translators always have the opportunity of reproducing a few—true, not all—peculiarities of colloquial speech, of extraliterary language, and consequently, the matter is not at all as hopeless as it seems" (1984, 136). For Chukovskii, translation was a high art, in practicing which "it is impossible to apply sweeping rules [...]. Precisely because it is a matter of art, such rules do not generally exist. There are no universal recipes here. Everything depends on individual circumstances. In the final analysis the fate of a translation is always decided by the translator's talent, his cultural level, his taste, his tact" (141).

Chapter 4

Translating *Skaz* as a Whole-Text Realium: From *Skaz* to Swaggering Pizzazz (English-to-Russian)

> Each epoch deserves the translation that it either tolerates or admires.
> — Ivan Kashkin[1]

J. D. Salinger's short novel, or novella, *The Catcher in the Rye* (1951), has been on the required reading lists in American high schools for the last half-century or so. It is an integral part of the American literary canon. Since it first appeared in Russian translation in the *Inostrannaia literatura* (Foreign Literature) literary journal in 1960,[2] the novel has also been very popular in the Soviet Union and now Russia.

Three "Catchers in the Rye": From Ideology to "Cool-Dude-Speak"

There are three available and easily accessible Russian translations of *The Catcher in the Rye*: the first—a "canonical" one—is by Rita Rait-Kovaleva (1960), the second is by Maksim Vladimirovich Nemtsov (2008), and the third—by Iakov Kalmanovich Lotovskii (2010). *The Catcher in the Rye* is a first-person, "unreliable narrator" story told by a troubled, 17-year-old youth, Holden Caulfield, the main character, from some sort of a sanatorium or psychiatric facility, where he finds himself after having a nervous breakdown. The story is a *skaz*-like description of Holden Caulfield's three-day "odyssey" that takes him from his Pencey Prep school in Pennsylvania, from which he is expelled for failing academically, through New York, where he spends some time psyching himself up to return home and face his parents, to the specialized institution from which he is telling his story.

The reasons for Rita Rait-Kovaleva's choosing this particular novel to translate, as well as the "official" reasons why a major Soviet literary journal selected it for translation are obscure. It may be that following the official acceptance of Hemingway as a "progressive-minded" modern author, the Soviet literary establishment was looking for another "progressive" American writer with a skeptical view of the American way of life. Maksim Nemtsov

---

[1] Quoted in Kornei Chukovskii's *Vysokoe iskusstvo* (1966, 524)

[2] *Inostrannaia literatura*, no. 11 (November 1960).

does not give any reasons for his retranslation either in his blog or in his interviews, but an analysis of the pragmatic effects of his translation provides a good indication of what he has achieved in comparison with Rait-Kovaleva. As for Iakov Lotovskii, he explains in his translator's preface that, much as he admires Rait-Kovaleva's canonical translation, he offers his own version in order to correct some inaccuracies in the Rait-Kovaleva translation caused by Soviet censorship, the translator's isolation from the *realia* (culture-specific concepts) of the Western world, and her own aesthetic preferences.[3]

Before I get to the fundamental CTDA issues of this case study, I will get a relatively minor issue out of the way. Out of a sense of professionalism—and not by way of nit-picking criticism—I have to note that, despite the high quality of the three translations, Rait-Kovaleva, Nemtsov, and Lotovskii do commit occasional minor mistranslations of denotative and connotative meaning and culture-specific concepts (*realia*). For example, Rait-Kovaleva and Lotovskii translate *dinner* as "obed" (2010a, 9; 2010b, 5 respectively), where it is clear that an evening meal is meant (Nemtsov translates it correctly as "uzhin" [2008, 12]); both Rait-Kovaleva and Nemtsov mistranslate "were chucking a football around" (Salinger 1991, 4) as "goniali miach" (2010a, 9) and "miachik pinali" (2008, 12), where it is clear that Holden and his two friends were throwing an American football around (to each other)—they were not "kicking a ball around" as when playing soccer (Lotovskii gets it right by saying "perebrasyvalis' miachom" [2010b, 5]); Rait-Kovaleva is somewhat wide of the mark when she translates Holden's prep school's ad *Since 1888 we have been molding boys into splendid, clear-thinking young men* as "S 1888 goda v nashei shkole vykovyvaiut smelykh i blagorodnykh iunoshei" (2010a, 6), where her "smelykh i blagorodnykh" sounds more like "bold and noble" than "splendid," [and] "clear-thinking"; Nemtsov offers the somewhat awkward "S 1888 goda my lepim iz mal'chikov velikolepnykh zdravomyslia-shchikh iunoshei" (2008, 10), where the choice of "lepim" conjures up images of Play-Doh figurines and has a slightly pejorative connotation in Russian that is absent in the original, while Lotovskii has "S 1888 goda my formiruem blestiashchikh i blagorodnykh molodykh liudei" (2010b, 5), where it is still not clear where "blagorodnykh" (noble) has come from. There are other little mistranslations, but they are not a big issue: they do not skew the translations in any significant way, and, besides, to put it cynically, the readers of the translations would be oblivious to them unless they compared the original and its translations and knew the two languages and cultures well enough to draw any conclusions.

---

[3] For a more detailed rationale for Lotovskii's retranslation, see his translator's preface in Appendix 2.

For an initial comparative foretaste of how the three translators cope with Salinger's text, here are the first five sentences of the novel, with some distinctive characteristics of the original text and its translations underlined:[4]

J. D. Salinger (1951)
The Catcher in the Rye

If you really want to hear about it, the first thing you'll probably want to know is where I was born, and (1) what my lousy childhood was like, and how my parents were occupied (2) and all before they had me, and (3) all that David Copperfield kind of crap, but (4) I don't feel like going into it, if you want to know the truth. In the first place, that stuff bores me, and in the second place, my parents would have about two hemorrhages apiece if I told anything pretty personal about them. They're quite touchy about anything like that, especially my father. They're nice and all—I'm not saying that—but they're also touchy as hell. Besides, I'm not going to tell you my whole goddamn autobiography or anything. (1991, 1)

Рита Райт-Ковалева (1960)
Над пропастью во ржи

Если вам на самом деле хочется услышать эту историю, вы, наверно, прежде всего захотите узнать, где я родился, (1) как провел свое дурацкое детство, что делали мои родители до моего рождения (2 --), словом, (3) всю эту дэвид-копперфилд-овскую муть. Но, (4) по правде говоря, мне неохота в этом копаться. Во-первых, скучно, а во-вторых, у моих предков, наверно, случилось бы по два инфаркта на брата, если бы я стал болтать про их личные дела. Они этого тепеть не могут, особенно отец. Вообще-то они люди славные, я ничего не говорю, но обидчивые до чертиков. Да я и не собираюсь рассказывать свою автобиографию и всякую такую чушь […]. (2010a, 5)

Максим Немцов (1998)
Ловец на хлебном поле

Если по-честному охота слушать, для начала вам, наверно, подавай, где я родился и (1) что за погань у меня творилась в детстве, чего предки делали (2) и всяко-разно, пока не заимели меня, (3) да прочую Дэвид-Копперфилдову херню, (4) только не в жилу мне про все это трындеть, сказать вам правду. Во-первых, достало, во-вторых, предков бы по две кондрашки хватило, если бы я стал про них чего-

Яков Лотовский (2010)
Над пропастью во ржи

Если вы и в самом деле непрочь услышать обо всем об этом, вам сперва, наверно, захочется узнать из каких я мест, (1) как прошло мое сопливое детство, род занятий моих родителей (2 --) (3) и прочую муру в духе Давида Копперфильда. Но, (4) честно говоря, неохота в этом ковыряться. Во-первых, скучно, во-вторых, моих предков, наверно, хватил бы инфаркт, если б я стал трепаться

---

[4] For the full text of the first paragraph of the novel and its three translations, see Appendix 3.

нибудь личное излагать. Они насчет такого чувствительные, особенно штрик. Не, они *нормальные*, всяко-разно, я ничего не хочу сказать, но чувствительные, как не знаю что. А кроме того, так я вам и выложил всю автобиографию, ага. (2008, 9)

про их *личные дела*. Они у меня жутко осторожные насчет этого, особенно отец. Нет, родители прекрасные и все такое, никто ничего не говорит, но осторожные до предела. Короче, я не собираюсь излагать свою дурацкую автобиографию от и до. (2010b, 2)

A close reading of the three translations, and already the above passage, show that Nemtsov, Lotovskii, and, to a limited extent, Rait-Kovaleva, in fact "liven up" the original. This raises the question: What reasons do the translators have and to what extent are they warranted to enliven the original text by using language stylistically more marked than the language of the original? The other overarching characteristic of the original is that it is a whole-text *skaz*, evincing a clearly discernible recurrent set of stylistic devices used by Salinger to impersonate the narrative voice of Holden Caulfield, the first-person narrator. This, in turn, raises the question: To what extent has each translator succeeded in conveying this American version of *skaz* in the form of a first-person, whole-text *skaz* narrative in Russian? These are questions of translatorial pragmatics. In this chapter, I will attempt to answer these questions.

Defined very broadly, translation pragmatics is the tasks that the translator sets for himself or herself consciously or, in fact, fulfills unconsciously; it is the overall effect that he or she produces through the translation, oftentimes without realizing and/or admitting what he or she is doing. Each of the three translators pursues a pragmatics of their own, but Nemtsov and Lotovskii are closer to each other than either of them is to Rait-Kovaleva. As already mentioned, in the case of Rait-Kovaleva, we can see a mild tendency to liven things up through the choice of vocabulary and syntax. Rait-Kovaleva does tone down some coarse language in some places of Holden Caulfield's narrative, most likely in order to avoid the strictures of Soviet censorship and, presumably, to satisfy her own inner censor (at the time of translating she was a Soviet lady aged 62), but she compensates for that in other stretches of the text by resorting to what in Russian creative circles is called *ozhivliazh*, meaning enlivening or accentuating some features of an artistic object or activity. This is most likely done in order to emphasize—consciously or subconsciously—"the otherness" of the narrator, Holden Caulfield, who is a representative of "their" teenagers and who, therefore, speaks in a way ostensibly alien to that of the Soviet youth of the late 1950s and early 1960s. Without this "otherness," the Russian reader would mistrust the narrative while, without the toning down, the Russian censorship system would not have let the translation be published. That was the double bind Rait-Kovaleva had to operate in. And she acquitted herself remarkably well, especially given the fact that she had previously never been to an English-speaking country and the genre of street language was not at all encouraged and did not exist in officially printed Soviet publications. It was only with the arrival of *glasnost'* and *perestroika* in the late 1980s that youth slang rapidly began to become voguish and started to seep inexorably into mainstream literary publications.

So how exactly does *ozhivliazh* manifest itself in the three translations? As mentioned earlier, *ozhivliazh* (from the Russian *ozhivliat'*—to make more lively or to bring [back] to life) means enlivening or "sexing up" the text of the translation, as compared with the original, through use of stylistic devices. I submit that a "sexing-up" trend has become quite prominent in Russian translations of American texts in the last quarter-century and deserves a comprehensive sociolinguistic evaluation. The seeds of *ozhivliazh* were sown by the Kashkintsy group of translators already in the 1930s (see chapter 1). As shown earlier, *ozhivliazh* manifests itself in the text of a translation in the form of its semantic, syntactic, and pragmatic parameters. Syntactically *ozhivliazh* is embodied in more emphatic sentence structures; semantically, it is realized through the choice of words; and pragmatically, it involves the whole of the text from the perspective of how its receivers react to it. The most noticeable "bearer" of text enhancement is vocabulary. I have already discussed this in some detail in chapters 1 and 2. By way of a reminder, a vocabulary item—a word or a phrase used in a text—is usually perceived as either emotionally neutral (not expressing or implying any emotion) or as expressing a certain (1) emotion, (2) the extent of that emotion, and, quite often (3) an implied or overt evaluative judgment (an attitude of the speaker toward what is being said). Besides these properties, a particular expression belongs to a more or less clearly felt (4) functional style (or register)—from neutral to poetic at one extreme and from neutral to vulgarly obscene at the other. The expression may also belong to a (5) regional, social, or age-specific (temporal) dialect, (6) enjoy a more or less clearly felt frequency of occurrence in a particular register, and (7) conjure up more or less similar associations—as assumed by the translator—in the minds of the receiver of the original text and the receiver of its translation(s).

An experienced translator is usually able to convey the basic denotative meaning (the cognitive, dictionary word sense) accurately; it is the connotative elements of word senses indicated above that prove quite intractable or plain invisible, depending on the level of expertise or professionalism of the translator. I will now briefly illustrate the concepts I have introduced and the extent of *ozhivliazh* or non-*ozhivliazh*, using examples from the three translations of *The Catcher in the Rye*.

Holden Caulfield: "Anyway, I kept standing next to that <u>crazy</u> cannon, looking down at the game and <u>freezing my ass off</u>" (Salinger 1991, 4). Rait-Kovaleva translates this sentence like this: "Slovom, stoial ia u etoi <u>duratskoi</u> pushki, <u>chut' zad ne otmorozil</u>" (2010a, 8–9). The intensity of the emotion expressing discontent and discomfort in "chut' zad ne otmorozil" (literally: "I almost froze my backside off") is perceptibly lower than that of "freezing my ass off," and the choice of "zad" ("backside" in Russian) to translate *ass* is arguably dictated by Rait-Kovaleva's fear of being castigated by her editors as vulgar and corrupting the crystal-clear morals of the contemporary Soviet youth. *Zad* is a colloquial-bordering-on-slang word that was marginally permissible in polite company in those times. In this instance, Rait-Kovaleva tones the coarse part of the narrative down.

By contrast, Nemtsov does not tone the idiom down; he chooses to use a more colloquial sentence structure and more slangy vocabulary in the rest of the sentence. He translates the sentence as follows: "Ladno, stoiu riadom s <u>dolbanutoi</u> pushkoi, gliazhu vniz, gde futbol idet, a <u>zhopa podmerzaet</u>" (2008, 12). In my perception as a native Russian speaker and sociolinguist, the word "zhopa" as a translation of *ass* sounds about right, especially today, although the phrase *zhopa podmerzaet* (literally, "The ass is getting somewhat frozen") is not a "smooth" idiom in Russian the way "freezing one's ass off" is in English. It is an example of a pragmatic inconsistency. *Dolbanutoi pushkoi* is slightly more emotionally charged in Russian than "crazy cannon" in English. Besides, Nemtsov's version of the sentence sounds a little more "staccato" or irregular than the standard syntax of the original sentence. The prosody of this single sentence could be further commented on but I think my illustration is sufficient. Lotovskii translates the same sentence in a spirit similar to Nemtsov's: "Koroche, stoial ia u etoi <u>duratskoi</u> pushki, smotrel na igru i <u>chut' zhopu ne otmorozil</u>" (2010b, 5). With their *chut' zhopu ne otmorozil* and *a zhopa podmerzaet*, respectively, Lotovskii and Nemtsov finish neck and neck. How would *I* translate it? I would suggest something like this: "Koroche, poka ia stoial u etoi grebanoi[5] pushki i smotrel, kak rebiata vnizu igraiut v futbol, ia chut' zhopu sebe ne otmorozil." It is another variant of a translation, if not an improvement.

As I have already pointed out, what Rait-Kovaleva tones down in one place she makes up for by jazzing the text up a little bit in other places. This is already noticeable in the opening sentences of the book quoted at the beginning of this chapter, and a "combing-through" of the whole of her translation shows that Rait-Kovaleva tends to somewhat "overfulfill" the reasonably expected quota of enlivened elements in her translation. Here is a random example of Rait-Kovaleva's penchant for mild *ozhivliazh*:

Salinger	Rait-Kovaleva
I remember around three o'clock that afternoon I was standing <u>way the hell up</u> on top of Thomsen Hill, right next to this crazy cannon that was in the	Помню, в тот день, часов около трех, я стоял <u>черт знает где</u>, на самой горе Томпсона (sic!), около дурацкой пушки, <u>которая там торчит</u>, кажется, с

[5] I use *grebanoi* here as an intensifier to convey the slangy intensity of "that crazy cannon."

Revolutionary War and all. (1991, 2)   самой войны за независимость. (2010a, 7)

Chert znaet gde (literally, "the devil knows where") and especially *kotoraia tam torchit* (roughly, "that has been a conspicuous fixture there") are obviously overcompensations for something the translator felt was lost in her translation elsewhere. The two phrases could arguably also be classified as a mild case of *otsebiatina* (from the Russian *from oneself*—"fromoneselfness")—the translator's not entirely justified or warranted additions to or recasting of the original content of the text.

I will complete tracing the trajectory of the trend of *ozhivliazh* in the three translations with the help of one final example:

Salinger	Rait-Kovaleva	Nemtsov	Lotovskii
And yet I still act sometimes like I was only about twelve. Everybody says that, especially my father. It's partly true, too, but it isn't *all* true. People always think something's *all* true. I don't give a damn, except that I get bored sometimes when people tell me to act my age [Salinger's italics]. (1991, 9)	И все-таки иногда я держусь, будто мне лет двенадцать. Так про меня все говорят, особенно отец. Отчасти это верно, но не совсем. А *люди всегда думают, что они тебя видят насквозь.* Мне-то наплевать, хотя тоска берет, когда тебя поучают – веди себя как взрослый. (2010a, 15)	Но я все равно иногда себя веду так, словно мне лет двенадцать. Это все говорят, особенно мой штрик. С одной стороны так и есть, только не *совсем.* Часто думают, будто что-то *совсем* бывает. Мне надристать, вот только достает иногда, если мне говорят, чтоб вел себя как полагается. (2008, 16)	И все равно веду себя иногда, будто мне лет двенадцать. Все это говорят, особенно отец. Отчасти это правда, но не вся. Люди всегда думают, что знают про тебя все. Мне-то начихать, просто бывает тошно, когда тебе твердят – веди себя, как взрослый. (2010b, 10)

Of the three above translations, Nemtsov's is the most "enlivened" due to his harshly slangy "shtrik" for *father*, harshly vulgar "mne nadristat'" (literally, "I don't give a runny shit") for *I don't give a damn*, and the slangily enhanced "dostaet" (something like "it gets my goat") for the neutral *I get bored*.

Lotovskii's version is practically "unenlivened," although "byvaet toshno" ("I sometimes feel nauseous/sick") is slightly more emotionally charged than the straightforward "I get bored." If I were translating this, I would use the arguably more common slang version "mne nachkhat'" instead of the somewhat literary "mne nach_i_khat'" for *I don't give a damn*. On the whole,

Lotovskii's version of this passage is very close in tone and style to that by Rait-Kovaleva, down to the slight mistranslation of the sentence *People always think something's* all *true*, where Holden Caulfield is making a general philosophical statement and not saying that people generally tend to believe that they see through him.

As for Rait-Kovaleva, the only perceptible enlivening in this extract is her translation of *I get bored* as "toska beret" (literally, "melancholy/ennui over-comes me").

It should be noted in passing that back-translations are not, of course, a perfect way to do a comparative analysis of translations but sometimes they do help to throw into relief some nuances that would otherwise go unnoticed by less linguistically proficient audiences.

The net result of this "original-in-hand," close comparative analysis of the three translations leads me to the following conclusions. Nemtsov has an ex-cessive tendency to liven things up, believing, it would seem, that the kind of language Rait-Kovaleva used in her translation would be too bland and alien to Russian Generation "Y." Lotovskii is not far behind, professedly fulfilling his goal of eliminating the "inaccuracies" in Rait-Kovaleva's translation.[6] Rait-Kovaleva signals the 1940–50s U.S. teenage slang (minus the coarsest turns of phrase) through creative stylization (slight deviations from the usual socialist realist style of writing) and mild foreignization. I submit that Rait-Kovaleva's translation follows the Kashkintsy's lead in creating a special field, or "zone" in Russian-language literary texts that became reserved specifically for Russian-style "Americanese"—the Russian "Amerikanskii" literary substyle. Although accepted by the Soviet literary establishment, this style of trans-lating was shaping up as a distinctive mode of verbal expression that was not exactly "ours" (*nash*—Soviet). In contrast to the mainstream writing of the time, it was subtly alluring, attractive, and voguish because, in an Aesopian sort of way, it half suggested the idea of freedom, the idea of democracy, the state of being able to say and do what you wanted to say and do in opposition to the totalitarian constraints of life and self-expression in the Soviet Union of the 1960s.

Rait-Kovaleva—most likely unbeknownst to herself—was developing the trend initiated by Vera Toper with her trend-setting translation of Heming-way's *Fiesta* (*The Sun Also Rises*) in 1935 and Evgeniia Kalashnikova with her translation of *A Farewell to Arms* in 1936; she was continuing to create an "Amerikanskii" substyle in Russian literature, which—even in its innocuous-ness—was already something marginally subversive, given the Cold War adversarial politics of the Soviet Union and the USA. She later stylistically developed and reinforced this emergent "American" sub-canon in Soviet lit-

---

[6] See his "Translator's Preface" at http://7iskusstv.com/2010/Nomer2/Lotovsky1.php.

erature in her translation of Kurt Vonnegut's *Breakfast of Champions* (1975) and other works.[7]

In his novel-in-notes *Solo na undervude* (Solo on an "Underwood"; 1980), Sergei Dovlatov[8] tells the following two anecdotes:

> At one time I was Vera Panova's[9] secretary. Vera Fedorovna once asked me, "Whose Russian is the best, do you think?" I probably should have answered, "Yours." But I said, "Rita Kovaleva's." [Panova]: "Who's this Rita Kovaleva?" [Dovlatov]: "Rait." [P]: "Would she be the one who translated Faulkner?" [P]: "Faulkner, Salinger, and Vonnegut." [P]: "So Faulkner sounds in Russian better than Fedin?"[10] [D]: "Without a doubt." Panova paused and said, "How terrible!"
>
> With reference to Vonnegut, there is this story about Gore Vidal. While visiting Moscow, he was reportedly asked by some fans of Vonnegut what he thought of Vonnegut's writing. "Kurt's novels are terribly inferior in the original to their translation..." was his response.[11]

Ivan Kashkin once famously remarked that "each epoch deserves the translation that it either tolerates or admires."[12] When Maksim Nemtsov and Iakov Lotovskii offered their retranslations of *The Catcher in the Rye*, in 2008 and 2010, respectively, it was as if they were channeling the zeitgeist of the "wild" 1990s and the 2000s. Nemtsov's and Lotovskii's translations came roughly two generations later than Rait-Kovaleva's. They no longer carry any ideological subtext or political implications that the Soviet-era Aesopian-language adepts would have uncovered and appreciated. In the era of the Internet, the Soviet-style "Aesopian language" and the need for its creation or decryption are, for all intents and purposes, dead. Any subversive implications that Nemtsov's or Lotovskii's translations might have would be lost on or irrelevant for Russian Generation "Y." Nor would present-day Russian youth be

---

[7] Rait-Kovaleva's other translations of Kurt Vonnegut that achieved cult status in the Soviet Union include *Kolybel' dlia koshki* (Cat's Cradle; 1963), *Dai vam Bog zdorov'ia, mister Rozuoter* (God Bless You, Mr. Rosewater; 1965), and *Boinia nomer 5* (Slaughterhouse-Five, or the Children's Crusade; 1969).

[8] Sergei Dovlatov (1941–90) was a Russian writer who lived and wrote in New York from 1979, when he emigrated there, to his death in 1990.

[9] Vera Fedorovna Panova (1905–73) was a famous Russian Soviet writer. For several years, Sergei Dovlatov was her private secretary.

[10] Konstantin Aleksandrovich Fedin (1892–1977) was a famous Russian Soviet novelist and literary functionary.

[11] The Russian text of *Solo na undervude* is available at http://lib.ru/DOWLATOW/dowlatow.txt.

[12] Ibid.

enticed by the relatively tame—although once perceived as "hot"—language of Rait-Kovaleva's translation. In the first decade of the new millenium, the "buzz" had to come from somewhere else. And it did come, largely in the form of "sexing up" the American original. The translators' pragmatics is stylization through harsh modernization and domestication; the two new translations are, in large part, executed in the sociolect of present-day young Russian speakers. Both translations exude an aura of undisguised *ozhivliazh*.

Nemtsov's translation of 2008 has created quite a stir in the Russian blogosphere. Numerous bloggers reacted in a very acrimonious way to Nemtsov's translation, comparing it with the canonical one by Rait-Kovaleva (Iakov Lotovskii's translation is as yet little known). The reactions split the online audience along generational lines. There are many defenders of the Rait-Kovaleva translation: after all, in addition to its distinctive style and perceived initial ideological subtext or message, it is also canonical because it has been read by at least three overlapping generations: the fathers and mothers of the 1960s, their sons and daughters of the 1990s, and their grandsons and granddaughters of the "Aughts." But the Rait-Kovaleva text is no longer a social rebel manifesto in "special Russian Americanese." Its ideology is gone. To Russian youth today Rait-Kovaleva's Holden Caulfield sounds tame; his quest for fairness and protest against "phoniness" need a punchier verbalization. Nemtsov's and Lotovskii's translations supply just that: they offer the American novel the chance to gain traction in new conditions owing to its "real cool-dude" kind of vernacular, a variety of Russian with which many Russians—and not necessarily teenagers—can identify. Lotovskii's translation is the more nostalgic one because he belongs to the generation that was able to be impressed by the implied rebelliousness of Rait-Kovaleva's text, and he himself admits as much in the preface to his translation. While giving no indication of being aware of Nemtsov's translation, Lotovskii has produced a version of a translation that tends to steer a middle course between Kovaleva's and Nemtsov's. The ideology has dissolved into a present-day Russian "cooldude kind of speak."

Three "Catchers in the Rye": From *Skaz* to Pizzazz

Skaz as a distinctive *embedded* narrative style of a literary character was already discussed in chapter 3, where I dealt with the different strategies of translating *skaz* into English by different translators of *War and Peace*. In this section, I will examine and illustrate the notion of *skaz* as a *whole-text* narrative technique by considering the ways *skaz* is dealt with in the three translations into Russian of *The Catcher in the Rye*.

By way of refreshing the reader's knowledge of this literary phenomenon, I will repeat here that the word *skaz* is of Russian origin; it literally means "a tale" and is derived from the Russian *skazat'* or *rasskazat'*, that is, "to say" or "to tell." *The Encyclopaedia Britannica* defines *skaz* as "a written narrative that imitates a spontaneous oral account in its use of dialect, slang, and the peculiar idiom by a particular persona."[13] The Russian *Concise Literary Encyclopedia* defines *skaz* as "a special type of narration by a specifically named or unnamed person dissociated from the author and possessing a distinctive manner of speaking."[14]

Those are very broad definitions but they should be sufficient for present purposes. How does *skaz* relate to Salinger's *The Catcher in the Rye*? *The Catcher in the Rye* is a first-person, unreliable-narrator, "spontaneously"-told story characterized by the narrator's distinctive choice and use in speech of the then contemporary youth sociolect, general slang, preferred idioms, digressions, illogicalities, tedious repetitions of "filler words" (or "parasite-words" as they are called in Russian), as well as occasional deviations from the linguistic norm (grammar and vocabulary "errors"). Holden Caulfield's speech peculiarities or preferences are not random—they comprise a unified system, the elements of which are consistently repeated throughout the narrative. This system of reprised stylistic devices constitutes what I submit is a "whole-text realium" that coincides with the whole authorial narrative, as opposed to embedded *skaz* (considered in chapter 3) that constitutes part of the authorial narrative—an import into the narrative of a stylized imitation of a character's oral speech. In other words, I argue here that *The Catcher in the Rye* is an example of an American kind of whole-narrative *skaz* that presents serious difficulties in translating into Russian. In this case, I consider the ways the three translations of the novel into Russian incorporate the translation-resistant components of *skaz* as one manifestation of the intricately composite cross-cultural "other." More specifically, the question I pose is "To what extent does each of the three translators of *The Catcher in the Rye* manage to convey this particular aspect of hard-to-convey 'otherness'?" Let us try to work this out.

Holden Caulfield's set of consistently used and clearly distinguishable linguistic and stylistic means (characteristic turns of phrase) is already deployed in the very first chapter of the novel.[15] The reader begins to recognize and anticipate Holden's trademark "cool-guy" manner of speaking already after the first chapter, and this quality is consistently maintained from the very first to the very last sentence of the novel.

By far the most frequently used expressions are "and all," "damn" or "goddamn," "this" (in the familiar-phatic sense), "kind of" or "sort of," "old"

---

[13] *Encyclopaedia Britannica Online*, s.v. "Skaz," accessed 14 August 2013, http://www.britannica.com/EBchecked/topic/547338/skaz.

[14] Chudakov and Chudakova 1971; translated from a quote from Shmid (2010, 186).

[15] For the differences in the translations of the main skaz-forming elements by Rait-Kovaleva, Nemtsov, and Lotovskii, see Appendix 4. The numbers following the examples given in the appendix indicate the pages where they can be found in the respective translations.

(in the familiar-phatic sense), "boy" (introducing a declarative or interrogative sentence in order to make an emphatic statement), "hell" or "heck" (for emphasis), hyperboles (exaggerated statements, often including unrealistic amounts expressed by numerals, also for emphasis), emphatic syntactic constructions in complex sentences in clauses beginning with "if" or "what"), occasional moderate vulgarisms like "ass," and occasional deviations from standard grammar like: "He didn't talk to you at all *hardly* [my italics] unless you were a big shot or a celebrity or something" (Salinger 1991, 142).

Practically all of the enumerated language means are used redundantly, as "parasitic expressions"—to use the Russian phrase—in order to mark the narrative as spoken speech. Interestingly and characteristically, the use of vulgarisms is very limited, with the "f"-, "c"-, and "s"-words not used at all, except for one episode at the end of the novel where the phrase "fuck you" is used five times, in a mediated way, as a vulgarism written on a school wall and an Egyptian tomb in a museum (Salinger 1991, 201, 202, 204). Rait-Kovaleva translates it in a euphemistic "protocol" way as "pokhabshchina" (2010a, 254, 255, 257, 258), Nemtsov as the vulgar "khui vam" (a cock to you) (2008, 194, 195, 196, 197), and Lotovskii as "fuck you," written in English (2010c). Also interestingly, the incidence of general-purpose slang is relatively low, while the active vocabulary of the protagonist—despite his thinly veiled literary pretensions—is rather limited, too.

Given those distinctive features of the text, one of the translators' main challenges was to preserve the *skaz*-like effect of the narrative by using and maintaining a similarly identifiable set of linguistic and stylistic means throughout the Russian translation. Based on my analysis of the whole text of the novel, I believe that the *skaz*-like qualities of the original, as expressed in its vocabulary and syntax, find their equally consistent expression in the translations by Lotovskii and Nemtsov, with Rait-Kovaleva being a close second.[16]

Of course, Nemtsov and Lotovskii had much more leeway than Rait-Kovaleva—socially, politically, and culturally—because the Soviet Grande Dame Censorship was not constantly breathing down their necks, and they could be pretty certain that their work would reach the masses, if only via the Internet. The only concern they were bound to share would be the effect of their work on their professional reputation, especially as compared with that of Rait-Kovaleva. In this respect, Nemtsov's translation ran into a minor critical storm in the Russian blogosphere, with quite a few readers—supposedly, the older contingent of Internet users—accusing him of overloading his translation with present-day Russian "community-college" (*proftekhuchilishche*, or *PTU* in Russian) kind of youth slang. Lotovskii's translation is still waiting on its being read by a wider audience so it has not yet drawn enough comments to make generalizations about.

---

[16] For comparisons of their translation styles, see Appendix 3.

There is another important but difficult-to-convey parameter of *skaz*, and that is its overall prosodic[17] effect on the reader. In other words, apart from special vocabulary and syntax, *skaz*-styled texts are distinguished by their unique rhythmic flow of speech—particular types of *oral* speech—which *skaz* is supposed to imitate. To get a comparative sense of the rhythms and cadences of the three different texts of *The Catcher in the Rye* in Russian, I kept reading some correlated parts of them out loud to myself. To my ear, Nemtsov's translation has a somewhat bumpy, staccato, and at times stilted kind of feel and sound to it. Lotovskii's text reads more smoothly, although it, too, has its share of "speed bumps." Rait-Kovaleva's version reads a little more fluidly than Nemtsov's—its prosody is close to that of Lotovskii. In other words, in terms of the aural smoothness of the flow of text, it seems to me that—on the whole—both Rait-Kovaleva's and Lotovskii's versions are slightly closer to the original than Nemtsov's version.

Although the overall sense of fit between original and translation is one of those "soft" metrics that are very difficult to pin down, I will venture to say that, on balance, all three translations represent Holden Caulfield's narcissistic account of post-adolescent self-absorption and rebelliousness against the phoniness of life quite well. I would give them equal grades for overall impression—a kind of overall artistic performance—despite the noticeable differences in the "ideological," lexical, grammatical, and prosodic solutions the three translators adopt to cope with the "translatorial other." That said, I cannot help feeling that Nemtsov and Lotovskii strain a little too hard to speak a 2000s variety of youth slang. As a result, their types of youth vernacular and *skaz* morph into a kind of verbal "pizzazz" that tends to overshadow the perceived original literary and ideological aspects of the novel.

From a wider perspective—that of cross-cultural literary and translational pragmatics—there is one other question that has to be posed by the translator and the translation critic alike, namely: "Who exactly is Salinger's Holden Caulfield addressing in English, and how does that addressee correlate with the addressees of Rait-Kovaleva, Nemtsov, and Lotovskii in Russian?" My answer is that, through his protagonist, Salinger is addressing that most elusive of audiences—the broad reading public, not just teenagers. His use of language, though provocative and unusual for the prose fiction of the time, was embraced and identified with by a wide cross-section of American society—the American young adults and adults of the 1960s and later years. Rait-Kovaleva's translation is also general reader-oriented—perhaps, out of necessity rather than choice—and that is why, judging by the blogs, her translation still enjoys wide popularity, even with the current "new-generation" of young adults. Thus Rait-Kovaleva speaks to a wider cross-section of sociocultural constituencies, whereas Nemtsov and Lotovskii speak through their

---

[17] Prosody is the set of speech variables, including rhythm, speed, pitch, and relative emphasis, that distinguish vocal patterns (*American Heritage Dictionary*, 5th ed., 1414).

translations in a language commonly used by the teenagers and young adults of the "Naughty Aughts" and today. They stylize their translations by modernizing the language quite deliberately through anachronisms (for example, *blin* in Lotovskii: "Blin, zamerz kak sobaka" [6]; *vsiako-razno* in Nemtsov: "V obshchem, dekabr' i vsiako-razno kolotun" [12]), choppy syntax, and more than a few vulgarisms (*zhopa* in Nemtsov [12]; the same *zhopa* in Lotovskii [5]; *Mne nadristat'* for "I don't give a damn" in Nemtsov [16], and the like). In other words, their prevailing method of translation is modernization through *ozhivliazh* ("sexing the text up") based on current young people's slang. As a result, their translations—judging by the blogs—seem to engage predominantly the sociocultural identities or constituencies of high school and college students. Thus, with reference to the perceived readership of the three translations, I would distinguish two consistently-followed pragmatics of translation: on the one hand, that of Rait-Kovaleva and, on the other, the one shared by Nemtsov and Lotovskii, with two different target audiences in mind: respectively, the general readership, however vague that concept may seem, and the young "cool-speaking," rebellious-without-a-compelling-cause learning and entrepreneurial social contingents. In the end, each individual reader selects—or, most likely, runs into accidentally and quite unconsciously—their own translation, which will become their accidental original.

Concluding Remarks

To conclude, Rait-Kovaleva's translation conceals a mild ideological subtext while Nemtsov's and Lotovskii's overshadow any ideology with present-day youth slang—what I referred to in the first section of this chapter as "cool-dude speak."

With regard to vocabulary and syntax, the *skaz* elements come through in Nemtsov's and Lotovskii's translations more prominently than in Rait-Kovaleva's, most likely because Nemtsov and Lotovskii were not as constrained by the need for public propriety in the use of language as Rait-Kovaleva was. As for prosody, Lotovskii's and Rait's translations are somewhat closer to the original than that by Nemtsov. At the same time, Nemtsov's and Lotovskii's translations go a little overboard with the arguably vulgar aspects of youth slang and modernizing stylization of the whole narrative. It seems that, in order to make their new translations of the Salinger novel attract new, young readers, the translators had to shift their focus and concentrate on the harsher slang elements of present-day Russian. One might say that the traditional qualities of *skaz* have thus been reinforced with verbal pizzazz.

As far as the elusive category of overall artistic effect is concerned, I would rank the three translations on the same level, prefacing the ranking with Kashkin's maxim that "each epoch deserves the translation it either tolerates or admires" (Chukovskii 1966, 524). Kashkin's pithy saying calls for some clarification, though, especially today, when translators continue to be all but "invisible" to the reading public and when there may exist several translations of the same literary work. With reference to *The Catcher in the Rye*, I would say that it is very important for the cross-cultural educator (professor or reviewer) to make the textual differences of the three translations visible to their readers, thus confronting especially the millennial reader with the intellectual challenge of figuring out why the three translations of the same original are so different and speak to different temporal and sociocultural identities. The question to begin answering that would be: "Did the translators actually intend their translations to have the effects that I have tried to pin down?" There is no way of knowing for sure, of course, but, whatever the translators' professed or latent intentions may have been, a classic of Russian literary criticism, Iurii Tynianov, provides at least a partial answer to that question: "it is [...] absolutely clear that there is no such thing as an *entirely separate* work of fiction [in this case each of the three translations], that each work of fiction enters an already existing system of literature, correlating with it in genre and style (while differentiating itself within the system), and that a work of fiction has a special function to fulfill in the literary system of a given epoch. A work of fiction, torn out of the context of the given literary system and transferred to a different one [the way any translation usually is], acquires a different coloring, develops new properties, and enters another genre while losing its own; that is to say, its function shifts. The new environment causes a shift of functions within the given work of fiction itself: in a given epoch, what was auxiliary in the past becomes dominant in the present" (1967, 48–49).

Chapter 5

Translating Postmodernism: A Translator's Modus Operandi

An iconic figure in the field of translation, Vladimir Nabokov, once wrote:

> What is translation? On a platter,
> A poet's pale and glaring head;
> A parrot's screech, a monkey's chatter,
> And profanation of the dead. (1975a, 9)

Nabokov, who felt very strongly about achieving high-quality literary and poetic translations, knew what he was talking about. He spent nearly ten years on his translation of and commentary to *Eugene Onegin*. What he produced is a uniquely indispensable two-volume linguistic and cultural aid (Pushkin 1975) to any English speaker of Russian who wants to gain a deep understanding of this "encyclopedia of Russian life," as the famous 19th-century Russian literary critic Vissarion Belinskii put it. The problems that Nabokov tried to resolve in his two-pronged approach arise in translating highly evocative texts (fiction and poetry), where, to quote Tim Parks, the focus of the text shifts away from the "object of evocation" (characters, plot, and setting) to the "medium of evocation"—the language (Parks 2007, 95). Parks proposes gaining a better understanding of the original text and the other culture by examining perceived divergences between original and translation (1975, 140).

In this chapter I will focus on the only existing at the time of this writing translation of the novella *Day of the Oprichnik* (*Den' oprichnika*) (Sorokin 2011b). The novella is by a popular contemporary Russian writer and dramatist, Vladimir Sorokin (b. 1955). Sorokin's 2006 dystopia is a very much translation-resistant text, projecting a controversial vision of Russia in 2028. I will navigate the different "tributaries" of the "translatorial other" with the help of Jamey Gambrell's translation that came out in 2011 (Sorokin 2011a). There were three main reasons why I chose *Day of the Oprichnik* for the present analysis. First, Sorokin is now one of the few 21st-century Russian writers well known in the USA. Second, the English translation of *Oprichnik* came out very recently and has been reviewed in various prestigious publications.[1] And

---

[1] See, for example, Tony Wood, "Howling Soviet Monsters," *London Review of Books*, 30 June 2011, pp. 32–33; and Rachel Polonsky, "Violent, Ecstatic Russians," *The New York Review of Books*, 22 March 2012, pp. 28–30.

third, the authorial style of the novella is a unique pastiche of linguistic means and intertextuality that are very difficult to convey in translation. Most importantly, the *Oprichnik* is a good illustration of what I mean by "the other in translation," and the way I examine it is an illustration of comparative translation discourse analysis applied to a postmodernist text.

As emphasized in the introduction, I undertake such analyses in order to counteract the tendency in translation reviews to assign a translation an aesthetic autonomy from the source text and to judge it "not according to a concept of equivalence, but according to the 'standards' by which [the critic] judges original compositions. [...] this approach [is] belletristic because it emphasizes aesthetic qualities of the translated text itself. It is also impressionistic in the sense that it is vague or ill-defined" (Venuti 2011).

I will start off my analysis with another quote from Tim Parks: "[I]n the literary text an awful lot of things can be happening at once, perhaps contradicting each other, perhaps qualifying each other; as a result the translator may find that it is not possible to express all of these complications simultaneously in his or her language" (2007, 14). For myself, I will add that today nobody can afford ten years like Nabokov to examine every cultural nook and cranny of Sorokin's multilayered, deeply culture-embedded text. Therefore, in my analysis, I will, of necessity, bring the range and complexity of the translator's tasks down to a relatively manageable level, considering the ways Gambrell performed them through the prism of only the key translation-resistant "components" of "the other" in Sorokin's text.

Sociocultural Context

Sorokin's title *Day of the Oprichnik* immediately brings to mind James Joyce's *Ulysses* (1922) and Aleksandr Solzhenitsyn's *One Day in the Life of Ivan Denisovich* (*Odin den' Ivana Denisovicha*, 1962). The two classics describe in great detail—respectively, in a modernistic and a realistic way—one day each in the life of a particular personage: in the former case, the middle-aged Jewish advertising salesman Leopold Bloom's activities in the city of Dublin, Ireland, between 8 a.m. and 3 a.m. on 16–17 June 1904, and, in the latter case, the horrors of surviving one routine day of the brutal realities in a Stalinist Siberian labor camp in the 1950s. In this latter story the protagonist Ivan Denisovich Shukhov is serving his eighth year of a ten-year sentence.

The novella (*povest'*)—as Sorokin himself prefers to call his *Oprichnik*[2]—is set in the new Russia of 2028, by which time a government system has been

---

[2] In this podcast of Sorokin's workshop at Stanford University on 19 October 2011, Sorokin presents and discusses his *Day of the Oprichnik*. The question-and-answer session that followed his talk was consecutively interpreted by Jamey Gambrell (website of Stanford University's Division of Literatures, Cultures, and Languages, https://www.stanford.edu/dept/DLCL/cgi-bin/web/news/dlcl-writer-residence-vladimir-sorokin).

established that closely resembles the system of *oprichnina* that existed in the time of Ivan the Terrible (1530–84), the Russian tsar associated with extreme violence in dealing with his real and imaginary opponents. In 1565 he set up what many historians believe was the prototype or archetype of the Soviet state secret police, most widely known outside Russia as the KGB, with its current successor being the FSB (the Federal Security Bureau/Service), to combat sedition among the class of high Russian nobility, the boyars. This Russian-style "praetorian guard" was known as *oprichniki* (plural of *oprichnik*), from the old Russian preposition *oprich* (except for, besides, i.e., exceptional, special people). The system itself, including the oprichniki and the lands that were allotted to them, came to be called *oprichnina*. Ivan the Terrible declared oprichnina in contradistinction to that part of Russia that began to be called *zemshchina* (from the Russian *zemlia*—land), or the rest of Russia, supposedly disloyal to the tsar. Oprichnina existed until 1572, when Ivan the Terrible himself abolished it.

The first-person unreliable narrator of the story is the hard-drinking, exotic-drugs-taking, high-ranking oprichnik Andrei Danilovich Komiaga. Komiaga is the first deputy head of the oprichnina department of the Russian government. His immediate superior and head of oprichnina is a man whose nickname is Batya. Batya is directly accountable to His Majesty (the Sovereign), who is the supreme leader of the country. In present-day Russian, *batya* is both a criminal-world and military-slang sobriquet for a respected male or commander, roughly corresponding to words like *gov(ernor)* (in British English), *boss*, *the Man*, etc. In familial contexts, it is equal to the respectfully polite *Dad*. Batya is the futuristic avatar and projection of Ivan the Terrible's head of the oprichniki Malyuta Skuratov, who was known for his exceptional cruelty, sadism, and deviousness. The book opens with a "respectful" dedication to "Grigory Lukyanovich Skuratov-Belsky, nicknamed Malyuta." As the story unfolds, the narrative voices of Komiaga, Batya (Komiaga's immediate superior), and the extra-diegetic narrator "Sorokin" intermingle, becoming difficult to disentangle and thus complicating the translator's tasks.

In many senses, the novella is a *roman à clef*, with many names reminiscent of specific political, public, and cultural figures. In particular, at different points in the novella, I associate Komiaga, Batya, His Majesty, and their rhetoric with Putin and his government. *Day of the Oprichnik* was published in 2006, half-way into Putin's second term as president of Russia and at a time when his alleged policies of increasing totalitarianism and clamping down on the political gains of the late 1990s were drawing pointed criticism both from the Western media and from the inchoate Russian neoliberal opposition. The Russian government began to be routinely referred to as the "Putin regime." Now that Putin has been reelected as president, Sorokin's *Oprichnik* anti-utopia can arguably be read as a possible projection into the future of the current Russian powers that be. Indeed, it is hard not to view Komiaga, Batya, and His Majesty as a thinly camouflaged, collective caricature of Putin. Will

Sorokin's intimation of Putin's reincarnation prove prophetic in the foreseeable future? Was it an intimation? Will this boost the popularity of the *Oprichnik* novella and its translation? Did the translator see her task in translating Sorokin's novella as a political lampoon or serious literature? These are interesting questions. Time will show. In the meantime, the author himself sheds some light on the nature of his work in his interviews, blog, and workshop on the Stanford campus referenced earlier. In his own words, Sorokin is only interested in a single theme—violence:[3] "What is violence, and why are human beings incapable of renouncing it?" he asks (Polonsky 2012, 30). As for attempts to deconstruct his texts and brand them postmodernist, Sorokin, according to Polonsky, is "ridiculing [Slavists'] attachment to the theorists of deconstruction, Gilles Deleuze and Jacques Derrida," and [...] asks rhetorically: "'Is the feeling of terror also a text? Is love a text? Is backache also a text?'" (Polonsky 2012, 30).

In his talk about the novella at Stanford University on 19 October 2011,[4] Sorokin makes three distinct points: number one—it is the first time that oprichnina has been made the centerpiece of a major literary work; number two—he aimed to show that, over the centuries, the mindset of the oprichnik (Komiaga) has been a distinct feature of Russian life; and number three—he is fascinated by the nature and persistence of violence in human affairs.

A skillfully executed text does excite certain emotions—love, hate, pleasure, disgust, a sense of exhilaration and being inspired, or a sense of depression and being discomfited—otherwise it is not verbal art. To use Tolstoy's primary qualification of art (incidentally, Sorokin holds Tolstoy in high esteem), *Day of the Oprichnik* is "infectious," or "contagious," the quality Tolstoy ascribes to powerful works of art in his extended essay of 1896 *What Is Art?*: "The stronger the infection the better is the art, as art."[5] But Tolstoy famously differentiates between "good art" and "bad art." It seems to me, that, from a Tolstoyan perspective, *Oprichnik* would not be considered good art—it would be bad art. But, of course, by that token—and in his own words—most of

---

[3] See also Sorokin's interview with Tatyana Voskovskaia at http://lib.misto.kiev.ua/SOROKIN/interv01.txt.

[4] https://www.stanford.edu/dept/DLCL/cgi-bin/web/news/dlcl-writer-residence-vladimir-sorokin

[5] Here is a longer passage from *What Is Art?* Lev Nikolaevich Tolstoy: "The feelings with which the artist infects others may be most various—very strong or very weak, very important or very insignificant, very bad or very good: feelings of love for one's own country, self-devotion and submission to fate or to God expressed in a drama, raptures of lovers described in a novel, feelings of voluptuousness expressed in a picture, courage expressed in a triumphal march, merriment evoked by a dance, humor evoked by a funny story, the feeling of quietness transmitted by an evening landscape or by a lullaby, or the feeling of admiration evoked by a beautiful arabesque—it is all art. If only the spectators or auditors are infected by the feelings which the author has felt, it is art." http://babel.hathitrust.org/cgi/pt?view=image; size=100;id=mdp.39015007053500;page=root;seq=11;num=v.

Tolstoy's works belong in the category of bad art. Speaking for myself, *Oprichnik* strikes me as a masterfully executed deeply intertextual work of verbal art; it arouses—in me, personally—a mixed reaction of alarm and a sense of emotional unease. The pragmatic question is—Do I get a similar emotional reaction after reading the Gambrell version of *Oprichnik*? I will answer this question later. At this point I will confine myself to defining Sorokin's sociocultural profile as that of a neo-Slavophile who does not believe that Russia may have any livable future.[6]

Translating the "Untranslatable": A Foretaste of the Narrative

At this point I have to restate the seemingly obvious but—curiously—usually glossed over fact that it is the original literary text itself[7] that constitutes the core of "the other" in translation and that it is a very deep knowledge of the pair of languages and their respective cultures that is an absolute *sine qua non*

---

[6] Sorokin's 2012 New Year's greetings posted in his blog commingle Komiaga's and the author's narrative styles to such an extent that the blog entry reads like a passage from *Day of the Oprichnik*: "I have to admit that, regrettably, I'm not a great believer in the future of the Postsovietistan that grandly calls itself the Russian Federation. Rather, it's not so much that I don't believe in its future as that I can't envision it from a broad perspective that would encompass a degree of freedom. And the reason for this is not in the KGB-cum-gangsters' state control, nor is it in the unburied state of the old Soviet Union, whose decomposition has been poisoning the present with its putrid stench for nearly two decades,—(The other day, I zapped through the New Year's TV channels: all I got was the across-the-board retro-Soviet trash, large-boobed pop bimbos belting out Stalin-period hits, nausea-inducing, wretched, Soviet-style comedies, Brezhnev-era New Year's Eve television parties, stand-up comedian Raikin's socialist-minded obtuse jokes, the fuck-up of a movie *Irony of Fate*, etc., etc.)—the reason for this Russian non-future is the human material. Alas, the genetic degeneration of our population has stopped being a metaphor" (A.B.) (Я признаться, грешным делом не очень верю в будущее Постсовка, громко именующего себя Российской Федерацией. Даже, не то что – не верю, а совсем его не вижу как некую развернутую перспективу, как степень свободы. И дело тут не в лубянско-бандитской власти, даже не в Совке, непохороненность которого уже второе десятилетие отравляет своим трупным ядом настоящее [я тут прошелся по новогоднему телеящику: сплошная советская ретруха, сисястая попса распевает сталинские песенки, идут тошнотворно-убогие совковые комедии, брежневские «Новогодние Огоньки», социалистические шуточки Райкина, уебищная «Ирония судьбы», и т.д.], а в человеческом материале. Увы, генетическое вырождение населения нашего перестало быть метафорой). *VLDMR SRKN: Ofitsial'nyi sait Vladimira Sorokina*, http://www.srkn.ru/blog/2012-01-03.html.

[7] Here I won't discuss the relatively rare cases when there are more than one original, sometimes in different languages, for example, Samuel Beckett's own English and French versions of *Watt* and *Murphy*, or Nabokov's various self-translations, which can be viewed as "parallel" originals.

required of the literary translator. Unfortunately, such a restatement is necessary in view of the errors in translating even some basic language that are so common in English translations of Russian literature and films.

But "the other" in translation is not only the text as a general manifestation of the foreign language in all of its incredible complexity and versatility; more specifically, it is the mutual "organic" inability of a given pair of languages to engage, on an equal footing, in certain linguistic and cultural games that imaginative authors set up and play in their texts. The expert literary translator is aware of this and either goes for broke in waxing "superimaginative" or "sucks up" the inevitable losses and pretends that nothing serious has happened, the façade of translatorial authority being impenetrable to the general readership by default. Many translators tend to steer a middle course by neutralizing or "normalizing" the text of the translation. That is what, to a certain extent, Gambrell has had to resort to, faced with some intransigent linguistic and cultural incompatibilities between Russian and English.

Here is a foretaste of the general tone of Sorokin's narrative that gives an initial idea of some of the problems Gambrell had to deal with. The passage, which is part of Komiaga's interior monologue, is used as a summary of the book on the flyleaf of the Russian original (Sorokin 2011b) and can be found on page 30 of Gambrell's translation (Sorokin 2011a):

<u>Супротивных</u> много, это верно. Как только восстала Россия из <u>пепла Серого</u>, как только осознала себя, как только шестнадцать лет назад <u>заложил</u> Государев <u>батюшка</u> Николай Платонович первый камень в фундамент Западной стены, как только <u>стали мы</u> отгораживаться от чуждого извне, от бесовского изнутри – так и <u>полезли</u> <u>супротивные</u> из всех щелей, <u>аки сколопендрие зловредное</u>. Истинно великая идея порождает и великое сопротивление ей. Всегда были враги у государства нашего, внешние и внутренние, но <u>никогда так яростно не обострялась</u> <u>борьба</u> с ними, как в период Возрождения Святой Руси. (2011b, 4)

There are plenty of <u>opponents</u>, that's true. As soon as Russia rose from the <u>Gray Ashes</u>, as soon as she became aware of herself, as soon as His Majesty, <u>Father Nikolai Platonovich, laid</u> the foundation stone of the Western Wall sixteen years ago, as soon as <u>we began</u> to fence ourselves off from the foreign without and the demon within—<u>opponents began to crawl</u> out of the cracks <u>like noxious centipedes</u>. A truly great idea breeds great resistance. Our state has always had enemies inside and out, but <u>the battle was never so intense</u> as during the period of Holy Russia's Revival. (2011a, 30)

Gambrell's excellent translation shows certain lexical and syntactic "neutralizations" that tone down the historical-archaic flavor of the original. Thus she uses some neutral vocabulary instead of bookish and archaic words (for example, the neutral "opponents" for the bookish-archaic *suprotivnykh*, which is more like "seditionists," or the neutral "like" for the archaic *aki*, which does not have a correspondence in English); puts adjectives in front of nouns, being unable to keep them in postposition in English (thus *pepla Serogo* is translated as "Gray Ashes," and *skolopendrie zlovrednoe* as "noxious centipedes"); puts predicates after subjects, for the same reason (*zalozhil batiushka*—"Father laid," *stali my*—"we began," *polezli suprotivnye*—"opponents began to crawl out"); and, finally, neutralizes the emphatic construction *nikogda tak iarostno ne obostrialas' bor'ba* by using a direct word order—"the battle was never so intense." Such neutralizing modifications modernize the text in minor ways, and this is, in fact, the general, hardly avoidable, strategy of the translator throughout the text. By negotiating the "organic" and cultural incompatibilities of the two languages through modernization, Gambrell produces a less historically stylized text as compared to the original. Granted, there was not much Gambrell could do about the adjective-noun and subject-predicate word order, but she could have translated *suprotivnye* as "seditionists," for example, using a more bookish word, or preserved the emphasis in the last sentence by saying "never has the fight against them been so fierce (or ferocious)." She could also have used a more "intense" adjective like "fierce" or "ferocious" instead of "intense" for *iarostno*, which is arguably more emotionally charged and bookish than "intense." But, of course, the translator was guided by her own sense for the text, and I am not criticizing—just suggesting alternative translation variants.

A lot is happening at the same time in Sorokin's text: it is an explosive mixture of ponderous, homily-like syntax, archaic vocabulary, cultural *realia*, and prosodic riffs that reads like a bombastic, pontificating sermon. This is quite appropriate for the Ivan the Terrible period and the postmodernist nature of Sorokin's novella, but it is an overwhelming challenge for the translator. Could the translator perhaps have used the King James Bible (1611) as a source for archaizing her translation and making the stylistic choices easier and more "authentic"? I do not really think so, as the familiarity of the Bible diction in the English-speaking world would have made the translation overly domesticated, i.e., sounding more Anglo-Saxon than Russian. Bottom line: with Sorokin, any translator is way out on a limb.

Fairy Tale-cum-Bylina Style

What kind of text is Sorokin's story? Sorokin regales the reader with the most jarring descriptions of unconventional sexual behavior, exotic drug abuse, and scenes of violence such as the graphic gang rape episode at the beginning of the novella and the lengthy description of group "caterpillar" sodomy at the end. Graphic imagery and sensibilities aside, Sorokin's text uses the grammar, prosody, and, partially, vocabulary of Russian fairy tales and *byliny*, epic tales that were sung in olden times to the accompaniment of psalteries.[8] It is much more "musical" than Platon Karataev's or Holden Caulfield's narratives (discussed in chapters 3 and 4) in that it appeals to the Russian reader by its song-like, alliterative, and rhyming cadences, strongly reminiscent of childhood and calming bedside readings. What comes into a clanging collision with the anodyne linguostylistic qualities of the narrative is the coarseness, violence, and sexism of its subject-matter. The text is skillfully crafted to shock, fascinate, and amuse. In places, it sounds like gangsta rap, and Gambrell's translation often does justice to this quality of the text. By way of example, here is a description of Komiaga's rap-like cell phone tone that he hears continually throughout the day:

Моё мобило будит меня:	My mobilov awakens me:
Удар кнута – вскрик.	One crack of the whip – a scream.
Снова удар – стон.	Two – a moan.
Третий удар – хрип.	Three – the death rattle.
[…]	[…]
Комяга слушает, – прикладываю	I put the cold mobilov to my warm,
холодное мобило к сонно-тёплому уху.	sleepy ear. "Komiaga speaking."
(2011b, 6)	(2011a, 3)

Of course, the prosody of a stretch of text in Russian cannot be replicated in full in English. The alliterations and assonances in the above Russian fragment evoke the sounds of strong Russian swearing—note the consonants *b* as in *bliad'* ("ho," as in lady of very easy virtue) and *ebat'* (to fuck), *kh* as in *khui* (cock), and *p* as in *pizda* (cunt). These do not have the same associations (or "phonological distributions") as the English bilabials *m*, *b*, *p*, and *w*, which are not present (except for *b*) in the most common swear words in English. Generally speaking, given the "material" differences between Russian and English phonologies and phonetics, the evocative effect of the Russian in the novel is impossible to reproduce in full, and in some instances at all, in a translation. Because of the aural and associative divergences of the two languages, the overall "aural effect" that Gambrell achieves in most of her translation is somewhat milder than that of the original. That said, I think Gambrell did as good a job of translating prosody as can possibly be expected, and I will give some more illustrations of this later.

Sorokin's novella is a prime example of narrative stylization. A stylized text is an authorial imitation of a particular style of writing and/or speaking, based on a particular genre or mixture of genres and set in an identifiable

---

[8] by·li·na *noun* \bəlēnə\ *pl* byli·ny \-nē\ *or* bylinas \-nəz\: a Russian folk epic or ballad. Russian, from *bylina* (what has been), from *byl* (was), past of *byt'* (to be); akin to the Sanskrit *bhavati* (he is). *Merriam-Webster Unabridged Dictionary*, http://www.merriam-webster.com/dictionary/bylina.

temporal setting (historical period). Sorokin's text is a combination of poetic elements typical of the Russian folk genres of fairy tales and byliny. Consequently, the text deploys a lot of historical *realia*, i.e., archaic or archaic-sounding words and turns of phrase that, arguably, are associated by the Russian reader, if not directly with the period of Ivan the Terrible, then vaguely with some bygone age.[9] In describing the salient attributes of the oprichniks, Sorokin archaizes the text. But the novella is also a futuristic dystopia set in 2028. Many technological advances have been made in Russia, and they are described using authorial neologisms such as *puzyr' vestevoi*, translated as "news bubble,"[10] which is a kind of combination television-holographic-iPhone information-exchanging device, or *mobilo*, translated as "mobilov"[11] (cell videophone with holographic imaging), or *merin*, translated as "Mercedov"[12] (a Mercedes car filled with electronics and creature-comfort devices).

---

[9] In fact, the style of describing the scene of the rape of a "new Russian" aristocrat's wife and the subsequent bloody fistfight between the toughest oprichnik and the toughest member of the aristocrat's household at the beginning of the novella is strongly reminiscent of Mikhail Lermontov's stylized bylina "Lay (Ballad) of the Tsar Ivan Vasil'evich, a Young Oprichnik, and the Daring Merchant Kalashnikov" (*Pesnia pro tsaria Ivana Vasil'evicha, molodogo oprichnika i udalogo kuptsa Kalashnikova*; 1837). There is no question in my mind that Sorokin, who, judging by his age, learned excerpts from this epic poem as a middle-school student, imitates Lermontov's "old-fashioned" style, and many Russians will "hear" this. Despite Sorokin's own protestations, his style is typical of postmodernist prose. Galina Rylkova provides a penetrating analysis of Russian postmodernism in her book *The Archeology of Anxiety* (Pittsburgh: University of Pittsburgh Press, 2007), writing, among other things, that "on the one hand, in order to legitimize their subversive and often overtly offensive writings within the Russian cultural tradition, they [Russian postmodernists] had to show that they in fact took their roots from one of the most vital periods in cultural history [in this case, the Golden Age of Russian poetry]; on the other, to acquire and preserve their own voice they had to distinguish themselves radically from their progenitors. In any case, 'strong writers do not choose their prime precursors: they are chosen by them, but they have the wit to transform the forerunners into composite and therefore partly imaginary beings'" (199). Rylkova quotes Harold Bloom's *The Western Canon* (New York: Riverhead Books, 1995), 10.

[10] Here the Russian chain of associations with the words *puzyr'* and *vesti* is comparable with the associations triggered by the words *bubble* and *news* in English.

[11] This is an excellent Gambrell solution as it highlights the Russianness of the text— many Russian surnames end in "-ov." On the other hand, there are losses in the range of associations a Russian will most likely have, as the word *mobilo* in the original Russian evokes other slang words ending in *o: mudilo* (asshole), *murlo* (bruiser), and *chmo* (trash, as in despicable person).

[12] *Merin* is also a "normal" Russian word meaning "male horse," a means of transportation in olden times. Translating *merin* as "Mercedov" is an ingenious translation solution. It is very funny for an English-speaking Russian reading the translation, be-

As a fairy tale-bylina kind of stylized narrative, *Oprichnik* is an ingeniously powerful, eclectic text that reads like an affirmation of Russia's traditionality and indestructability.[13] But let us get down to specific cases, i.e., the linguistic means of stylization, in the original and its translation, with the understanding that I will be able to point out only some of the most salient features of the text. Among the most translation-resistant elements of the text are realia.

Realia

Realia (plural of *realium*) is a technical term (already briefly discussed in chapter 3) that, in its most general sense, means words and phrases denoting objects, phenomena, and practices that are to be found in one culture but are conspicuously absent in another. By way of an initial example, let me consider briefly a quite "transparent" case—the Russian army and countryside clothing accessory *portianka*. Portianka is a piece of cloth wrapped around the foot instead of or on top of a sock and worn inside a jackboot. This accessory for keeping one's feet warm is still widely used in the Russian military and in the countryside.[14] At one point in Sorokin's novella, portianki are advertised on an electronic billboard. Gambrell translates it as "leggings" (2011a, 133), which in English normally means a tight-fitting stretchable garment that covers the body from the waist to the ankle.[15] It would have been fine if the word *portianka* was randomly used in a casual description or enumeration in the *Oprichnik* text for some local color, but in the instance I am about to describe, it is densely contextualized in an advertisement that Komiaga is examining and is important as cultural characterization:

> На здании «Детского мира» огромное стекло с рекламою живой: байковые портянки «Святогор». Сидит на лавке кучерявый молодец, девица-краса в кокошнике опускается перед ним на колено с новою портянкою в руках. И под треньканье балалайки, под всхлипы гармоники протягивает молодец босую ногу свою. Девица оборачивает ее портянкой, натягивает сапог. Голос: «Портянки торгового товарищества "Святогор". Ваша нога будет как в

cause the Russian suffix "-ov" actually means "the son of." In this instance Gambrell out-Sorokins Sorokin.

[13] An iconic Russian writer, Aleksandr Solzhenitsyn, throughout his long life, was anxious to "Russify" the Russian language. I think his wildest dreams get fulfilled in Sorokin's style.

[14] One needs special skills to wrap a portianka around one's foot properly in order to avoid blisters. Comfortable socks would do much better, but they would be a concession to the "Western ways."

[15] The translation of *portianka* as "leggings" does not convey the sense of how cumbersome portiankas can be.

люльке!» И сразу – колыбельная, люлька плетеная с ногой, в портянку завернутой, покачивается: баю-бай-бай... И голос девицы: «Как в люльке!» (2011b, 198–99)

On the Children's World department store building there's an enormous frame with a live advertisement: for Sviatogor flannel leggings. A curly-headed youth sits on a bench; a beauty of a girl in a traditional Russian headdress kneels down in front of him with new leggings in her hands. The young man extends his bare leg to the strum of a balalaika and the sobs of a harmonica. The young lady wraps it in the leggings, and pulls on his boot. A voice declares: "Sviatogor Trading Company leggings. Your foot will feel like it's in a cradle." Right away you hear a lullaby, and see a wicker cradle rocking gently with leggings-wrapped legs in it: rock-a-bye baby ... And the girl's voce says: "they'll cradle your legs!" (2011a, 133)

The translation conjures up an ambiguous, eroticized image of a possibly cross-dressing couple or a transvestite young man, which—judging by the Russian text—is not at all what Sorokin is trying to say. In fact, the translation distracts the reader from Sorokin's satirizing the absurdly archaized, militarized, and tackily patriotic mass culture. The central misleading lexical element is the translation of *portianki* as leggings. "Puttee" or "foot wrap"—as possible functional equivalents—would seem to work better here. Another way of dealing with the realium of portianki would be to go in for a little foreignization via transliteration, followed by a translation by paraphrase: "Flannel *portianki* from Sviatogor—the number one foot-warming wraps (or foot-huggies) maker!" instead of "Sviatogor flannel leggings." Then, in the other two instances, toward the end of the passage, one could use "portianki" and "portianka" as an already established localism. Although wordier, such a translation would avoid any misleading chains of associations.

Historical and present-day realia are one of the major challenges Gambrell had to deal with. The methods of translating realia are: 1) finding a functional equivalent close enough to the source language concept (like "leggings" above); 2) calquing (creating a loan-word)—"State Snarl," meaning a special security police honking siren; 3) transliterating and/or transcribing a realium and relying on its context to illuminate its meaning (*kissel* [2011a, 6], *zakuski* [2011a, 141] or *portianka* in the example above); 4) importing the realium into the translation unchanged (Gambrell does this very rarely), 5) replacing the realium with a generic term ("headdress" for "kokoshnik" in the above example), 6) translating it by paraphrase (circumlocution); 7) creating an original metaphor through a literal translation ("I turn on my State Snarl" [132] for the literal "I honk my state hypertone horn" ["Signaliu *gosgiperton-om*," where *gosgiperton* is an authorial new-technology neologism] [198]; 8) introducing explanatory footnotes and endnotes (Gambrell uses them very sparingly); and, finally 9) leaving the realium out altogether (a translator's surrender).

But sometimes realia are much less obvious. Here is an example of an unexpected pitfall concealed by a realium-like cultural allusion. In the original we have "Ud ego so vshitym rechnym zhemchugom palitse Il'i Muromtsa podoben" (2011b, 40). Gambrell's translation: "His [Posokha's] member has freshwater pearls sewn in it; the pattern resembles Ilya Muromets's diamond-shaped vestments" (2011a, 24). This may read all right to somebody unfamiliar with Russian culture, but it is, in fact, a serious mistranslation. In the original, Posokha's penis is being compared to the fighting club that Il'ia Muromets, the Russian folk-epic hero, used to bash his foes. The heavy medieval war club (or mace) with a spiked metal head was used by medieval Russian fighters to crush armor and enemies. The mace can be seen hanging from the right wrist of Il'ia Muromets in Viktor Vasnetsov's iconic 1898 painting *Bogatyrs (Three Russian Warriors).*[16] (Il'ia Muromets is the warrior in the middle of the threesome.) Hence the comparison, which cannot fail to conjure up an association with the Vasnetsov painting in most native Russians' minds. The translation should have been something like this: "Posokha's member with its pearl-studded head resembles epic warrior Il'ia Muromets's fighting cudgel." Gambrell was misled by the dictionary, which does have the right word sense, but also the wrong one for the given context.

The troublesome realia in the Sorokin text can be grouped into several categories. In the following sections, I will discuss the more relevant ones.

New Russian Terms

By *new Russian terms* I mean authorial neologisms—words and meanings of words that were invented by Sorokin to signal the future time of the narrative. These also include "ordinary" words and phrases with new meanings, for example: *chitat' s bumagi* (to read from paper as opposed to on an electronic screen; 2011b, 218); *novostnoi puzyr'* (news bubble, an electronic news-streaming gadget; 2011b, 218); *golyi* (naked, meaning "compromised," stripped of all means of existence as a result of falling foul of the authorities; 2011b, 243), and others. It is noteworthy that Sorokin studiously avoids any use of "Anglicized" vocabulary, i.e., new words and phrases borrowed from English, which has been a major feature of lexical innovation in Russian over the last quarter-century or so; the occasional foreign borrowings in Sorokin's text come mostly from Chinese, with China being the dominant global power in 2028. For example: *sha bi* (asshole; 2011a, 108); *diao da lian!* (no fucking way; 2011a, 121); *hao hai zi* (attaboy; 2011a, 137); *min min* (splendid; 2011a, 137); and others. As seen from the above examples, Gambrell usually calques and transliterates borrowed and invented vocabulary, on occasion coming up with some ingenious solutions, such as *Merinov* for *merin* (a Mercedes car) or

---

[16] *Wikimedia Commons,* http://commons.wikimedia.org/wiki/File:Die_drei_Bogatyr.jpg?uselang=ru.

mobilov for *mobilo* (a cell phone). This fits in very well with Sorokin's tendency not to use Anglicized slang. In the last two examples, the suffix *-ov* mimics the typical Russian endings of male surnames like Ivanov, Petrov, or Sidorov. With *merin*, there is a minor loss: Sorokin's play on the Russian meaning of *merin*, which is "gelding"—a castrated male horse, does not come through.

Sovietisms

Occasionally, Sorokin resorts to Sovietisms (Soviet-era political-ideological clichés), and quite often to turns of phrase that—while not being overt Soviet-isms—still ring some terminological bells reminiscent of the Soviet era. An example of an overt Sovietism would be *gorstka zlobstvuiushchikh otshche-pentsev* (2011b, 215), translated by Gambrell as *just a handful of malicious dis-senters* (2011a, 143). While Gambrell's translation is fine, my sense is that in *gorstka zlobstvuiushchikh otshchepentsev*[17] the Russian active present participle *zlobstvuiushchikh* is more emotionally charged (intense and dynamic) than the adjective *malicious*, and *otshchepentsev* is a more harsh-sounding and Soviet-era-evoking word than *dissenters*. In my mental search for a weightier, harsher and more unusual vocabulary solution, I came up with *a bunch of venom-spewing seditionists*—just as a possible variant.

Archaic Vocabulary

Archaic vocabulary or archaisms are words and expressions that are no longer generally used in everyday conversation, but may be used by speakers or authors for stylistic purposes—in order to create an atmosphere of past times or produce a comic or ironic effect. Archaisms are ubiquitous in the novella, sometimes combining the three kinds of effects simultaneously. Of necessity, Gambrell is often forced to replace archaic vocabulary with neutral- or formal-register items: *zelo*—"strongly," *koshel'*—"bag," *smradnyi*—"stink-ing," *tokmo*—"only," etc., because 16th-century English correspondences would be incomprehensible to present-day readers or because such corres-pondences are simply not available.

"Talking Names"

"Talking names" are names that have preserved some denotative, metaphori-cal, or emotional connotations evoking special associations in the minds of the speakers of a given ethnic and/or sociocultural community. Originally, names were like that—they referred to some salient characteristics of their bearers. In Russian such names are known as "talking names" (*govoriashchie imena*). Names in general—and "talking names," in particular—are especially deeply embedded in a given culture. For example, the "emotionality," familiarity, and evocativeness of diminutive Russian names formed by suffixes (Mikhail—Misha, Mishen'ka, Mishulia, and the like) are beyond the linguistic

---

[17] This is a piece of Soviet journalese typical of the 1960–70s.

and cultural grasp of English, which is an "analytic" and not a "synthetic" (relying on inflections) language.

Sorokin uses names of people to fit the illusion of the back-to-the-future bylina-cum-fairy tale he is narrating. On the one hand, the names of his characters sound like pristinely Russian names well suited to evoke the ambience of the 16th century. They are rough, character-defining names: Komiaga (from the Russian *kom* + the aggrandizing suffix *-aga*—"lump," or "chunk," i.e., something ragged, rough-hewn, coarse; it also associates with *komissar*, *Komsomol*, *kommunist*, *komuniaka*—the last one being a pejorative nickname for a Communist Party member, etc.), Pravda (truth), Potrokha (offal, gut, tripe, giblets), Ziabel' (ploughed land; a chaffinch; but mostly an echoic word triggering associations with such strong swear words as *ebat'* [to fuck] and its past perfective, masculine, singular *zaebal*, formed from the infinitive *zaebat'* [meaning to exhaust by sexual intercourse or, by extension, by continuous persecution or fault-finding]), and others. On the other hand, Sorokin introduces a special twist to this array of fake old Russian-sounding names. These names are created and chosen in such a way that they simultaneously sound like prison or underworld nicknames ("handles"). By setting up associations with the "handles" one expects to hear in the speech of convicts or the criminal element, Sorokin is thus subtly implanting into the reader's mind the idea that the Russian state, its rulers, and their protectors—the oprichniki—operate like a criminal gang. In this case, neither quality of these "talking names" can be replicated in translation, and even if Gambrell was aware of the second connotational layer of these names, there was nothing she could do about them. Thus the nickname Batya belongs to Komiaga's boss and patron, whose real first name and patronymic is Boris Borisovich. Incidentally, it was Boris Berezovskii (BB), a Russian oligarch recently deceased in England under mysterious circumstances, who allegedly suggested Vladimir Vladimirovich Putin as a successor to Boris Nikolaevich Yeltsin in 1999. Obviously, President Yeltsin's first name was also Boris, and it was he who appointed Putin as his successor and interim President of Russia on 31 December 1999. Yeltsin's own nickname in his inner circle was *Ded*, or "Grampa," which in certain contexts may be synonymous with Batya. These are just a few examples of the chain-of-associations-triggering tricks and allusions Sorokin uses in making his novella similar to a *roman á clef*. Some other evocative, prison-like monikers of the characters are Posokha, Sivolai, Pogoda, Okhlop, Nagul, and Kreplo.

Russian Food and Drinks
Russian food and drink items are also translation-resistant realia. I will give just one example, although, throughout the novel, the names of dishes and drinks are a frequent challenge to the translator. At the very beginning of the novel, Komiaga wakes up with a debilitating hangover, and his first order of business for the day is the Russian-style "hair of the dog," consisting of "stakan belogo kvasu, riumka vodki, polstakana kapustnogo rassola" (2011b, 8)—

in Gambrell's translation "a glass of white kvass, a jigger of vodka, a half-cup of marinated cabbage juice" (2011a, 5). Gambrell's is a good translation, even though it may sound somewhat exotic in English, whereas the Russian description of the way Komiaga begins to deal with his hangover is quite commonplace. There is nothing exotic or original in the traditional folk hangover remedy of having *kvass* (which would be vaguely recognizable by English speakers as something Russians drink), pickle brine, or *rassol* (the Russian word for what is translated as "marinated cabbage juice"), and a good shot of vodka. The English-language reader may wonder about the exact nature of the two beverages, besides the vodka, and may even get the impression that Komiaga is some kind of a food nut or "foodist." In actual fact, *rassol* is the salty and spicy water in which not only cabbage but also pickles have been preserved. It is not a juice. My point is that the cultural understanding of the situation would be crystal-clear and dead easy for any Russian, but it is partially obscured and "exoticized" by the translation for the English-language reader. And this cannot be helped, because such a reader would not have the experience of the drinks in question, nor does English have the corresponding words. The translations of the names of the oprichniks' food and drinks inevitably sound somewhat unusual and end up emphasizing the local color and the seemingly exclusive nature of the oprichniks' meals, whereas, in most cases, what is being talked about is pretty common Russian food. In other words, through no fault of the translator, the English-language reader's perception of the food-and-drink items mentioned in the text will inevitably be skewed, if ever so slightly, because of the semantic and pragmatic opacity of the food-and-drink realia in the translation. This is just another "little" example of the impossibly difficult tasks of the literary translator. How does the translator usually deal with food-and-drink realia? Just like Gambrell does throughout the novel: by foreignizing the translations using transliteration and calquing (for example, cranberry *kissel*[18] in "Tanyusha serves cheese pancakes, steamed turnips in honey and cranberry *kissel*"; 2011a, 6); by neutralizing lexical items (using stylistically neutral vocabulary), i.e., making them culturally unmarked; and by domesticating them, using vocabulary marked by the translation-receiving culture. How would I translate the above hair-of-the-dog recipe? I would suggest "a glass of kvass, a shot of vodka and a half-glass of rassol."[19]

Period Clothing and Furnishings
Period clothing and furnishings present similar difficulties for translation and lend themselves to solutions similar to those used in translating the other historical realia. A specific illustrative example will suffice (this is an episode at

---

[18] *Kissel* (*kisel'*) is a sweet drink resembling thin jelly, made by boiling pureed fruit and thickening the liquid with arrowroot starch.

[19] A fermented beverage made from black or rye bread.

the beginning of the story when Komiaga's servant Fedka is helping him on with his attire of the day):

Он вынимает платье из шкапа, начинает одевать меня: белое, шитое крестами исподнее, красная рубаха с косым воротом, парчовая куртка с куньей оторочкой, расшитая золотыми и серебряными нитями, бархатные порты, сафьяновые красные сапоги, кованные медью. Поверх парчовой куртки Федька надевает на меня долгополый, подбитый ватою кафтан черного грубого сукна. (13–14)

He takes a <u>robe</u> out of the <u>wardrobe</u> and begins to dress me: first, a white <u>undergarment</u> embroidered with crosses, a red shirt with collar buttons on the side, a brocade jacket with weasel trim, embroidered with gold and silver thread, velvet <u>pants</u>, red boots of Moroccan leather <u>fashioned with wrought copper soles</u>. Over the brocade jacket, Fedka places a black, floor-length, wadded cotton caftan made of rough broadcloth. (8)

In Russian, the above clothes sound very "old Russia," rich, and exotic; in English they seem less so. In other words, the Russian text is more archaized (stylized) than the translation: the underlined items, except for the last one, are old-fashioned Russian, whereas their translations are neutral English. As for the boots, they most likely did not have copper soles (that would be quite impractical and inconvenient)—what is likely meant are decorations (maybe, some folk pattern) made with copper rivets and studs on the tops of the boots. The rule of thumb in translating such descriptions is to try to signal the archaic character of the items by using one or two in the translation, and this is exactly what Gambrell does throughout the text. The problem, however, remains: it is the absence of mirror-like correspondences between comprehensible archaic vocabulary in English and Russian. Using neutral vocabulary is often the way out.

Titles and Forms of Address
Titles and forms of address are another source of possible "associational" displacements in the minds of the English-speaking reader: *oprichnik* (a member of the elite part of the state security police), *pod"iachii* (clerk), *brat Komiaga* (brother Komiaga), *gospodin oprichnik* (Sir Oprichnik), *ovechina moia* (my dear little lamb), *babechina moia* (Grandmama dear), *anokhi moi svet-rodimye* (2011b, 272) (my dearest Enochs—most likely Batya's mispronunciation of "eunuchs"; 2011a, 180), *volki vy sopatye* (2011b, 274) (you sniveling wolves; 2011a, 181), etc. These the translator either translates using the existing English correspondences (*Gosudar'*—Your Highness), leaves out (which Gambrell practically never does), neutralizes ("clerk" for *pod"iachii*; 2011b, 274), or transliterates ("the Strel'tsy" [2011a, 195] for "Streletskii Prikaz" [2011b, 139], which is the old name for the government department in charge of the "rifle-armed infantry"—in this context, "the Defense Ministry").

Slogans, Exhortations, and Interjections

Slogans, exhortations, and interjections can be neutralized by using inconspicuous language or by not being translated at all; domesticated by using translating language functional equivalents that bear some marks of the receiving culture; calqued (translated word for word); or imaginatively reinvented. Gambrell practically never omits anything in her translation, resorting to one or another method of translating these clichéd, incantation-like elements of the text. Some of them are easy to deal with: *Gosudarynia moia—*Your Highness; *pod"iachii—*clerk, etc. Others are realia-like folkloric interjections like *okhtish li okh*, or *okhtish mne okh*, for example (2011b, 190). The last two are used to signal anticipation of something unpleasant, difficult, or bad happening; express commiseration and sympathy; or are just used as discourse markers, segmenting folk verses into separate sense units. Gambrell translates them as "ay ay is me!" or "oh woe is me ay ay!" (2011a, 126), making them sound as strange in English as do their counterparts in Russian. Another trademark Sorokin/Komiaga incantation-discourse marker is the phrase *i slava Bogu* (and thank God), often used at the ends of paragraphs as a sign of Komiaga's self-censorship and conformity. The oprichniks are fond of shouting *"Goida!"*—which is their rallying cry, a call for resolute action, or an expression of strong approval of a course of action. This is consistently translated by Gambrell as "Hail!" *Slovo i delo!* (Word and deed!) is another interjection of approval (probably invented by Sorokin by analogy with the KGB/FSB emblem and motto *Shchit i mech—*shield and sword), emphasizing the principled character of the oprichniks' actions and the unswerving correspondence between their words and deeds.

Grammar and Prosody

Another difficulty for the translator is Sorokin's textual stylizations involving grammar. As far as morphology is concerned, the relatively infrequent obsolete Russian word forms are "neutralized" or conveyed by paraphrase. Thus *dragotsennye kamenia* (*kamenia* is the obsolete-poetic form of *kamni*) is translated by Gambrell as "precious stones," where the obsolete form *kamenia* is subsumed under and disappears in the translation "precious stones," with the "historical flavor" of the word lost in translation. Or *voditsa* with its diminutive suffix *-its*, typical of a folkloric style, is translated as just "water." Such neutralizations are in most cases unavoidable, inevitably resulting in a text that is slightly more "smoothed-over" and less evocative than the original. But morphological archaisms are rare in the Sorokin text, so they do not affect the general tone of the narrative. It is syntax, however, used by Sorokin to produce the stylized fairy tale-cum-bylina prosody of the narrative, that is extremely translation-resistant because of the "organic" incompatibilities in this respect between Russian and English. The core difficulty is in the post-positional strings of attributes (usually adjectives and occasionally adverbs) that are a hallmark of the entire Russian text and that are mostly impossible to duplicate because English rigidly favors adjectival attributes preceding the words that they modify, whereas the Russian bylina-style folk epics are heavily marked by post-positional adjectives and adverbs, which makes them easy to recite or sing. In fact, that is exactly how these originally orally transmitted tales existed in the past: in olden times they were sung by *bayan*s (traveling epic-poem singers–raconteurs) to the accompaniment of *gusli*—psalteries (ancient stringed instruments).

Sorokin's text is a bizarre verbal symphony: it alliterates, rhymes, has assonances, is euphonious and rhythmic—it alternately sings and raps. Does it read like that in English? Can or should it read like that in English? It is hard to make it do so in translation, but in many instances Gambrell succeeds in conveying some significant elements of the Russian prosody. Here is an example of how Gambrell recreates the rap-like style of Komiaga's interior monologue (this becomes more obvious if the two passages are read out loud one after the other for comparison):

Хорошо из Москвы суровой после дня рабочего полноценного в родное Подмосковье возвращаться. А с Москвой прощаться. Потому как Москва – она всей России голова. А в голове имеется мозг. Он к ночи устаёт. И во сне поёт. И в этом пении есть движенье: суженье, растяженье. Напряженье. Многие миллионы вольт и ампер создают необходимый размер. Там живут энергетические врачи. Там мелькают атомные кирпичи. Свистят и в ряды укладываются. Друг в друга вмазываются. Влипают намертво на тысячи век. И из этого построен человек. Дома молекул с ладкою в три кирпича. А то и в четыре. Кто шире? А иногда и в восемьдесят восемь. Мы их об этом потом расспросим. И все дома за заборами крепкими, все с охраной, твари крамольные, гниды своевольные, во гресех рождённые.
(2011b, 280–81)

After a full day of work it's good to leave the stern capital behind and return to my dear Moscow woods. To say farewell to Moscow. Because Moscow is the head of all Russia. And the head has a brain. By night the brain tires. And sings in its sleep. And in the singing there's motion: contraction, expansion. Tension. Suspension. Millions and millions of volts and amps create the necessary rate. Energy doctors dwell there. Nuclear bricks flicker. They whistle and bind. Stick fast forever and evermore. And man is made from this store. Molecule houses of three rows. Even four or five. Which is wide? Sometimes of eighty-eight. We'll ask them later. And all the houses are behind sturdy fences, they all have guards, the subversive vermin, willful worms, born with silver spoons, for execution doomed.
(2011a, 187)

Granted, in the final sentence, Gambrell mistranslates *vo gresekh rozhdennye*, which means "born in sin," as "born with silver spoons"—but that is most likely to make the phrase partially rhyme with "for execution doomed." Such tricks are acceptable, if used consciously for a specific purpose.

Of course, any translation of an intricately constructed literary text always has its limitations, and the translator usually knows what has been or is to be lost in translation. On the level of the whole text, Gambrell is quite successful in stylizing the prosody of her translation to fit the Russian original. This works well with the other ingenious stylistic solutions in her translation: the result is a bizarre and somewhat disorienting—not to say, Orientalizing—English text. Just what Sorokin may well have ordered, given that the effect of the original is also bizarre, disorienting, and artificially "overly Russian."

Intertextuality

Alongside the historic archaization, futuristic neologisms, and epic-fairy tale prosody, the Sorokin text is imbued with intertextuality. It is another defining characteristic of *Oprichnik*. David Lodge, the author of *The Art of Fiction*, defines intertextuality as the "many ways by which one text can refer to another: parody, pastiche, echo, allusion, direct quotation, structural parallelism" (1992, 98). Thomas Foster, the author of the books *How to Read Literature as a Professor* and *How to Read Novels as a Professor*, describes the effect of intertextuality:

> What happens if the writer is good is usually not that the work seems derivative and trivial but just the opposite: the work actually acquires depth and resonance from the echoes and chimes it sets up with prior texts, weight from the accumulated use of certain basic patterns and tendencies. (2003, 187)

Sorokin's text is indeed rich and resonant—it bristles, brims, bleeds, and blasphemes with allusions. What the story lacks in terms of a compelling plot Sorokin compensates for by verbal pyrotechnics and calisthenics. The narrative is a carnival of linguocultural exuberance. At the same time Sorokin's intertextuality has a characteristic twist: it consists of a series of extensive parodic-satirical allusions that vulgarize recognizable positivity-charged texts. The parodies sound shocking and perversely amusing. Thus Sorokin takes a piece of writing—for example, the late 1960s–70s school-curriculum poem "A Story about an Unknown Hero" by Samuil Iakovlevich Marshak (1887–1964) in our illustration below—and upends it: In this case, the unequivocally selfless, life-endangering heroic deed to save somebody else's life on the part of a strapping young man is reworked into a prurient story of a sex-obsessed 33-year-old high-ranking Russian bureaucrat (part of the new *nomenklatura*) who can only get complete sexual satisfaction if he has sexual intercourse with someone in the middle of a major fire, which he himself has started with the aim of having a satisfying sex act. The message that I draw from this is that in the new Russia anything that looks like a selfless, self-sacrificing act is false because, at bottom, the motives are base, self-seeking, or sexually oriented. Here are the first three stanzas of the Russian original, Sorokin's parody, and Gambrell's translation:

Самуил Маршак	Доброжелательный аноним	By Well-Meaning Anonymous
Рассказ о неизвестном герое	Оборотень на пожаре	Werewolf at a Fire

Ищут пожарные,	Ищут пожарные,	Firemen are looking,
Ищет милиция,	Ищет полиция,	The police are looking,
Ищут фотографы	Ищут священники	Even priests are looking
В нашей столице,	В нашей столице,	Throughout our capital city.
Ищут давно,	Ищут давно,	They are seeking a Count,
Но не могут найти	Но не могут найти	Whom they haven't yet found,
Парня какого-то	Графа какого-то	Nor ever have seen,
Лет двадцати.	Лет тридцати.	A Count round about age thirty-three.

Среднего роста,	Среднего роста,	Of medium height,
Плечистый и крепкий,	Задумчиво-мрачный,	Pensive and glum,
Ходит он в белой	Плотно обтянут	He's smartly attired,
Футболке и кепке.	Он парою фрачной.	In tails and cummerbund.
Знак ГТО	В перстне	Cut in the signet ring
На груди у него.	Брильянтовый ёж у него.	On his finger,
Больше не знают	Больше не знают	A hedgehog of diamond gleams and glims,
О нём ничего.	О нём ничего.	But not a whit more is known about him.

Многие парни	Многие графы	Nowadays,
Плечисты и крепки,	Задумчиво-мрачны,	Counts are oft
Многие носят	Стильно обтянуты	Pensive and glum,
Футболки и кепки.	Парою фрачной,	Stylishly garbed,
Много в столице	Любят брильянтов	In tails and cummerbund.
Таких же значков –	Заманчивый дым, –	They adore the alluring
Каждый	Сладкая жизнь	Dazzle of diamonds,
К труду-обороне	Уготована им!	The dolce vita
Готов!		Is just waiting to find them.
(1930s?)	(2011b, 58–59)	(2011a, 37–38)

In the Marshak story, the young man, on seeing a little girl waving her arms in a window of an apartment house engulfed by fire, climbs up the rainwater pipe, brings the girl down to safety, hops onto a street car and disappears into the workday turmoil of Moscow without leaving a name. Hence the search for him in order to reward his heroic deed with a medal or some other symbol of public recognition.

In the Sorokin story, the generously-endowed young Count climbs through the window of a burning house that he himself set on fire, has rough sex with a generously-endowed young lady amid the conflagration and in full view of the crowd down on the sidewalk, and then gets away from the scene in his Rolls Royce, running over a stray dog in the process and leaving the crowd wondering where the lady has disappeared to. A search is on for the Count in order to punish him for cheating on his wife, who is the Russian Sovereign's daughter. The motive is revenge.

Marshak's "A Story about an Unknown Hero" is a lively, easy to remember Soviet hymn glorifying selfless heroism for the sake of other people. High school kids in Soviet Russia had to learn most of the poem by heart and then recite it from memory in class for a grade. Sorokin's intertextual appropriation highlights the perverse nature of the new Russia. The parodic text resonates with the original Marshak verses stored in the Russian collective cultural memory, adding to the narrative an extra layer of signification and making it fun to read. Gambrell's ingenious translation of the poem preserves the surface layer of signification and is also fun to read, but the text is less deep than the original. The English-language reader will take it at face value.

To add another brushstroke to the picture of intertextuality in Sorokin's novella, here is another example. It is seriously politically incorrect because it creates a morally painful juxtaposition of Jews and Hitler. It may be argued, I suppose, that it reinforces a dimension in Komiaga's character—that of thinly veiled anti-Semitism:

Vladimir Maiakovskii	Vladimir Sorokin	Jamey Gambrell
Да будь я хоть негром преклонных годов, И то б, без унынья и лени, Я русский бы выучил только за то, Что им разговаривал Ленин! (http://www.anekdot.ru/id/143206/)	Да будь я евреем Преклонных годов, И то – nicht zweifelnd und bitter, Немецкий я б выучил только за то, Что им разговаривал Гитлер. (2011b, 209)	Were I a Jew Late in life, Even then— *Nicht zweifelnd und bitter* I'd learn German If only because, 'Twas German spoken By Hitler. (2011a, 140)

To help the reader with the intertextuality above, both Sorokin and Gambrell provide their respective passages with footnotes: Sorokin gives the original Maiakovskii verse in Russian and the Russian translation of the German phrase "nicht zweifelnd und bitter," which is "bez somneniia i gorechi"; Gambrell gives the English translation of the German phrase as "without

doubt or bitterness" and her own translation of the original text by Maiakovskii, which goes: "Were I even a Negro late in my life, even so, without dawd-
ling or dreariness, I'd go and learn Russian simply because, 'twas in Russian
that Lenin conversed" (2011a, 140). As with the previous piece of verse, in Soviet times, every Russian knew those lines. They were memorized and recited
in school as a celebration of the world-historic importance of the Russian language because Lenin, the founder of the Soviet state, spoke it. In Komiaga's
case, the lines are a paraphrase of the Maiakovskii lines by Komiaga's mathematician grandfather, who recited his version of the quote in order to force a
reluctant Komiaga to apply himself more vigorously to learning German. The
effect is jarring and funny because the juxtaposition is so starkly unPC.

These are just two examples of the several extensive segments of the
Sorokin text playing on the cultural background and perceived high school
knowledge of the reader. The latent problem of the text extracts quoted above
is that they are no longer part of the school literature curriculum, probably
because they are too Soviet, which means that the multilayered resonance of
Sorokin's intertextuality may well be already lost on part of Russian readers
younger than Sorokin and will certainly be increasingly unrecognizable as
time goes by. This is the time bomb ticking away inside any postmodernist
text, and a usually insurmountable difficulty for the translator. How does
Gambrell cope with the pervasive intertextuality of the novel? With difficulty,
as any translator would, because the required cultural background of the
English-speaking audience is not there. However, as with the problem of
prosody discussed earlier, she generally succeeds in conveying the disorienting, alien aura of Sorokin's story and the sense that the Russians are a strange
breed, just as the received stereotype has it.

Dimensions of Pragmatics Revisited

The translator's imprint on the text of the translation is determined by his/her
educational, linguistic, and translation expertise levels, manifesting themselves within a given sociocultural context. A comparative translation discourse analysis usually reveals, first, mistranslations which are the result of
deficiencies in the translator's knowledge of the foreign language, and, second, the cultural misconceptions verbalized in the translation. But the translator's unique traces in the text are also left by the specific pragmatics applied
by the translator to the whole text. This pragmatics consists in utilizing the
five modes or modalities of translation outlined in chapter 3. The degrees of
application of these modes of translation are determined by the overall,
central pragmatic strategy that the translator has to decide on from the very
beginning, with the prospective, assumed audience and the purpose of translation being the determining factors. In this section, I will retouch and further

specify the five pragmatic strategies as deployed by Gambrell in translating Sorokin's text.

Neutralization vs. Domestication (Naturalization)

Neutralization and domestication (or naturalization) are viewed by some writers as synonyms. I differentiate between them by treating them as two distinct concepts, techniques, and outcomes. Neutralizing a stretch of language involves giving up on duplicating any distinctive features that it has in the original and using instead "undistinguished" language in the translation. For example, Gambrell translates the Russian archaic *opuskaiu ochi dolu* (2011b, 255)—which stands out in the Russian text as an instance of historical stylization—as the neutral (indistinguishable from the rest of the text) "I lower my eyes" (2011a, 168). Some other examples: the Russian slangy and vulgar *pod"eldykivat'* (2011b, 215), which, in this context, means "to fawn on someone" or "to curry favor with someone" (it is derived from the obsolete *elda*—penis) is translated by the neutral and unnoticeable "to pretend" in "They know how to pretend" (2011a, 143). I would suggest: "They know how to brownnose you" or something along similarly harsh lines; *tolkovishche*, a historically stylized slang term for "meeting" (2011b, 139), is just that in the translation—"meeting" (2011a, 95); the non-standard (dialectal) *tapericha* (2011b, 244) becomes "now" (2011a, 162), etc. The translation is filled with instances of neutralization that are—in the majority of cases—unavoidable due to the differences in the etymological trajectories of the Russian and English vocabulary and grammar.

In contrast to neutralization, I define domestication (or naturalization) as the creation of a translation that is clearly marked as belonging to the receiving (target) culture. A domesticated translation fits into the text as something integrally belonging to the receiving language and culture. It is different from the "neutral" parts of the text. Translating Russian expletives (*mat*), which is discussed in chapter 2, may serve as a graphic illustration of domestication. Here is an extract from the *Oprichnik*, in which Komiaga is listening on his car radio to a subversive broadcast by the Voice of America aimed at undermining the norms of decency in Russia, where *mat* is forbidden and punishable by law. The broadcast is called "Russian 'Mat' in Exile," and it is a vulgarized retelling of the famous murder scene in Dostoevsky's *Crime and Punishment* (i.e., another piece of intertextuality):

Охуенный удар невъебенного топора пришелся в самое темя триждыраспронаебаной старухи, чему пиздато способствовал ее мандаблядски малый рост. Она задроченно вскрикнула и вдруг вся как-то пиздапроушенно осела к непроебанному полу, хотя и	The un-fucking-believable blow of the butt-fucking axe hit the goddamn temple of the triply gang-banged old bag, facilitated piss-perfectly by her cunt-sucking short height. She cried out cumly and suddenly collapsed on the jism-covered shit-paneled floor, although that

успела, зассыха гниложопая, поднять
свои злоебучие руки к хуевой, по-
блядски простоволосой голове…
(2011b, 103–04)

rotten pussy-hole of a hag had time to
raise both of her ass-licking hands to her
fuckin' bare-ass pimped-up head.
(2011a, 66)

Of course, both passages above sound contrived because nobody swears like that in real life, although the "swearing material" both in Russian and English is authentic and used very imaginatively. The translation is the result of defamiliarizing domestication, which utilizes standard swear vocabulary in imaginative ways. To me it sounds as perversely funny as the original. Perversely, because this is a "desacralization" of a tragic and gory scene from a canonical Russian novel. From my perspective, the perceived authorial purpose of making the broadcast sound comically absurd has been achieved. But the bottom layer of the harrowing Dostoevsky text is lost on the English language reader. I suspect that the feeling of unease I experienced when I read the parody of the pawn-broker's murder scene will not arise in a reader from another culture.

Foreignization

As was pointed out in chapter 3, the five strategies of "pragmatizing" the original, i.e., bringing it in line with the perceived expectations of the audience, overlap and inter-penetrate. The above example of defamiliarizing domestication bears witness to this in that it is socioculturally strange, not to say ridiculous, even though it does rely exclusively on genuine English expletives. Now suppose I wanted to foreignize the extract to the full in order to bring the reader as close to the Russian text as possible. I would have to imitate the Russian morphology, syntax, lexis, style, and imagery to the point of seriously straining the resources and boundaries of English. This should supposedly bring the English reader closer to the imagery of the original. A foreignized translation of the extract might go something like this:

Охуенный удар невъебенного топора
пришелся в самое темя триждырас-
пронаебаной старухи, чему пиздато
способствовал ее мандаблядски малый
рост. Она задроченно вскрикнула и
вдруг вся как-то пиздапроушенно
осела к непроебанному полу, хотя и
успела, зассыха гниложопая, поднять
свои злоебучие руки к хуевой, по-
блядски простоволосой голове…
(2011b, 103–04)

The cock-boggling blow of the no-fucking-joke axe landed smack on the top of the head of the triply-fucked-inside-out old hag, which blow was cuntingly facilitated by her twat-hoe short height. She gave out a jerked-off cry and suddenly kind of slumped all of a heap, like a saggy-eared cunt, onto the underfucked floor, managing for an instant, like the rotten-assholed, knickers-pissing bitch that she was, to raise her fierce-fucking arms to her cock-like, whorishly plain-haired head… (A.B.)

In my attempt at foreignizing the Russian text above, my translation bursts at its semantic seams, so to speak, due to the semantic, morphologic, and syntactic incompatibilities of the two languages. In fact, what I have ended up with sounds absurdly stilted, or "stiltedly" absurd. More so than Sorokin's text does. In this particular case, Gambrell's domestication-cum-defamiliarization solution seems to work better because it relies on the defamiliarized usual, whereas mine depends too much on the foreignized and the unusual. But either approach arguably has its merits.

Stylization

Stylization is imitation of a particular author's style, recognized functional style, specific genre of writing, or the language of a particular historical period. In translating complex texts, stylization may involve creating a style of writing that does not exist in the translating language and that will necessarily eclectically combine existing expressive means with something invented. Sorokin's text is a dystopia that combines stylized archaization of lexis and syntax, vulgar slang, authorial sociocultural and technological neologisms, and double entendres based on intertextuality. What makes Sorokin's novella serious literature is the polyphony, or heteroglossia (*raznorechie*), to use Bakhtin's term, of the various texts and styles it creates. At the same time this is what makes Sorokin's text pretty much "inimitable" in translation. I would say that in Sorokin's novella everything is stylization. It would follow that Gambrell's task was to replicate this stylization and make it as comprehensible to the English audience as possible. The problem is that postmodernist writing, with its interplay of styles, is most comprehensible within the medium of the original language and against the background of the original literary trends and brands. In a translation, such stylization is possible only to a limited degree because of the readers' lack of the cultural background that postmodernist texts aim to engage. In fact, no matter what the translator could do with Sorokin's text, short of wholesale neutralization, it would still be perceived, to the exclusion of everything else, as a distinctly Russian story. Its foreignness would overshadow the novella's distinctive "clangor" and clash of styles in Russian and so the claim of any translation of this very postmodernist text to being serious literature would be partially undermined. It is a brave translator who undertakes such a thankless task.

Contamination

This brings us finally to the issue of contamination. As was already briefly described in chapter 3, contamination is the use of grammatical forms and lexis that are generally considered by the majority of the native speakers of a language community and also by the scholarly institutions of that community (dictionaries, educational bodies, etc.) as "non-normative" or non-standard. Contamination is used by the author in order to signal the speaker's different sociocultural status relative to the other characters in the piece of writing.

Contamination is a salient marker of the sociolect the speaker uses. As such it is usually impossible to duplicate exactly, so it is normally signaled and compensated for by irregular usages in the translating language in the parts of the text that often do not exactly coincide with the "contaminated" stretches of language in the original. The cross-cultural reader gets the general idea. In *Oprichnik*, however, we have a special case where contamination as a translation strategy is not a significant factor because the original is not "contaminated" in the traditionally defined sense of the word. Nevertheless, the translation still gets somewhat "contaminated" in the sense that the text is full of loan translations (calques) and "barbarisms"[20]—"contaminants" that have not been neutralized. These culturally and linguistically less visible items of the original are more noticeable in the translation. The translation is contaminated by its foreignness.

Concluding Remarks

The major difficulties in Sorokin's text can be grouped under two broad rubrics: cultural-historical realia and peculiarities of authorial style—diction, text prosody, and intertextual allusions. Gambrell deals with realia in the well-established ways, with the predictable result that their salient presence in the translation makes the translation a more alien text to its English readers than it is to Russian audiences, whose cultural experience makes many of the realia inconspicuous or invisible. The peculiar authorial diction mixes together archaisms, vulgarisms, and neologisms resulting in a very eclectic, graphic, "shock-and-awe" style that triggers semantic chains of associations impossible to replicate in a translation. As a result, I expect the Russian reader to be more appreciative of Sorokin's individual style than is the English-speaking reader, who lacks the native linguistic and literary basis for comparison. Prosody (the text's cadencies, rhythms, assonances, alliterations, and not infrequent rhymes) is rendered by Gambrell surprisingly well; surprisingly, because there is little "organic" correspondence between Russian and English phonological resources and because of the very limited ability of English to appropriate the numerous instances of the Russian word order with post-positional adjectives and adverbs, typical of Russian folk epic narrative poems (*byliny*) and fairy tales. Sorokin's text "sings," Gambrell's "swings," which is no mean achievement. Intertextuality proves more problematic. With his across-the-board monocultural intertextuality, Sorokin sets himself up to be hoist with his own petard in any translation: the parodied Russian literary works and cultural experiences are impossible to evoke in the collective memory of the English-speaking audience because such an audience simply does

---

[20] Barbarism—the use in a language of forms or constructions felt by some to be undesirably alien to the established standards of the language (*Dictionary.com*, http://dictionary.reference.com/browse/barbarism).

not have a comparable educational and cultural background. As for the question which I ask at the beginning of this chapter—do I feel the same level of emotional unease when reading the translation that I feel when reading the original?—my answer is "Not entirely." I find the translation somewhat more detached—less affectively poignant and compelling than the original, most likely, because I am a product of Soviet-Russian culture. Overall, Gambrell's is a highly commendable translation reinforcing, as it does, "Western" stereotypical views of Russian culture as crude, violent, and hopelessly undemocratic—exactly the views Sorokin himself publicizes in his blog.[21] This last point needs some additional attention. According to Parks, "the central irony of much modern international literary celebrity" is the fact that "however much the writer may prize his individual identity, his book is not the same book in another context" (Parks 2007, 243). It is

> notoriety, non-conformism, and assault on received opinion at home [that] encourage publication in other languages, since nobody is more avidly sought after than a rebel from another land; indeed, this is a crucial factor in the internationalization of literature, going back as far as the exiled Catullus [and] the exiled Dante [...]. Depending on the content and structure of the book, the author may still appear to the foreign reader as a rebel, but at the linguistic level, the level that, as Juan Gelman claimed, is most determining, the individual element in his work is lost. It threatens no one in the country of consumption [...]. We enjoy vicariously without being challenged or threatened. (Parks 2007, 244)

One might add that we are also likely to adopt a patronizing attitude toward the cultural other because we are incapable of appreciating the more subtly disturbing aspects of the narrative. Given these potential constraints, is it possible to translate Sorokin's novella as a very complex piece of postmodernist writing, i.e., serious literature, or would the translator be wiser to render it as a political-ideological lampoon, which it also is, resonant with the easy stereotypes of Russia entertained by foreign audiences? In the former case, the translator would focus on the "untranslatable"—uniqueness of linguistic choices, intertextuality, and prosody; in the latter—on the shock effect of the characters' extraordinary behavior. Sorokin's text is both serious postmodernist literature and a political lampoon. Gambrell goes for broke and pursues both literature and entertainment. I think her translation is a *tour de force*. I do not see how one can succeed better, always knowing, of course, that one can succeed differently.

---

[21] *VLDMR SRKN: Ofitsial'nyi sait Vladimira Sorokina*, http://www.srkn.ru/blog/2012-01-03.html.

Finally, although the translator's tasks are formidable and may be too "artistic" to verbalize, I firmly believe that it is supremely important for the translator to understand and formulate for oneself his or her *modus operandi* in tackling a particular piece of writing. To quote Parks, it is "important to understand the strategy of the work as a whole, its rhythms, its imagery, its stylistic techniques; only then can we reconstruct it as a coherent whole, and thus, as Beckett liked to say, 'fail better'" (2007, 248).

By Way of a Coda

There is an intersemiotic aspect of *Oprichnik*'s intertextuality that is impervious to effective translation. It is the graphic imagery of the novella that feeds, to a large extent, on the emblematic visual impact of Eisenstein's film *Ivan the Terrible*, especially its second part, which contains bacchanalian scenes of rampaging oprichniks.[22] To me, the final homosexual orgy and some other important episodes in the book read like a sexed-up intersemiotic translation of sequences from the Eisenstein film. Thus, on top of everything else, the whole novella reads like a series of separate cinematic episodes, which makes it all the more compelling for the native reader and that much more frustrating for the translator.

---

[22] In his interview with Tat'iana Voskovskaia, originally posted online on 4 April 1998 (http://lib.misto.kiev.ua/SOROKIN/interv01.txt), Sorokin talks in some detail about the more important formative influence on him of Soviet films, rather than literature. It should also be added that Sorokin is a professionally trained artist (see the same interview), which implies an acute visual perception of reality. I think this seeps through into his texts.

Chapter 6

Translation as a Political Weapon:
Having a Riot Translating "Pussy Riot"

Imagine living in a world without translators. [...] The human brain has evolved to permit the learning of just a single language; translation is thus out of the question. The resulting world [...] is radically and starkly diminished. [...] the Arabs, the Assyrians, the Egyptians, the Greeks, the Hebrews, and the Romans learned nothing from one another. There has been no New Testament, no Renaissance, no Reformation, no Enlightenment, no scientific or industrial revolution. There is no [...] United Nations Charter [and] no European Union. Works of literature, philosophy, scholarship, and science that may have been produced in other linguistic contexts are forever inaccessible to speakers of English—and of course the English language itself has not developed in anything like its present form.[1]

This is a thought experiment portraying a dystopian situation, of course, but it makes a point whose relevance is only matched by its being generally ignored. The point is that, while the complexity and significance of translators' work is routinely underappreciated, translation plays a central role in a vast range of human activities. The case study in this chapter shows how different translations, mistranslations, or "non-translations" of an idiomatic expression betray one's political and socio-cultural preferences. I illustrate my argument with a recent globally reported incident involving a group of young Russian women who call themselves "Pussy Riot." I do not adopt either a pro or a contra attitude toward Pussy Riot themselves, but—to reiterate—examine the incident to illustrate the use of translation as an important means of socio-political discourse.

"Musical" Backstory

Pussy Riot is a Russian self-designated punk-rock collective based in Moscow. Its members are women wearing brightly colored balaclavas and staging

---

[1] Catherine Porter, "Why Translation?" *MLA Newsletter* (Fall 2009), reprinted in the Modern Language Association blog, accessed 27 February 2013, http://www.mla.org/blog?topic=130.

unauthorized provocative performances in unusual public locations. The performances are then edited into music videos and posted on the Internet. Pussy Riot's lyrical themes include feminism, LGBT rights, opposition to Russian president Vladimir Putin, whom they regard as a dictator, and denunciation of links between the leadership of the Russian Orthodox Church and the Putin administration.[2]

On 19 February 2012, Pussy Riot attempted a performance at the Epiphany Cathedral at Yelokhovo in Moscow, but after having some sound problems with the amplifiers, were led out of the church by security guards.[3] On 21 February 2012, five members of the group staged a performance in front of the iconostasis in Moscow's Cathedral of Christ the Savior. After less than a minute, their actions were stopped by church security officials. By evening a music video entitled "Punk Prayer—Mother of God, Chase Putin Away!" appeared on the Internet.[4] The English Wikipedia provides the following description of the contents of Pussy Riot's Internet posting:

> The song, which they [Pussy Riot] described as a punk *moleben* (supplicatory prayer), borrowed its opening melody and refrain from Sergei Rachmaninoff's *Bogoroditse Devo, Raduisya* (Ave Maria), from the *All Night Vigil*. In the song, they invoked the name of the Virgin Mary, urging her to get rid of [the then] Russian Prime Minister Vladimir Putin and to "become a feminist," claiming that she would support them in their protests. They alluded to close ties between the church and the KGB[5] ("Black robes, golden epaulettes"), criticized the subservience of many Russians to the church ("Parishioners crawl bowing") and attacked the church's traditionalist views on women ("So as not to offend His Holiness, women must bear children and love"). They used the crude epithet *"Sran Gospodnya,"* literally "shit of the Lord" but usually translated as "holy shit" [...]. They referred to Russian Orthodox Patriarch Kirill I, as a *"suka"* (bitch)[6] and accused him of believing more in Putin than in God.[7]

---

[2] See Wikipedia, accessed 12 December 2012, http://en.wikipedia.org/wiki/Pussy_Riot.

[3] For more details, see http://en.wikipedia.org/wiki/Pussy_Riot.

[4] The version that is widely disseminated online can be watched and heard here: "Pank-moleben 'Bogoroditsa Putina progoni' Pussy Riot v Khrame," YouTube video, 1: 53, posted by "Garadzha Matveeva," http://www.youtube.com/watch?v=GCasuaAczKY.

[5] This government agency's official name since 1995 has been Federal Security Service (usually abbreviated as FSB for "Federal'naia sluzhba bezopasnosti").

[6] In Russian prison slang (*fenia*), *suka* is a deeply derogatory term for a prisoner who is collaborating with the prison authorities, informing on other prisoners, and also a prisoner who has been sodomized in prison and is held in total contempt and treated as somebody "untouchable."

[7] Wikipedia, http://en.wikipedia.org/wiki/Pussy_Riot (accessed 29 December 2012). At this point in its entry, Wikipedia gives three references: (1) [Khristina Narizhnaya], "Pussy

Three group members—Nadezhda Tolokonnikova (b. 1989), Maria Alekhina (b. 1988), and Ekaterina Samutsevich (b. 1982)—were arrested in March and charged with hooliganism (a variety of disorderly conduct in the Russian penal code). Denied bail, they were held in a pre-trial detention center until their trial began in late July. The defendants pleaded not guilty, saying that they had not meant their protest to be offensive. "We sang part of the refrain 'Holy shit' [*sran' gospodnia*]," Tolokonnikova said in court. "I am sorry if I offended anyone with this. It is an idiomatic expression, related to the previous verse—about the fusion of Moscow patriarchy and the government. 'Holy shit' is our evaluation of the situation in the country. This opinion is not blasphemy."[8]

On 17 August 2012, the three members were convicted of hooliganism motivated by religious hatred, and each was sentenced to two years' imprisonment. On 10 October, following an appeal, Samutsevich was freed on probation, her sentence suspended. The sentences of the other two women were upheld. In late October 2012, Alekhina and Tolokonnikova were separated and sent to prison camps.[9] Interviewed at her prison camp by the *Novaia Gazeta* journalist Elena Masiuk in late January 2013, Tolokonnikova said: "Our action was rather a pro-religion than an anti-religion one. I'm absolutely clear about that. [...] For me, the Bible is, like, an integral part of my life."[10]

Riot Trial Nears Verdict in Moscow," *Rolling Stone*, 7 August 2012, http://www.rollingstone.com/music/news/pussy-riot-trial-nears-verdict-in-moscow-20120807; (2) Carol Rumen, "Pussy Riot's Punk Prayer Is Pure Protest Poetry," *The Guardian*, 20 August 2012, http://www.guardian.co.uk/books/2012/aug/20/pussy-riot-punk-prayer-lyrics; (3) "What Pussy Riot's 'Punk Prayer' Really Said," *The Atlantic*, 8 November 2012, http://www.theatlantic.com/international/archive/2012/11/what-pussy-riots-punk-prayer-really-said/264562.

[8] Narizhnaya, "Pussy Riot Trial Nears Verdict in Moscow."

[9] http://en.wikipedia.org/wiki/Pussy_Riot (last accessed 11 December 2012).

[10] Elena Masiuk, "'Dvushechka': Zona ispravleniia dlia Pussy Riot," *Novaia Gazeta*, no. 7, 23 January 2013, p. 4, http://www.novayagazeta.ru/issues/2013/ 1988.html. The full relevant segment of the interview is as follows: "Масюк: Честно вам скажу, вы говорите 'Библия', и у меня это вызывает вопрос: почему Библия? Толоконникова: У вас вызывает вопрос, потому что, мне кажется, вы тоже оказались немного совращены этой государственной пропагандой. Поскольку *наше действие было скорее прорелигиозное, чем антирелигиозное. И для меня это очевидно совершенно.* Для меня это вытекало очень органично из всего того, о чем я думала раньше в своей жизни, и я достаточно серьезно интересовалась русской религиозной философией, и одно время я ее очень долго и упорно читала — Бердяев, Соловьев, Мережковский, эти кружки, которые собирались в начале XX века, Розанов, — они встречались с представителями официальной православной церкви и требовали модернизации православной церкви. И уже тогда представители официальной православной церкви воспринимали это все в штыки. Модернизации не случилось. И я чувствую себя просто продолжателем традиций этих русских философов, поэтому *Библия для меня является достаточно органичной частью моей жизни.* Кроме того, мне достаточно симпатичны протестантские идеи о том, что

It should be added, by way of clarification, that in the pre-montage video of the Pussy Riot performance in the Christ the Savior Cathedral, the only phrase that is clearly audible is indeed "Sran' gospodnia!" It is shouted out many times. The video that first appeared on the Internet[11] did not contain any clearly audible anti-Putin or feminist rhetoric.

The phrase *sran' gospodnia* deserves a brief discussion here as it is an example of how a sloppy translation of an English idiom—"Holy shit!" in this case—may go viral. I attribute the origin of *sran' gospodnia* to Leonid Volodarskii's widely popular voiceover translations of American movies in the 1990s. I have a distinct recollection of hearing Volodarskii translate the interjection *Holy shit!* as "Sran' gospodnia!" Thus, originally, it was a neologistic, foreignizing mistranslation—a typical piece of voiceover translationese. *Holy shit!* does not translate literally as "God's shit," "the Lord's shit," "Godly shit," "Lordly shit," etc. Back-translating these would indeed produce something like "sran' gospodnia." Based on the pragmatics of its usage, *Holy shit!* has good approximations in the vulgar "Ni khuia sebe!" and the euphemistic "Ni khera sebe!" which, for some reason, Volodarskii did not use. Various other voiceover translators picked up the newly-coined unusually-sounding idiom, making it widely known. As is often the case with punchy, unusual language used by voiceover translators, the expression has entered the Russian language and even acquired some "virtual" lexicographical status.[12] Today it is sometimes used—mostly by younger people—as an interjection expressing strong emotions or shock and also as a vulgar reference to a contemptible or detestable person or something disgusting. Pussy Riot's notoriety has arguably contributed to the spread of this expression.[13]

нужно обращаться в первую очередь к первоисточникам, не столько к церкви как иерархии, а именно к первоисточнику как откровению, данному изначально."

[11] The original, one-minute-thirty-five-second video can be watched here: http://www. youtube.com/watch?v=FoJqzGG7u_k (accessed 2 January 2013). I think it is significant that this pre-montage (without the singing) sequence at the Christ the Savior Cathedral was readily accessible online immediately after 21 February 2012, but today, in the overwhelming majority of attempts, one is taken to the one-minute-fifty-three-second video (with the superimposed singing and an added visual sequence from the Yelokhov Cathedral) that is erroneously widely believed to be the original recording of the performance. Whether this latter video was prepared beforehand or after Pussy Riot's Christ the Savior performance is immaterial for the purpose of the present argument. But one thing seems to be clear: it was meant for widespread consumption on the Internet.

[12] For the definitions of the phrase in Russian, see the online dictionary *Vikislovar'* at http://ru.wiktionary.org/wiki/%D1%81%D1%80%D0%B0%D0%BD%D1%8C_%D0%B3%D0%BE %D1%81%D0%BF%D0%BE%D0%B4%D0%BD%D1%8F.

[13] Quite rightly, interestingly, and significantly, Jeffrey Taylor of *The Atlantic* magazine back-translates the idiom Pussy Riot creatively used in their "prayer" as "Shit, shit, the Lord's shit!" ("What Pussy Riot's 'Punk Prayer' Really Said," 8 November 2012,

The Unbearable Lightness of Translation

A certain Mr. Ugrik, testifying as a prosecution witness at the Pussy Riot trial in Moscow on 1 August 2012, said the following: "Pussy Riot is a horrible name. 'Pussy' literally translates as 'exuding pus, pussy,' and 'riot' is 'debauchery.'"[14] Among the first to react to Mr. Ugrik's translation exercise was the translation sociologist Sergei Tyulenev, who wrote in his blog: "Obviously [a] truthful translation was not the goal. The goal was to translate the word 'pussy' together with another word, 'riot', [...] so that the band would look worse than it was and [so as] to mask the political nature of the action."[15] Indeed, the case of Pussy Riot shows that the translation of *Pussy Riot* can be tweaked in a variety of politically and culturally engaged ways. What follows is a discussion of the various translations of the band's name invoked by different high-profile personages in different media.

It is noteworthy that until the final stages of the trial, the punk band's name, "Pussy Riot," had usually not been translated—it had been embedded into discourse in its original English spelling. The name itself was a clever choice, arguably, aimed at audiences capable of understanding the double entendre in English. Criticizing the ineptness of the prosecution and Pussy Riot's own defense team, Michael Idov wrote in *The Guardian*:

> The only professionals anywhere in sight are Pussy Riot themselves. From their name, perfectly pitched to both shock and attract the western media, to their instantly recognisable look; from their message (concise bursts of feminist agitprop with just enough of a tune to pass as a song), to their method of distributing this message via social networks; from their initial punk posturing in interviews, to their point-

---

http://www.theatlantic.com/international/archive/2012/11/what-pussy-riots-punk-prayer-really-said/264562/).

[14] The complete relevant passage from the article "Svidetel' perevel v sude nazvanie Pussy Riot" (Witness Translates "Pussy Riot" in Court), posted on the site Lenta.ru on 1 August 2012, at 17:54:05, goes as follows: "Свидетель со стороны обвинения Олег Угрик, 1 августа дававший показания по делу участниц Pussy Riot, попросил суд обратить внимание на название группы, сообщает Интерфакс. 'Pussy Riot – жуткое название. Pussy переводится дословно как "гноевидный," "гнойный," a riot – "разгул,"' – сказал Угрик. Стоит отметить, что вариантов перевода у слов pussy и riot достаточно много. Например, pussy может переводиться как "кошка" или "соблазнительная женщина." В английском языке нередко употребление слова pussy в значении "женские наружные половые органы." Слово riot может, в частности, употребляться в значении "мятеж," "бунт," "изобилие," "бесчинства," accessed 20 August 2013, http://lenta.ru/news/2012/08/01/riot3/.

[15] See Sergey Tyulenev, "A Wrong Translation for a 'Right' Cause: A New Type of Translation Discovered," *Translation Studies and Its Turns* (blog), 14 August 2012, accessed 20 August 2012, http://translation.tyulenev.org/#post44.

edly academic statements to the court, which no less than David
Remnick called "a kind of instant classic in the anthology of dissi-
dence"; these women, and they alone in this mess, know exactly what
they are doing.[16]

Granted, "Pussy Riot" is a suggestive English name, which is quite under-
standable in an age of globalization, with English being the global lingua
franca.[17] And it is true that names of bands are traditionally not translated but
transliterated, transcribed or embedded into the receiving language in their
original form,[18] even though these "non-translation" translations often obfuscate the emotional connotations or the imagery of a proper name in their original language. The translator's justification and rationale in such cases are
that, whatever the losses in translation, the advantages lie in avoiding extra-
neous associations, bizarre connotations, and absurd language. Using a foreign name or an untranslated transliteration/phonetic transcription is the
translator's shield against practically unavoidable criticism. And yet, time and
again, translators are pressed into translating such names by the audience,
context, or specific circumstances. In such cases, translators often have to
hedge their translations with various cultural comments and defensive re-
marks. The defining factors in calibrating specific translations would normally be the audience and the direction of translation. Thus it is reasonable to
assume that the members of The Beatles or Iron Maiden did not count on the

---

[16] Mikhail Idov, "Pussy Riot Prove the Only Professionals in Sight," *The Guardian*, 17
August 2012, 11.59 EDT. http://www.guardian.co.uk/commentisfree/2012/aug/17/pussy-riot-
only-professionals-in-sight (accessed 12 December 2012).

[17] It is interesting to note that the Russian Pussy Riot have all but ousted the other
PusSy RiOt band from the Internet space, even though the latter seems to have been
formed much earlier: "Pussy Riot was born in Summer 2004 when Katerina and Ana-
stasia met Luisa. The three girls were soon on the same wavelength and began to play
in some music pubs and festivals. Pussy Riot is inspired by the nineties Riot Grrrl
movement, but they are always searching for more aggressive and modern sounds.
Pussy Riot's songs are prickly and they convey inner suffering into a mixture of hys-
terical and distorted screams together with dissonant sounds. The band recorded its
first official demo 'ThisTroy' on September 2006" (http://us.myspace.com/pussyriot).

[18] When I "naively" addressed the question of whether *Pussy Riot* should be translated
to the famous Russian lexicographer and translation theorist Dmitrii Yermolovich, his
response was unequivocal: do not translate. Here is our exchange: "А.В.: Уважаемый
Дмитрий Иванович, следует ли переводить на русский язык название группы
Pussy Riot, и если да, то всегда ли и как? Д.И. Ермолович: Иноязычные названия
групп, ансамблей и других музыкальных коллективов, как правило, не перевод-
ятся на русский язык. Вспомним, например, 'Роллинг стоунз', 'Дип перпл' и т.д.
Поэтому и Pussy Riot не переводится, а может только транскрибироваться на
русский язык ('Пусси Райот')." Aleksandr [Burak], 8 September 2012, "Perevoditsia li
'Pussy Riot'?" discussion on *Sait D. I. Ermolovicha*, http://yermolovich.ru/board/1-1-0-167.

names of their bands being translated into Russian. The evocative names were originally meant for English-speaking audiences. Translating these names into Russian would require some glosses. And this also holds true for translating the name *Pussy Riot*. But the fact is that, while aiming at global recognition, Pussy Riot remains a Russian band, and so—especially given the notoriety of their various performances—the question of how to translate their name into Russian acquires some extra legitimacy. In fact, this question has become inevitable and surfaced again and again in various media—even at the highest level.

Translation Battles

On 6 September 2012, the question of how to translate *Pussy Riot* into Russian was raised by none other than President Vladimir Putin himself. He was being interviewed by Kevin Owen of the Russia Today English-language television channel. The interviewer was obviously being coy and trying to entrap Putin, while Putin challenged the interviewer to translate the name into Russian himself:

VLADIMIR PUTIN: You've been working in Russia for a while now and maybe know some Russian. Could you please translate the name of the band into Russian?

В. ПУТИН: А Вы могли бы перевести название группы на русский язык? Вы ведь уже не один год живёте в России.

KEVIN OWEN: "Pussy Riot" the punk band, I don't know what you would call them in Russian, Sir, but may be you could tell me!

К. ОУЭН: Не могу сказать, как "Пусси Райот" переводится на русский, может быть, Вы подскажете?

VLADIMIR PUTIN: Can you translate the first word into Russian? Or maybe it would sound too obscene? Yes, I think you wouldn't do it because it sounds too obscene, even in English.

В. ПУТИН: А Вы можете перевести само слово на русский язык или нет? Или Вам неудобно это сделать по этическим соображениям? Думаю, что это неудобно сделать по этическим соображениям. Даже в английском языке это звучит неприлично.

KEVIN OWEN: I actually thought it was referring to a cat, *but I'm getting your point here*. […] (My italics—A.B.)

К.Оуэн: Я бы перевёл это слово как "кошечка", *но может быть, я чего-то не понимаю* [sic!].[19]

---

[19] There may be three reasons for the mistranslation of "but I'm getting your point here" as "no mozhet byt', ia chego-to ne ponimaiu": the translator's ignorance (unlikely); an instance of the translator's "misspeaking" without a chance to "unspeak" it

VLADIMIR PUTIN: I know you understand it perfectly well, you don't need to pretend you don't get it. It's just because these people made all of you say their band's name out loud too many times. It's obscene—but forget it.[20]

В. ПУТИН: Всё Вы понимаете, Вы всё прекрасно понимаете, не нужно делать вид, что Вы чего-то не понимаете. Просто граждане эти навязали общественному мнению своё название и заставили всех вас произносить его вслух. Ведь это неприлично, но бог с ними.

Immediately following this interview (in fact, on the same day), the *Moskovskii komsomolets* newspaper addressed the question of how to translate *Pussy Riot* to some translation experts. Their responses were published by the paper on the same day. Here is an excerpt from the *Moskovskii komsomolets* interview with Simon Shuster, the Moscow *Time Magazine* correspondent and apparently a heritage speaker of Russian:

> **MK:** Here's a question for experts: How do you translate "Pussy Riot"?
> **Shuster:** Most likely, "the riot of pussy cats." That's the only correct [translation].
> **MK:** You mean "kitties"? Or something else?
> **Shuster:** Yes, "kitties."
> **MK:** But there is another translation, which is, putting it mildly—"the rebellion of vaginas" [*bunt vagin*]. Is it possible to say so?
> **Shuster:** This is a very funny conversation we're having here. Yes, it is possible to say so, too. But the phrase is very difficult to translate into Russian because English slang words that have similar meanings in Russian are swear words [*mat*] in Russian, whereas in English they have milder meanings. The meaning of the word "pussy" is "the female reproductive organ." But "pussy" is a mild word, which is much less coarse than the Russian word beginning with a "p" [*pizda*]. This is

---

(very likely in the heat of consecutive translation at such a high level); or the translator's political intention to provoke Putin into making one of his signature un-PC comments (extremely unlikely). "[B]ut I'm getting your point here" should have been translated as "no ia, [kazhetsia,] dogadyvaius', na chto Vy namekaete" or "ia ponimaiu, chto Vy imeete v vidu."

[20] Vladimir Putin, interview by Kevin Owen, Russia Today, 6 September 2012, http://rt.com/news/vladimir-putin-exclusive-interview-481/ (video of the interview with an English voice-over translation). The full Russian text can be found on the *bport.com* website at http://www.b-port.com/news/item/ 87560.html, while the full English text is available on the Kremlin website at http://eng.kremlin.ru/transcripts/4367.

really a very hard translation question. What the members of the band meant I cannot say.[21]

When asked how to translate *Pussy Riot* into Russian, the translator of children's literature Marina Boroditskaia said:

> The phrase *pussy riot* does not sound coarse. Some say that it should be translated as "p[izdo]revolutsiia" [*pizdorevoliutsiia*—cunt revolution]; that's a pile of hogwash! The word *pussy* has two meanings. The first, and the most frequent one, is part of the collocation "pussycat," that is, a "female kitty" [*koshechka zhenskogo pola*], or "pussy" [*kiska*]. The second meaning is "the female genitals," but without the vulgar connotation, that is, it is not the [Russian] word consisting of five letters [*pizda*]—it is a milder word. The word "riot" means "rebellion" [*vosstanie*], "mutiny" [*bunt*] or "protest" [*protest*]. *Pussy Riot* should be translated as "babii bunt" [petticoat mutiny/women's riot], "a nu-ka, devushki" [Go, girls!/Come on, girls!/Put your best foot forward, girls!], or "a nu-ka, babon'ki" [same as previous].[22]

The translation debates continued on Tuesday, 11 September, in the course of Arkadii Mamontov's show *Spetsial'nyi korrespondent* on the Rossia-1 TV channel. The show was devoted exclusively to Pussy Riot and included

---

[21] Here is the Russian text published by *Moskovskii komsomolets*: "ВОПРОС ЭКСПЕРТАМ: КАК ПЕРЕВОДИТСЯ PUSSY RIOT? Московский корреспондент издания 'Тайм' Саймон ШУСТЕР: Скорее, 'бунт кисок'. Это самое правильное. МК: Вы имеете в виду кошечек? Или что-то другое? Шустер: Очень смешной разговор у нас получается. Да, можно и так сказать. Но это очень тяжело перевести на русский, потому что сленговые слова, которые имеют похожие значения, на русском — это мат, а в английском языке имеют более мягкое значение. Значение слова 'pussy' — женский половой орган. Но это довольно мягкое слово и далеко не столь грубое, как слово на 'п' в русском языке. Это действительно очень тяжелый вопрос с переводом. И что имели в виду участницы этой группы, я не могу сказать," http://www.mk.ru/politics/article/2012/ 09/06/745487-perevod-slova-pussy-stal-temoy-diskussiy.html.

[22] "Perevod slovo 'Pussy' stalo temoi diskussii," *Moskovskii komsomolets*, 7 September 2012, accessed 17 December 2013, http://www.mk.ru/politics/article/2012/09/06/745487-perevod-slova-pussy-stal-temoy-diskussiy.html: Переводчик, детский поэт Марина БОРОДИЦКАЯ: "В словосочетании 'pussy riot' грубого звучания нет. Говорят, что это надо переводить как 'п...дореволюция', — это полная ерунда! Слово 'pussy' имеет два значения. Первое и наиболее частое — это часть словосочетания 'pussy cat', то есть 'кошечка женского пола', 'киска'. Второе значение — женский половой орган, но не с матерной окраской, не слово из пяти букв, а более мягкое наименование. Слово 'riot' — 'восстание', 'бунт', 'протест'. Pussy riot следует понимать как 'бабий бунт', 'а ну-ка, девушки', 'а ну-ка, бабоньки'".

Mamontov's two-part documentary about Pussy Riot, titled *Agents Provocateurs*. In the second part of the documentary and show, *Pussy Riot* was repeatedly translated as "vzbesivshiesia/vzbuntovavshiesia zhenskie polovye organy" or "vzbesivshiesia zhenskie genitalii" (female genitalia gone mad).[23] There was one other translation. A participant in the show, a writer and MGIMO[24] professor, Iurii Viazemskii, when asked what *Pussy Riot* meant, said the following: "I have sorted through quite a few translations, and the most decent one is sluts [*prishmandovki*] [...] I am answering your question and say, 'They're sluts.'"[25]

Even before Mamontov's show, Anatolii Vasserman, the controversial host of the NTV *Vasserman Reaction* show, had habitually referred to Pussy Riot as "the group whose name is politely translated as 'the rebellion of vaginas' [*bunt vlagalishch*]."[26] Another controversial TV personality, actor and film director, Aleksandr Gordon, translates "Pussy Riot" as "pis'kiny strasti" (roughly, "wee-wee agitation/fever").[27]

---

[23] Here is the relevant quote from Lenta.ru: "*Для тех, кто пропустил первую серию, ее основные тезисы были пересказаны еще раз (хороший прием и для укрепления их в сознании преданного зрителя). Вот эти тезисы: акция Pussy Riot была отнюдь не политической, а провокационной, призванной расколоть церковь и подорвать устои российского общества. Главным провокатором и революционером, как известно, является дьявол – неслучайно в глазах участниц группы мелькают 'искорки', а смех (не без помощи искусного монтажа) звучит да и выглядит демонически. По этой же причине название Pussy Riot переводится в фильме не иначе, как 'взбесившиеся/взбутовавшиеся женские половые органы' или 'взбесившиеся женские гениталии' – так и неприличных слов избежать получается, и корень 'бес' лишний раз ввернуть,*" http://lenta.ru/articles/2012/09/13/mamontov/, accessed 13 September 2012; http://ruskline.ru/news_rl/2012/09/12/video_ kto_ stoit_za_pussy_riot/, accessed 17 September 2012.

[24] MGIMO stands for Moscow State Institute of International Relations (Moskovskii gosudarstvennyi institut mezhdunarodnykh otnoshenii pri Ministerstve inostrannykh del Rossiiskoi Federatsii).

[25] In Russian: "*[Я] перебрал довольно много переводов, и самое приличное – это 'пришмандовки.' [...] Я отвечаю на ваш вопрос и говорю: 'Это пришмандовки!'*" Arkadii Mamontov, "Provokatory. Fil'm Arkadiia Mamontova ob aktsii Pussy Riot," YouTube video, 1:09:48, from Rossiia-1 broadcast *Spetsial'nyi korrespondent* televised on 11 September 2012, posted by "ThingsJust4Fun" on 26 April 2012, http://www.youtube. com/watch?v=aeT0dZbGkzc. Viazemskii's comments appear at 0:41:34–0:41:54.

[26] Anatolii Vasserman, "Vasserman o 'beshenykh pis'kaskh,'" YouTube video, 2:37, from NTV broadcast of *Reaktsiia Vassermana*, posted by "razuznaika," 29 June 2012, http://www.youtube.com/watch?v=hrPihcJsYec&feature=related.

[27] Aleksandr Gordon, "Pro 'Pussy Riot,'" YouTube video, 3: 32, from interview televised on 19 April 2012, posted by "1tvnetru," 26 April 2012, http://www.youtube. com/watch?v=Q-_VLnWFSwE.

The controversy around Pussy Riot continued to escalate. On 13 September 2012, during a widely popular topical social commentary talk show *Poedinok* (duel/mano a mano), hosted by Vladimir Solov'ev, the opponents of the punk band consistently translated "Pussy Riot" as "female genitalia gone mad" (*vzbesivshiesia zhenskie polovye organy* or *bunt vzbesivshikhsia zhenskikh genitalii*). The supporter of the group, Leonid Gozman, who is also the leader of the anti-Kremlin party Soiuz pravykh sil (Union of Right Forces), protested vehemently and resorted to detailed quotes from the Oxford and Cambridge English-Russian dictionaries, insisting that the word *pussy* actually meant "cat," "kitty," or "bunny" (*koshka, koshechka, zaika*) and emphasizing that it was only at the bottom of the dictionary entry that the "vulgar slang term" "the vulva" (*grubo: zhenskie polovye organy*) could be found.[28]

The *Online Slang Dictionary*, which—like Wikipedia—is continuously updated by its users, rates the vulgarity of its entries by crowdsourcing. We find that, on a 100-point scale of vulgarity, the average level of vulgarity of *pussy*, as perceived by 257 native speakers of English, is 71.[29] In other words, the word *pussy* is considerably closer to being vulgar than neutral. And this is exactly the assessment that 32 of my American students provided when asked in a questionnaire to rate the vulgarity of the word *pussy* on a 100-point scale. When asked to define the phrase *Pussy Riot* (30 of them never heard the expression), the students gave widely varying interpretations, some of them tongue-in-cheek.[30]

Do the punk band's members have a translation of their own? They usually say "Pussy Riot," but during the appellate court hearings on 10 October

---

[28] Vladimir Solov'ev, *Poedinok*, Rossiia-1, 13 September 2012, http://vipzal.tv/tv-peredacha/poedinok-smotret-onlajn-s-vladimirom-solovevym-61-vypusk-13-09-2012-rossiya-1.html.

For the record, under the headword "pussy," the second edition of *The Encarta Webster's Dictionary of the English Language* (2004) defines its sense number 3 (out of a total of 5) as "a highly offensive term for the vulva." The fifth edition of the *American Heritage Dictionary of the English Language* (2011) has a sense number 3a, which is defined as "vulgar slang: the vulva." The relevant entry in the *Free Online Dictionary* gives the following senses of "pussy": Pussy *n. pl.* pussies: (1) *Informal* A cat. (2) *Botany* A fuzzy catkin, especially of the pussy willow. (3) *Vulgar Slang* a) The vulva. b) Sexual intercourse with a woman. (4) *Offensive Slang* Used as a disparaging term for a woman. (5) *Slang* A man regarded as weak, timid, or unmanly, http://www.thefreedictionary.com/pussyonline.

[29] *Online Slang Dictionary*, s.v. "pussy," accessed 8 October 2012, http://onlineslangdictionary.com/meaning-definition-of/pussy#vulgarity.

[30] For example, "I do not really understand it. Is it a 'pathetic riot'? Or a riot against vaginas?" / "A mob of wimps; a mob of genitalia; or a mob of cats." / "It sounds like a very small riot that looked wimpy." / "Females rioting against leaders in European Asia [sic]." / "The phrase conjures a meaning having something to do with loose sexual morals." / "Nothing really comes to mind. Maybe, girls having fun?" / "It's either a strong show of feminine protest, or a bunch of civil disobedient-minded cats."

2012,[31] Ekaterina Samutsevich, one of the three punk band members who was given a separate court hearing, offered her own, "authorized" translation of *Pussy Riot*:

> In contrast to Putin,[32] I will have the courage to translate the band's name "Pussy Riot" out loud—it means "the rebellion of kitties."[33] And this is better and less indecent than his [Putin's] calls to "whack enemies in the outhouse."[34] [Я осмелюсь, в отличие от него, перевести вслух название группы Pussy Riot – это "бунт кисок". И это лучше и менее неприлично, чем его призывы "мочить в сортире" врагов.]

An important aspect of the ongoing debates about how to translate *Pussy Riot* into Russian is the attempt by the majority of the debating "translators" to work out their translations based on the polysemic dictionary senses of the *individual words* that make up the two-word neologistic set phrase *Pussy Riot*. The phrase has, in fact, to be translated at the level of the whole word collocation, in which, on the one hand, there is a simultaneous interaction of several connotations, creating a gestalt effect, and which, on the other hand, is actualized in multiple pragmatic contexts defined by different sociocultural expectations and translation consequences. The least that can be done before translating the name at all would be to realize that the meaning of a fixed

---

[31] See "Uslyshannye molitvy: Ekaterina Samutsevich vyshla na svobodu. Reportazh 'Lenty.ru,'" 11 October 2012, http://lenta.ru/articles/2012/10/10/pussyfree/.

[32] Samutsevich was referring to Vadim Takmenev's documentary "V gostiakh u Putina," shown on NTV on Putin's 60th birthday on 7 October 2012, in which Putin challenged Takmenev to translate the phrase *Pussy Riot* into Russian. Takmenev did not accept the challenge, nor did Putin suggest a translation out loud, http://www.ntv.ru/novosti/348821/. The episode was a replay of the unanswered challenge Putin offered the British journalist Kevin Owen on Russia Today on 6 September 2012, which I described earlier.

[33] Among other meanings, "kitty"—a smart, lovely, beautiful, and amazing person (http://www.urbandictionary.com/define.php?term=kitty).

[34] *Mochit' v sortire* (to whack/ice in the outhouse/in the latrine) is the expression that the then Prime Minister Vladimir Putin used during a televised press conference in Astana, the capital of Kazakhstan, on 24 September 1999, while commenting on the air bombardments of Grozny, the capital of Chechnya, by Russian planes the previous day. The exact quote, which went viral instantly, is as follows: "We will pursue terrorists everywhere. If it's an airport, then—in the airport. What I mean is, excuse my language, we will catch them in the bathroom, we will whack them in the outhouse, if need be. That's it, end of story" (Мы будем преследовать террористов везде. В аэропорту — в аэропорту. Значит, вы уж меня извините, в туалете поймаем, мы в сортире их замочим, в конце концов. Всё, вопрос закрыт окончательно). "Putin: V sortire zamochim!" YouTube video, 0: 10, posted by politota.ru, accessed 21 August 2013, http://www.youtube.com/watch?v=7VmakmVR4iQ.

word combination is not derivable from the simple summation of its component parts. From this perspective, Boroditskaia's translation of *Pussy Riot* as "Babii bunt" is not as far-fetched as it may seem at first glance. Nor is Gordon's "Pis'kiny strasti," for that matter. If I were forced to choose one translation for all audiences, I would be painfully torn between the two.

Granted, a word's emotional, evaluative, and offensive valencies are realized in context and have to be somehow taken into account. But translations and folk mistranslations work in a mysterious way. Mistranslations sometimes gain wide currency. Thus, in the midst of the raging "Pussy Riot" controversy, the Russian blogosphere was actively using the "folksy" transliterations "pussiraitki" (the plural of "pussiraitka"), "pus'ki" (the plural of "pus'ka"), and "pis'ki" (pis'ki—a term close to "pussy" but less evocative and used mostly when talking to small children].[35] The other "translations" of or references to "Pussy Riot" are "pizdiachii bunt" (cunts' riot), "bunt kisok" (pussycat mutiny), "dikaia pizden'" (wild cuntness), "pizdopogrom" (cunts on a pogrom/pogrom cunts or rampaging cunts], "buntuiushchie vaginy" (rioting vaginas),[36] and so forth.

Concluding Remarks

In conclusion I would argue that the name "Pussy Riot" was originally created as a self-advertising gimmick, whose marginal vulgarity was calculated to attract the attention of audiences that understand some English. In Russia, most people do not understand the non-translated connotations of the English name, but it has acquired wide currency and recognition owing to the intensive coverage of the Pussy Riot incident in the media.

The final statements of the three punk performers at the trial read like a political and philosophical indictment of the current Russian system of government (Nadezhda Tolokonnikova is, in fact, a former student of the Philosophy Department at Moscow State University).[37] Incidentally, in her address, Tolokonnikova used the untranslated name "Pussy Riot."

---

[35] For example, "Saliut u SIZO v den' rozhdeniia pussiraitki Samutsevich" (Fireworks Outside Pre-trial Detention Centre on "Pussiraitka" Samutsevich's Birthday), *Shans Online*, 10 August 2012, http://shans-online.com/news/2012-08-10/salyut_u_sizo_v_den_rozhdeniya_pussiraytki_samutsevich/.

[36] These are suggested translations of *Pussy Riot* into Russian sent by different people to Iurii Puchkov's (Goblin's) site, Oper.ru, accessed 23 February 2013, http://oper.ru/news/?page=9.

[37] The final statements made by the three Pussy Riot members at their trial on 8 August 2012 can be read here: "Zasedanie suda po delu Pussy Riot: Poslednee slovo obvinaemykh," *Ekho Moskvy* (blog), 8 August 2012, http://echo.msk.ru/blog/echomsk/917223-echo/. See also Tolokonnikova's "final statement" (which she was not allowed to make) at a hearing devoted to her petition to be released for good behavior on 6

In the meantime, the Russian participants in the continuing Pussy Riot discussions tend to choose a translation, or cunning mistranslation, of the name *Pussy Riot* that best fits their political and cultural identities. These translations/mistranslations range from the vulgar, unprintable "pizdobunt" (cunt/cunts' mutiny)—chiefly found on the Internet[38] and heard in the streets of Russia because the "three-and five-letter words" like *khui* (cock/prick) and *pizda* (cunt) are forbidden on television and in mainstream print publications—to the endearingly inspirational and empowering "A nu-ka, devushki!" (Come on, girls!/Go, girls!/Put your best foot forward, girls!).

The neutral, politically correct choice is to write and say "Pussy Riot" (Pussi Raiot), without translating the name and thus revealing one's attitude, and that is the name that is used in the court-ordered affidavit by the experts who evaluated the level of offensiveness and criminal intent of the Pussy Riot "actionist" performance.[39]

The crude versions of translating Pussy Riot (these are extreme examples of "sexed-up" translations or *ozhivliazh* in Russian) represent—through conscious choice or ignorance—a flagrantly sexist, patriarchally censorious, and harshly conservative view of the band. These include the borderline-acceptable on television "vzbesivshiesia / vzbuntovavshiesia zhenskie polovye organy" or "vzbesivshiesia zhenskie genitalii" (female genitalia gone mad), "prishmandovki" (sluts) (the Mamontov show), "bunt vagin" (the *Vasserman Reaction* show), or Zhirinovskii's "beshenstvo matki." In his book *Bogoroditsa, progoni!* (Mother of God, Chase Him Away!), the author Aleksei Chelnokov goes as far as translating the name of the band as "bunt lobkovykh vshei" (the rebellion of pubic lice) (Chelnokov 2013, 169).

Liberally-minded supporters of Pussy Riot, opposing alleged violations of civil liberties in Russia, tend to prefer toned-down translations like the above-mentioned "A nu-ka, devushki!", "A nu-ka, babon'ki!" (Basically, "Go. Girls!") (Boroditskaia), "bunt kisok" (pussycat riot) (Shuster and Samutsevich herself), "buntuiushchie koshechki" (rioting pussycats) (Gozman), and similar friendly appellations, but, in most cases, they just sound out "Pussy Riot" in Russian—"Pussi raiot."

In his widely publicized, above-quoted interviews with Owen and Takmenev, President Putin challenged his interviewers to translate "Pussy Riot" into Russian, which they would not do, and concluded openly that that was because the translation would sound indecent in Russian. This was a sly way

---

April 2013: "Neproiznesennoe poslednee slovo Tolokonnikovoi," *Radio Svoboda,* http://www.svoboda.org/content/article/24969820.html?nocache=1.

[38] A Google search for "pizdobunt" generates 1,570 Pussy Riot-related hits within 0.55 seconds (as of 11 December 2012).

[39] *Russkaia narodnaia liniia: Informatsionno-analiticheskaia sluzhba,* accessed 20 August 2013, http://ruskline.ru/analitika/2012/10/24/zaklyuchenie_komissii_ekspertov_po_delu_pusi_rajt/.

of denigrating the band by implication, a condemnation by omission, which seems to reflect the opinion of the majority of Russians.[40]

The domesticated, folksy transliteration "pus'ki," Gordon's choice "pis'-kiny strasti" (wee-wee fever or perhaps pussy fever) and Zhirinovskii's appellation of preference "beshenstvo matki" (madness of the womb) seem to be quite popular (193,000 results in 0.3 seconds, 481,000 results in 0.11 seconds, and 49,100 in 0.43 seconds, respectively, when Googled). I would interpret these as expressing an ambivalent attitude toward the band's incursion into the Christ the Savior Cathedral, when, on the one hand, speakers acknowledge that the band members may have been justified in trying to express their variety of truth, but on the other, imply some censure in the sense that the band may have gone too far by doing it in a rather vulgar way in the number one Russian Orthodox cathedral. The flippancy of these "translations" arguably promotes a mildly ironic, condescending attitude toward Pussy Riot that may well be the attitude of the none too liberal and none too conservative majority forming the basis of Putin's electorate. One should also bear in mind that what people are prepared to say and go on record with may be very different from what they say in the company they trust. In the final analysis, one can always hedge by asking, "What's in a name?" Only, when the Bard of Avon talked about naming a rose, he was not thinking in terms of translation.[41]

By Way of a Coda

The Pussy Riot political and cultural controversy has had far-reaching sociocultural consequences and interesting intersemiotic interpretations. For example, during an ASEEES roundtable discussion on 17 November 2012, one of the participants, Zakhar Ishov, suggested that Pussy Riot's "actionist" performance at the Christ the Savior Cathedral on 21 February 2012 was tantamount to the actions of Holy Fools for Christ in old Russia. Ishov's assessment is an example of an intersemiotic, arguably, politicized translation that legitimizes Pussy Riot as cultural rebels. In a similar interpretive mode, the head of the Russian branch of Amnesty International, Sergei Nikitin, has declared Pussy Riot to be prisoners of conscience, which is a political move of

---

[40] The results of public opinion polls, for example those published by FOM (Public Opinion Foundation) on 29 and 30 August 2012, indicate that 53 percent of respondents consider the court's decision just and 66 percent have a negative attitude to Pussy Riot's action in the Christ the Savior Cathedral ("Rezul'taty oprosov obshchestvennogo mneniia po delu 'Pussy Riot,'" website of Nika TV, accessed 23 February 2013, http://www.nikatv.ru/index.php/socity/7959-pussy-riot.html.

[41] "What's in a name? that which we call a rose / By any other name would smell as sweet" (William Shakespeare, *Romeo and Juliet*, 1600). *The Phrase Finder*, s.v. "A rose by any other name would smell as sweet," http://www.phrases.org.uk/meanings/305250.html.

international significance.[42] Artist Yoko Ono awarded Pussy Riot the "Lennon Ono Grant for Peace"—another political "translation."[43] The prestigious American magazine *Foreign Policy* has named the three convicted Pussy Riot members number 16 among the Top 100 Global Thinkers of the year.[44] The news portal Business Insider has included Pussy Riot in the list of the top 20 most impressive people of the year 2012.[45] Nadezhda Tolokonnikova has been declared a woman of the year by the French newspaper *Le Figaro*.[46] *Lenta.ru* reports that she is also on the *AskMen.com* list of the most desirable women of the year.[47] The television rights for the documentary *Pussy Riot: A Punk Prayer*, which debuted in January 2013 at the Sundance Film Festival, were bought by HBO Documentary Films[48] and widely released in June 2013.[49] I expect that there are other intra- and interlingual, as well as inter-semiotic translations-interpretations of "Pussy Riot" as an emblem and a phenomenon. In short, at the time of this writing, the show was going on—and a significant part of it was in translation.

---

[42] "Amnesty International: Devushki iz 'Pussy Riot' – uzniki sovesti," *Newsland*, accessed 19 December 2012, http://newsland.com/news/detail/id/930007/.

[43] "Peace to Pussy Riot: Yoko Ono Grants Award to Jailed Russian Band," *RT.com*, accessed 19 December 2012, http://rt.com/art-and-culture/news/yoko-ono-pussy-riot-770/.

[44] "2012's Global Marketplace of Ideas and the Thinkers Who Make Them," *Foreign Policy*, accessed 19 December 2012, http://www.foreignpolicy.com/2012globalthinkers.

[45] "The 20 Most Impressive People of the Year," *Business Insider*, 20 December 2012, accessed 25 December 2012, http://www.businessinsider.com/category/most-impressive-people.

[46] See, for example, "Russian Personalities: Nadezhda Tolokonnikova—first in Madame Figaro's List," posted 23 December 2012, accessed 25 December 2012, http://beautifulrus.com/nadezhda-tolokonnikova-is-the-first-in-madame-figaros-list/.

[47] "Pussy Riot popali v spisok samykh vpechatliaushchikh liudei goda," *Lenta.ru*, 23 December 2012, accessed 25 December 2012, http://lenta.ru/news/2012/12/23/businessinsider/.

[48] "HBO Buys Pussy Riot Documentary at Sundance," *Rolling Stone*, 21 January 2013, http://www.rollingstone.com/music/news/hbo-buys-pussy-riot-documentary-at-sundance-20130121.

[49] See also the HBO ad for the documentary *Pussy Riot: A Punk Prayer*, accessed 20 August 2013, http://www.hbo.com/documentaries/pussy-riot-a-punk-prayer/index.html#. At one point in the documentary, a Russian Cossack translates "Pussy Riot" as "vzbesivshiesia matki," which is back-translated in the subtitles as "deranged vaginas."

Chapter 7

Russian Translation Theory: Some Ongoing Discussions

The central distinguishing feature of Russian translation studies today is its focus on the interaction—the "dialectical unity"—of theory and practice.[1] In the Russian translation studies literature, the principles and methodology of translation, as well as translation pedagogy and criticism, are deeply embedded in concrete textual and sociocultural analysis. Texts on "pure theory" are rare: theory is inextricably intermingled with analyses of practice. Russian translation studies "refuses to divorce theory from practice and prefers to use terms that may be out of fashion but are more or less definite concepts" (Lanchikov 2011a, 42). Among such terms are "equivalence," "adequate translation," "literalist translation," "artistic translation," and others.

Buzadzhi

Defining Translation
Chair of the Department of English Language Translation at the Moscow State Linguistic University (MSLU), the leading translation and interpretation teaching center in Russia, Professor Buzadzhi defines translation in terms of relevance-in-communication theory as set out by Sperber and Wilson (1986; 1995; 2004) and as interpreted in an article by Ernst-August Gutt (1998). Buzadzhi's is a clear-cut definition: "a translation is a text in the translating language that is called upon to reproduce a maximum of communicatively relevant information contained in the source text, based on its relative value" (2011b, 52). Apparently to avoid being criticized for reductionism, Buzadzhi supplements his definition by adding that "the process of translation is not mentioned because if you have a text it implies that there has been a process" (52). What is important is "communicatively relevant information (CRI)," i.e., "information which is essential for achieving the aims of communication" (52). The aims of communication are "the aims set by the author of the text of the original (TO) ascertainable by the translator on the basis of the form and content of the text of the original" (52). In other words, the functional-communicative relevance of a piece of discourse is established by the translator, and

---

[1] For additional information about and examples of the ongoing reinstitutionalization of translation in Russia today, see Appendix 7, "Translation Think Tanks, Anti-Prizes, and Competitions."

this is done differently by different translators, which Buzadzhi's example from two very different translations into Russian of James Thurber's humorous story "The Owl Who Was God" illustrates very well (54).

Buzadzhi's definition of translation—and it seems, as far as I know, to be one of the latest variations on the theme in the Russian literature—presupposes the potential existence of multiple acceptable—"adequate," to use traditional Russian terminology—translations. He even admits that his definition presupposes the existence of "bad translations" because no translator arguably aims to produce bad translations (see 2011b, 55). I think this is a new development in Russian translation studies, because, in the past, while the possibility of several translations was tacitly accepted, it was never acknowledged openly as par for the course.

Bukvalistskii Perevod
Buzadzhi also makes an important clarification of the concept *bukvalistskii perevod* (literalist translation), which has been a staple fighting focus in Russian translation studies since the 1920s. Taking his cue from the famous Russian theorist of translation Vilen Naumovich Komissarov, who defined literalist translation as a "translation reproducing communicatively irrelevant elements of the original" (quoted from Buzadzhi 2011b, 52), Buzadzhi elaborates on Komissarov's definition by specifying that, in translation, "relevant information is the information that is new to the receivers [of the translation], that *is about* [my italics] the content and form of the original text (TO), that has a logical connection with the context, and whose processing does not involve excessive costs [effort] [...] A literalist translation violates the norms and usage of the translating language and conveys formal elements of the original text (TO) that are not relevant to the function of a given text" (53). Buzadzhi concludes that the "ability to differentiate communicatively relevant from communicatively irrelevant information is one of the key skills of a professional translator, the development of which takes years" (53). Thus "even top-notch professionals may disagree with each other as to the relevance of a particular element [of a text], as a result of which there will appear translations that are equally felicitous but that are different in the strategies that have been employed to produce them" (53).

Buzadzhi's amplification of Komissarov's definition of literalism in translation is an interesting new development in Russian translation studies because it helps differentiate literalist translation ("translating the letter of the text") from "translating the spirit of the text." The tenet of the Soviet school of translation, "Translate the spirit, not the letter of a text," has been bandied about in Russian translation discussions, without being defined in any reliable way, since the times of Chukovskii, the Kashkintsy, and Rita Rait-Kovaleva. Now it is being conceptualized in a more concrete way. It is being specifically suggested that translators adopt a relevance-theory approach. This development moves Russian translation studies closer to international translation studies, where Sperber and Wilson's relevance theory (1986), which builds on Grice's Relevance Maxims (1957, 1975), is regarded as probably the most important and influential theory of pragmatics in recent years.

The Ideology of Translation and Teaching Translation: An Anti-Postmodernist Manifesto
Another shift in Russian translation studies is the adoption of the concept of deconstruction—a form of semiotic analysis derived mainly from French philosopher Jacques Derrida's 1967 work *Of Grammatology*. In his recent article "Zakalka perevodom: Ob ideologicheskoi storone perevodcheskoi praktiki i prepodavaniia perevoda" (The Crucible of Translation: Some Considerations Concerning Translation Practice and Pedagogy; Buzadzhi 2011a, 55–66), Buzadzhi proceeds from the assumption that translation is a subtle instrument of ideological manipulation and a reflection of different kinds of power and domination. He defines his goal as that of "'deconstructing' his approach to teaching translation and—as far as possible—explaining why he plays his 'political role' in the classroom in the way he plays it" (56), in addition to the regular business of teaching the theory and practice of translation. As a result of his deconstruction exercise, Buzadzhi arrives at five "ideological" principles that underlie his own and his Maurice Thorez colleagues' practicing and teaching fiction prose translation from English into Russian. The term "ideology" is defined as "a set of interconnected ideas and requirements that forms the basis of specific actions, decisions, and so forth" (56).

The first principle is "enlightened linguistic conservatism": "sometimes conscious and sometimes unconscious rejection of poorly-assimilated-into-the-language borrowings, newfangled lexical constructions, and other such novelties" (Buzadzhi 2011a, 57). According to Buzadzhi, the proliferating English-derived "newspeak" (*iazykovoi novodel*) is not true language innovation, based on a creative use of the Russian language, but a "tasteless, kitschy neoplasm whose danger is in undermining the precision, richness and depth of the Russian language" (57). One of his examples is the overuse of the English borrowing *pozitivnyi* (positive)—as in "He's a very positive person." "What kind of characteristic is that?" Buzadzhi asks. "Does it mean 'optimistic,' 'a survivor,' or 'cheerful'? Or does it perhaps mean 'friendly,' 'kindly,' or 'fun to be with'?" (57). He concludes that such obfuscating usages are like "misshapen ink blobs spreading across the clearly-defined squares of a semantic field. The speaker 'kind of, like, said' and the listener 'kind of, like, understood,' while the actual sense has remained completely undefined" (57).[2] As result of such obfuscations, Buzadzhi goes on to say, the translating language itself becomes impoverished. Comparing the translating language

---

[2] I personally do not think that there is a problem with the adjective *pozitivnyi* if the speaker is aware of other synonymic possibilities and is using the word consciously to make a general "noncommittal" statement.

to a piano and the translator to a pianist who has worked long and hard to learn to play the instrument in such a way that the full compositional complexity and aesthetic and emotional meaning of a piece of music can be appreciated by the audience, Buzadzhi invites the reader to imagine a situation where most of the keys have been removed from the piano, leaving the pianist with only five or six keys called "problema," "aktsiia," "trend," "brend," and "dostatochno slozhno" [rather difficult]. "Such a set-up clearly won't do for Beethoven," Buzadzhi quips, "but it is fine for anyone capable of banging out a four-note ditty—for that, there is nothing to teach and nothing to learn" (57). The general conclusion Buzadzhi makes is this: "By giving in to mindless linguistic innovation translators are undermining their own position. They promote the creation of the kind of language [...] and the kind of translation quality criteria that make it impossible to differentiate between a masterly translation and a piece of hackwork. Unless translators want to find themselves out of a job, they need to take good care of their main work instrument" (57).

I find a lot of merit in Buzadzhi's position, but I have to admit that I also find it somewhat utopian: language happens through the agency of a wide and variegated cross-section of sociocultural contingents—it cannot be ruled by fiat, however noble or worthy. Language generally works in an unruly way.

Buzadzhi's second principle is that of the translator's "transparency," or modesty—modesty both in the general moral-ethical sense and in the sense of being invisible in the text, i.e., not leaving an identifiable translator's imprint on the translation. Buzadzhi denies that this is tantamount to "blandscript" (*gladkopis'*) because, according to him, the origin of "blandscript" is different. The origin of "blandscript," according to Buzadzhi, is the inability to differentiate between the authorial voice and the voices of the characters, manifesting itself in substituting for an authorially marked original a bland, easily-flowing text. The opposite of the translator's "transparency" is blatant literalness that highlights the translator's self, "as if it were not possible to create a non-trivial variant of translation that would correspond to the distinctiveness of the original without mutilating the translating language and thrusting upon the reader the translator's self" (58). In other words, it is "language mutilation" and the translator's obtrusive presence in the text that constitute the translator's unacceptable imprint on the text of the translation. These are familiar themes that the MSLU group of theorists have been discussing in *Mosty* since 2004.[3] As usual, the remedies are easier to prescribe than to implement.

---

[3] Based on their various publications, I have a pretty good idea who they hint at—primarily and specifically, at a team of two re-translators of Russian literature into English and a famous voiceover translator of English-language films into Russian, whom I mention in this book elsewhere.

Buzadzhi's third "ideological" principle is differentiation between cultures. According to Buzadzhi, "mixing together the cultures of the source and translating languages is more harmful [for the receiving culture] than excessive fondness of exotic usages" (2011a, 62). "In a nutshell," Buzadzhi continues, "the ideological orientation here can be formulated something like this: It is important to clearly see the differences between the cultures of the source language and the translating language and to translate for a reader who does not know a word in the source language and does not have any knowledge whatsoever of the source culture" (62). I somehow find this third principle an elaboration on the first—maintaining a balanced conservative attitude—besides, it seems to me overly isolationist with regard to the perceived background knowledge of the receivers of the translation. In my opinion, this principle comes into conflict with Buzadzhi's own conception of translation as a relevance-based communicative activity discussed earlier.

Thinking independently and standing one's ground, even as the majority around you may be critical of your position, is the fourth principle, and here Buzadzhi draws essentially on the writings of the Spanish philosopher José Ortega y Gasset (1883–1955), particularly on his programmatic work *The Revolt of the Masses* (1930). Buzadzhi discusses the global confrontation between opinion-driven majorities and scholarship- and skills-equipped professional minorities with regard to any artistic activity, translation included. As in his other writings, he is passionately emphatic: true professionalism in translation takes decades to acquire and should be respected as such. This may sound a little elitist, but this is essentially what "expert" literary translation is—an elitist occupation. I prefer to use the term "expert professionalism" in translation, a concept developed as the result of the latest cognitive "expertise studies," based on eye-movement tracking, keystroke logging, and talking-aloud protocols research that has made it possible to differentiate between professionalism, semi-professionalism, and "expert professionalism."[4]

The fifth principle—professional responsibility and diligence—stems from the fourth. "Since the 'mass-man'[5] has established himself in the world," writes Buzadzhi, [...] "and the written text has lost its reliability, the translator has to shoulder a double responsibility—his or her own and that of the "other guy"[6] (2011a, 65). Buzadzhi emphasizes that "the translator should be

---

[4] See Shreve and Angelone 2010.

[5] "Mass-man" is the term Ortega y Gasset introduced in his *La Rebelión de las Masas* (*The Revolt of the Masses*).

[6] In the 1970s and 1980s it became politically fashionable and ideologically commendable for Soviet production teams to include in their payrolls somebody ("the other guy") who was killed in the Great Patriotic War (1941–45) and to fulfill both the team's and "the other guy's" share of the production quotas. The extra money was used for charitable purposes. Hence Buzadzhi's cultural reference to "the other guy." The

exceptionally responsible for everything he or she writes in his or her translation and for everything he or she says about somebody else's translations; the translator must be totally responsible toward the author of the original, the readers of the translation, his or her colleagues, and, in the final analysis, toward the source and target cultures" (65). According to Buzadzhi, this "quadruple responsibility" extends as far as finding and correcting factual and stylistic errors even in the original source text, i.e., doing the work of the "other guy," and Buzadzhi provides some interesting examples of such cases. This is a moot point but I certainly share the general idea of extra professional responsibility.

Lanchikov

Buzadzhi's views are in large part influenced by those of his older colleague in the Department of English Language Translation at MSLU, Professor Viktor Konstantinovich Lanchikov. Today Lanchikov is one of the leading—if not *the* leading—translation theorists in Russia, in addition to being a well-known practicing literary translator and a sharp, uncompromising polemicist. He has written in practically every issue of *Mosty* (the leading translators' journal in Russia) since its launch in 2004 and publishes regularly in other venues as well. Since 2009, he has been *Mosty*'s editor-in-chief. Lanchikov is a vehement proponent of "enlightened linguistic conservatism," which I have already discussed in some detail in the context of Buzadzhi's work in the previous section.

General Use and Authorial Language
One of Lanchikov's signature themes is the inability of some translators to differentiate between an individual authorial style and standard idiomatic usage. Lanchikov and the American expatriate author and translator Michele Berdy were very brave and honest academically and intellectually when in 2006 they published an unsparingly critical article about the translation methodology of the husband-and-wife translation team Richard Pevear and Larissa Volokhonsky. The article is called "Success and Being Successful" ("Uspekh i uspeshnost'") and it critically examines numerous examples from the English retranslations of Russian classical literature by Richard Pevear and Larissa Volokhonsky. Berdy and Lanchikov demonstrate that, although the two translators claim to have a unique understanding of the true meaning of the Russian classics they retranslate, they cannot, in fact, differentiate between basic colloquialisms and unique authorial usages. This results in harsh literalist translations of standard Russian idioms, which, according to Berdy and Lanchikov, the translators confuse with individual authorial styles

---

phrase "za sebia i za togo parnia" (for oneself and for the other guy) is now used jokingly when some extra work is involved.

(Berdy and Lanchikov 2006). The article is still being hotly debated and contested.[7]

Archaization and Modernization

Lanchikov has also been the leading theorist in developing the conception of archaizing and modernizing in literary translation (see Lanchikov 2002; 2008).[8] In their recent definitive article on the subject, Lanchikov and his co-author, E. N. Meshalkina, make fun of some translators' misinformed, anach-ronistic archaizations and unwarranted modernizations, illustrating their point with the following example from 18th-century Russian history:

> Lady Rondeau[9] in her letters from Russia [...] describes a reception of Chinese ambassadors at the [Russian] imperial court. At a masked ball there, they are asked if they find the ball entourage strange. The Chinese reply, "No, because for us everything here is a masked ball."
>
> It is not difficult to understand the Chinese ambassadors: they found themselves in a situation where everything was alien, non-Chinese to them. How can one discern the difference between everyday clothing and behavior and the masquerade costumes and customs in a foreign country? Everything is equally strange.
>
> The literalist translator is just like a Chinese guy at a St. Petersburg masked ball: for him everything in the foreign language is strange, and he tries to reflect this strangeness in his translation, but he is unable to differentiate between the everyday way of expression and the truly unusual, authorial one. (Lanchikov and Meshalkina 2008, 12)

Lanchikov and Meshalkina define three general cases requiring "histori-cal stylization" on the part of the translator: "(1) when the time of the writing of the original is significantly removed from the time of the translation; (2) when the author of the original consciously resorts to the stylistic device of

---

[7] I briefly discuss this problem in chapter 3. Berdy and Lanchikov's article "Uspekh i uspeshnost'" can also be accessed on the Association of Lexicographers' site Lingvo: http://www.lingvoda.ru/transforum/articles/berdi_lanchikov.asp.

[8] The two key articles on the subject can also be accessed on the Thinkaloud and *Mosty* sites respectively: http://www.thinkaloud.ru/sciencelr.html; http://www.rvalent.ru/most19.html.

[9] Lanchikov is referring to *Letters from a Lady, Who Resided Some Years in Russia, to her Friend in England. With Historical Notes* (London: Printed for J. Dodsley in Pall-Mall, 1775). The 37 letters were written in the period from 1728 to 1739 by a certain Mrs. Vigor, who spent several years in St. Petersburg, Russia, being married twice to prominent representatives of the British government in the then Russian capital. After her second marriage, her name was Lady Rondeau. The letters are full of entertaining episodes and stories connected with the court of the Russian empress Anna Ioannovna (1693–1740; ruled 1730–40). See also http://www.jstor.org/discover/10.2307/4204849?uid= 3739600&uid=2129&uid=2&uid=70&uid=4&uid=3739256&sid=47699082590117.

historical stylization, and the translation is carried out at the time of the writing of the original; and (3) when the author of the original consciously resorts to the stylistic device of historical stylization, and the time of the writing of the original is significantly distant from the time of the execution of the translation" (2008, 20–21). The three types of situations correspond to three types of texts, which Lanchikov and Meshalkina call, respectively, "(1) archaic, (2) contemporary archaized, and (3) simultaneously archaic and archaized" (21). The task of the translator is "to simultaneously reproduce the culturally and temporally alien milieus in a way to make the reader appreciate the historical color without choking on the exotica" (12). "An effective historical stylization of the translator's text can only consist in an optimal combination of archaization and modernization that, on the one hand, should avoid an excessive modernization of the text and, on the other, the creation of an artificial and difficult to understand text. This optimal combination is determined in each particular case on the basis of the original text" (20).

Lanchikov and Meshalkina's general conclusion may sound banal, but the proof of the pudding is in the eating, and it is the numerous specific examples from Lanchikov's and other widely published translations that make the article highly instructive both for practicing translators and students of translation.

Overcoming the Law of Growing Standardization
In another of his recent articles, "The Topography of Searching" (2011b, 30–38), Lanchikov reinforces his and Berdy's ideas articulated in their article "Success and Being Successful" (2006). He begins by referring to the "law of growing standardization," first defined by the Israeli translation theorist Gideon Toury (1995, 267–68) and later restated by the British translation theorist Mona Baker in the form of four "universals" of translation that distinguish the language of original texts from their translations:[10]

1. Explicitation—the general tendency to express implied meaning directly;
2. Simplification—the tendency to simplify the language of the translation;
3. Normalization/conservatism—the tendency to exaggerate the characteristic features of the translating language, making the translation conform to the [translating language's] conventional models;
4. Leveling out—the tendency of the translated text to gravitate toward the center of a continuum. (Lanchikov 2011b, 31)[11]

---

[10] Mona Baker's conclusions are based on translation corpora research (Baker 1996).

[11] This quotation is my back-translation from Russian of the quotation from Mona Baker (see Baker 1996, 181–84) Lanchikov provides on page 31 of his article.

The last universal refers to cases when a whole-text *realium* like a regional dialect, for example, cannot be authentically reproduced in the translation but can be compensated for by using some "non-normative"—deviating from the generally accepted "correct" standard—language. Such a translation would tend to be somewhere in the middle of the continuum stretching from crude literalism to a translator's total *carte blanch*. Such a leveling-out may be illustrated by my version of a translation of a story told by the peasant soldier Platon Karataev in Tolstoy's *War and Peace*, which I adduce in chapter 3. It will be seen that, in my version, I try to avoid, on the one hand, the kind of wholesale domestication that characterizes the British translator Anthony Briggs's translation of the passage (his version sounds like the speech of an East End cockney) and, on the other, the jarring—in places—literalism of the translation of the passage by Pevear and Volokhonsky.

Polemicizing with unnamed opponents who would have us believe that the law of growing standardization is as relentless as a law of nature and inevitably leads to smoothed-over, easily flowing translations ("blandscript"), Lannchikov denies complete irreversibility of this law, arguing that it can, in fact, be counteracted in three ways. In some cases, it is possible to transfer "the form" of the original text into its translation directly. In other cases, it is not the form itself but the principle that can be replicated using a verbal play at a different language level (when, for example, a phonetic or orthographic phenomenon is re-enacted through lexical means). And in still other cases, the whole problematic stretch of language can be changed completely for the sake of achieving a comparable functional-communicative (pragmatic) effect. In fact, what Lanchikov does here is reaffirm the central tenet of the Soviet school of translation, according to which everything is translatable. As the Soviet-Russian linguist and translation theorist Leonid Stepanovich Barkhudarov famously put it: "There are only untranslatable particularities—there are no untranslatable texts" (1975, 213).

Lanchikov and Gasparov: Changing Functional Orientations

Lanchikov is also trying to redefine the periodization of translation styles suggested by the literary scholar Mikhail Gasparov, whose views I touch upon in chapter 2. Gasparov considers the development of literary translation in Russia from the perspective of changing literary trends. According to his theory, either a "literalist" translation style or a "free" translation style predominates depending on the prevalent literary trend of the time. Thus the classicism of the 18th century, the realism of the second half of the 19th century, and the socialist realism of the Soviet period are reflected in predominating "free" translations, whereas the romanticism of the early 19th century and the modernism of the late 19th century through the first third of the 20th century were conducive to the domination in translation of the literalist trend. In Lanchikov's view, this is a convenient oversimplification that does not take account of numerous discrepancies and overlaps between literary and translation trends resulting from the complexity of creating serious literature and the complexity of translation as a special kind of cross-cultural verbal interaction. According to Lanchikov, literary and translation trends do not coincide as neatly as Gasparov suggests. Lanchikov attempts to refine Gasparov's periodization by examining the evolution of translation styles from a functional-linguistic perspective. Drawing on the famous Russian literary translator Mikhail Leonidovich Lozinskii (1886–1955), he focuses on two functions of literary texts, translated texts included: the informative function that familiarizes us with different countries, cultures, epochs, and modes of thinking and feeling, and the aesthetic function that engages our emotions, tastes, and sense of beauty. Proceeding from the translation pragmatics advanced by the famous Russian translator and translation theorist Aleksandr Davydovich Shveitser, Lanchikov categorizes translated texts as those predominantly reflecting the aesthetic preferences of the translator, those geared to the expectations of the receivers of the translation, and those reflecting the communicative intent of the author of the original. From this perspective, translations done during a period generally dominated by a particular literary trend (like the Soviet socialist realism trend), in fact, turn out to have different functional-communicative orientations.

Lanchikov's conception is easier described than applied. It overlaps with that of Gasparov. If we compare, for example, Lozinskii's (1933) and Pasternak's (1940s–50s) translations of *Hamlet* from Lanchikov's perspective, we will find that Lozinskii achieves a precarious equilibrium between the aesthetic and informational functions, whereas Pasternak's translation leans heavily toward the aesthetic function and, in places, reads more like Pasternak's original creation than Shakespeare. On the other hand, proceeding from Gasparov's perspective, it can equally easily be argued that Lozinskii's translation bears the legacy of the modernism of the Russian Silver Age (c. 1890–early 1940s) and therefore is more literalist—even line-for-line—whereas Pasternak's translation is already located in the Soviet period and is, therefore, more artistic. Obviously, Lanchikov's conception of the historical development of literary translation in Russia is still a work in progress, but his is a more nuanced approach than Gasparov's. And of course it is too big a subject for one theorist and researcher to deal with definitively and quickly.

Ermolovich

Professor Dmitrii Ivanovich Ermolovich is a colleague of Buzadzhi and Lanchikov, working in the same department with them. I would expect his name to be recognizable to most people who are learning Russian or have anything to do with Russian-English translation. This is because he is the no. 1 Russian-English lexicographer (dictionary-maker) in Russia today, being—among other things—the author of the most up-to-date and comprehensive Russian-English dictionary, *The New Comprehensive Russian-English Dictionary* (2008), available in paper and digital forms (*Lingvo-12*). Besides being a sophisticated translation theorist and an inspiring translation teacher, Ermolovich has spent most of his life studying English and Russian proper names (personal and geographical) and religious terminology. These studies have resulted in a series of bilingual dictionaries of proper names and religious terminology as well as numerous scholarly publications in which he offers systematic ways of translating these special strata of vocabulary from English into Russian and Russian into English. All of his publications are listed on his website (http:// yermolovich.ru/), which is separate from the Thinkaloud site and which is a unique practical and theoretical resource for anyone involved with Russian-English translation.

Ermolovich vs. "Multitran"

Although less prominent on the polemical front as compared with Lanchikov or Buzadzhi, when it comes to expressing his assessments of publications on translation issues, Ermolovich does so very clearly and directly (see, for example, his comments on the prospects of automated translation later in this section or his assessment of Goblin's film translations in chapter 2). By way of an initial example of his style of criticism, here is his brief assessment of the widely known and used online multitran.ru dictionary, given under one of the rubrics of his site, "Questions, Answers and Discussions," in response to the question "Do you trust 'multitran.ru'?" by one of the readers of his site:

> "Multitran" is not really a dictionary in the strict sense of the term. It is a mechanical concatenation of all lexicographical resources that happened to be at the disposal of the creators of the site—meaning the large number of various, mostly specialized, dictionaries.
>
> The lexical mass that the creators of "Multitran" gained access to was superficially divided into thematic categories, but no unified lexicographical apparatus, such as a consistent system of word senses and markings or a system of describing contexts, has ever been developed. And it couldn't have been, as "Multitran" was not created by linguists. It is now being supplemented by individual translators sharing their outside-the-dictionary translation solutions on professional discussion forums.
>
> "Multitran" is like a large verbal dump, where a translator may sometimes dig out something valuable for a translation in a specialized field, find or recall a forgotten equivalent of a technical term or expression, or use a translation variant suggested by a colleague translating similar material. But there is plenty of "garbage" there. The main drawback of "Multitran," however, is the absence of a clear system of arranging translation variants. It's like looking for a needle in a haystack.

You may ask me, would I assign the leading role to such dictionaries among a translator's tools of the trade? Yes, I would, on the condition that such dictionaries are transferred to a professional lexicographical basis. (Ermolovich 2009)[12]

Ermolovich vs. the "Babel Fish"
In his recent article "The Blind Babel Fish"[13] (2011b) Ermolovich evaluates the prospects of automated translation, especially the "statistical approach" practiced by Google Translate (www.translate.google.com). He proceeds from Sir Roger Penrose's[14] perspective on the uniqueness of human intelligence and personal experience-based everyday interactions set forth in his famous book *Shadows of the Mind: A Search for the Missing Science of Consciousness* (1996). In this book Penrose argues that the multifaceted human consciousness is not comprehensively intelligible in terms of computational models. The brain's conscious and unconscious activity essentially transcends the forms or possibilities of computation. Penrose illustrates his thesis using mathematical logic, Kurt Gödel's proposition of incompleteness, Turing's machines, computability theory, quantum mechanics, and microbiology. Penrose's central point of departure is Gödel's incompleteness theorem, from which it is inferred that there are elements of human thinking that cannot be reproduced with the help of some provable rules or statements: there will always be statements or rules that are true but unprovable within a computational (algorithm-driven) system. Penrose concludes that artificial intelligence and computer-controlled expert systems are capable of assisting human expertise but will not be able to replace such expertise. Ermolovich extends Penrose's conclusion to translation and argues that a "robotic translator" cannot be fitted out with an ever-adjusting-to-communicative-circumstances store of emotional and intellectual information because, "in order to be able to use his or her experiential

---

[12] See also D. I. Ermolovich's site, http://yermolovich.ru/board/1-1-0-103, accessed 21 August 2013.

[13] The "Babel fish" is the fictional species of fish used as a biological universal translator in Douglas Adams's series of science fiction novels *The Hitchhiker's Guide to the Galaxy* (1979–92). A Babel fish is a small, yellow, leechlike creature that is inserted into the ear canal to allow the wearer to instantly understand anything said in any language and thus to communicate with both extraterrestrials and speakers of all the languages on planet Earth.

[14] Sir Roger Penrose (b. 8 August 1931) is an English mathematical physicist, recreational mathematician, and philosopher. He is an emeritus professor of mathematics at the Mathematical Institute at Oxford University and an emeritus fellow of Wadham College, also at Oxford University. He has received a number of prizes and awards, including the 1988 Wolf Prize for physics, which he shared with Stephen Hawking, for their contribution to our understanding of the universe. Apart from mathematical physics, he is widely known for his contributions to general relativity theory and cosmology.

knowledge, the subject must be cognizant of his/her life experience [*osoznavat' svoi zhiznennyi opyt*]" (Ermolovich 2011b, 62). Echoing Penrose's thesis, Ermolovich concludes that "the human ability of understanding and making conclusions is simply incapable of being formalized" (62). He backs this up with theoretical arguments and empirical studies. Part of his theoretical framework is based on Komissarov's thesis that the communicative situation of a translation episode (what I prefer to call a "translation discourse situation") can be reflected in translation at two levels of translating: the level of describing the communicative situation in superficial terms (this is the outward form of translation, based on dictionary entries, algorithms, statistics, etc.), and the deeper level of having a rationale for the particular language means used, dictated by being "inside the communicative situation," or translating "from within the situation." Komissarov calls this latter cognitive operation "identification of the communicative situation." A communicatively relevant identification of a translation situation often prompts a rethinking of the initial translation variant that comes to mind as a reflex action. In Penrose's and Ermolovich's terms, this means that an experiential understanding of the situation, i.e., its true content, determines the adequate language used to reflect it. Existing machines and the algorithms that they use cannot consciously gauge the true content of constantly varying situations.

To illustrate this conclusion with empirical data, Ermolovich conducted "a little experiment in order to establish to what extent the statistical approach (used by Google Translate, for example) can free the machine from the necessity to understand what is being translated under conditions of everyday interactions" (2011b, 63). As raw initial data for his empirical analysis Ermolovich chose the English transcript and its online Russian written translation by unidentified translators of the 149 parts of the American television series *Desperate Housewives*, comprising a total of 745,000 words in the English version. In this sample of common everyday American English, Ermolovich follows two phrases: *Good for you (her, him)* and *I'm good (We're good* and *Are we good?)*. In the Russian translation the phrase *good for you* is used a total of 23 times, with the top 12 identical translations using "molodets" (see the table below):

Переводы реплики (Translations of the phrase) Good for you (her, him, them)	Число употреблений (Number of times used)
Молодец (молодцы)! Вот молодец! Ты (он, она) молодец.	12
Рада за тебя. Рад за нее.	2
Хорошо. Это хорошо.	2
Так даже лучше.	1
Тем лучше для тебя.	1
Правильно.	1
Отлично.	1

Здорово.	1
Поздравляю.	1
Браво.	1
Всего (Total)	23

As can be seen from the table, the contextual variety of the translations is quite wide. Perhaps out of a sense of political correctness, Ermolovich does not run any of his "good for you" mini-dialogues through the Google online translator, but I will in order to find out how well "Google Translate" would cope with a very basic everyday English little dialogue from *Desperate Housewives*, in which the phrase "good for her" is used. The result is in the table below:

English Original	Google Translate
I just wanted to know if she was happy.	Я просто хотел бы знать, если бы она была счастлива.
I think she is.	Я думаю, что она есть.
Well… Good for her. (Ermolovich 2011, 2/30: 64)	Ну… Хорошо для нее.

Obviously, "Google Translate" does not do a very good job of it. The "statistical viability" principle proves a dismal failure in coping even with a ridiculously simple exchange. The translation should go: "Prosto khochu znat', schastliva li ona."—"Dumaiu, chto da."—"Rad za nee."

With the *I'm good* phrase Ermolovich gets an even wider array of translation variants (22 as compared to 10 in the previous example). The top four are: "Ia v poriadke" (9), "Khorosho/Eto khorosho" (5), "Spravlius'/Ia spravlius'" (4), and "Ia sam/Ia sama" (3) (2011b, 66). Again, Ermolovich is too tactful to give a little test to "Google Translate." But let us, just for the sake of consistency, get Google to translate the following simple exchange from *Desperate Housewives* with the phrase *I'm good* in it: "'You want to hear?' 'No, I'm good, thanks'" (season 2, part 8) (2011b, 66). In the Russian online transcript that Ermolovich examined, this is translated as: "Khochesh' poslushat'?' 'Net, ne stoit'" (66). Google comes up with the absurd: "Vy khotite uslyshat'? 'Net, ia khoroshaia, spasibo.'" It is obvious to a human translator that none of the top four "statistical favorites" would work here. (All right, the first one—"Ia v poriadke"—might, with a stretch.) But Google is not up to using any of them. The Google "statistical" approach is deficient in that it resolves the communicative situation based only on a superficial, frequency-of-use-based "trolling" of its database at the level of the available descriptions of situations (incidentally, originally supplied by human translators) that may or may not be intrinsically similar or identical to the communicative situation in question.

Granted, "Google Translate" did not do a very good job of translating very simple but communicatively circumscribed everyday dialogues above. Maybe it will do better translating a more extended literary, non-dialogic text? Unfortunately, in this case, too, Google performs true to its limitations, as described by Ermolovich. Even a relatively simple passage from Sorokin's *Day of the Oprichnik* becomes an insurmountable obstacle for "Google Translate":[15]

Супротивных много, это верно. Как только восстала Россия из пепла Серого, как только осознала себя, как только шестнадцать лет назад заложил Государев батюшка Николай Платонович первый камень в фундамент Западной стены, как только стали мы отгораживаться от чуждого извне, от бесовского изнутри – так и полезли супротивные из всех щелей, аки сколопендрие зловредное. Истинно великая идея порождает и великое сопротивление ей. Всегда были враги у государства нашего, внешние и внутренние, но никогда так яростно не обострялась борьба с ними, как в период Возрождения Святой Руси (Sorokin 2011b, 4).

Many opposite is true. As soon as Russia has risen from the ashes of the Grey, once conscious of itself as only sixteen years ago, my father laid the Czar Nicholas Platonovich the foundation stone of the Western Wall as soon as we began to isolate itself from the alien from the outside, from the demons within—and climbed opposite from all the cracks, like a skolopendrie malignancy. Truly a great idea, and produces great resistance to it. There have always been enemies of the state of our, external and internal, but never so hard not to escalate the struggle against them, as in the Renaissance of Holy Russia. (Google Translate)

The above translation speaks for itself: What makes this Russian text literature has been killed in the Google translation, no matter how pleasant the voice of the female reader of the translation, provided by Google, may be.[16]

The point of literature is to create artistic texts—works of verbal art, the uniqueness and pragmatic impact of which can be described from various perspectives. We talk about literature in terms of its expressive richness, complexity of language, individuation, investigating the human psyche, depicting consciousness, providing insights into the workings of the other's mind, exercising the imagination, creating a story about what it means to be human, vicariously setting up and resolving personal crises, and directly accessing the characters' thoughts, which is denied in our usual everyday interactions—basically superficial, self-promoting, less than authentic, and generally mis-

---

[15] Compare the Google translation with Jamey Gambrell's in chapter 5.

[16] One of the fun features of "Google Translate" is that the translation of the text you enter for translation into the available 64 languages can be immediately read out loud back to you by a native speaker of the translating language with a very pleasant voice.

leading. In other words, literature is a "trauma-free" testing ground for working out the human condition or our existential angst. Complex issues require complex approaches and usually complex solutions. They cannot be resolved on the basis of statistics alone.

It has to be admitted, for fairness' sake, that Google has done a tremendous job in the general scheme of translation, having become an indispensable aid to learners of Russian and English and to translators, especially beginning or technical ones. The problem is that, as with other things in life, the devil—or, rather, the phantom—of literature conceals herself/himself/itself/themselves in the conceptual, stylistic, aesthetic, communicative, intellectual, cultural and other details that are beyond the grasp of today's computing machines. Ermolovich's verdict is dire: "[E]ven if the 'Babel fish' from the Adams novels existed, it would translate exceptionally badly, especially in conditions of rapidly changing situations: located in the ear, the fish wouldn't be able to see anything and, having to operate exclusively from hearing, it would spew absolute translation garbage" (2011b, 71).[17]

Concluding Remarks

My research shows that, on the whole, the leading translators of imaginative fiction (prose and film) in Russia today maintain the traditional tenets of the Soviet-Russian school of translation that began to be established in the early 1930s. The basic tenet concerns translatability: Any text is translatable because human thinking is a phenomenon with universally comparable features. The Russian school of translation (represented by the specialists discussed in this chapter and elsewhere in the book) continues to maintain that anything that has been written or said by anybody in a different language can be adequately translated into another language. At the same time, it is generally admitted that there may be degrees of approximation to the original or, some would say, limits of translatability. In other words, Russian translation theorists and practitioners are redefining the romantic tenet of the Soviet school of translation that insisted on translating the vaguely defined "spirit of a text" in terms of the acceptability of multiple "adequate" translations of the same text that speak to a variety of sociocultural contingents and that reflect varying degrees of the translators' "professional expertise" or incompetence. This is a more sophisticated understanding of the principle of translatability as compared to the previously tacitly accepted but vaguely defined conception of some single "master translation." The updating of the tenets of translatability

---

[17] Another example of applying theory to practice is given in Appendix 5, which describes Ermolovich's translation of "supercalifragilisticexpialidocious."

and multiple representations of the "spirit of a text" brings the current Russian thinking on translation closer to global translation studies.[18]

Finally, the Russian translation school, represented by the MSLU/*Mosty* Group and other translators discussed in this book, is also a strong proponent of another longstanding tenet, first formulated by Kornei Chukovskii, that of translation as a "high art." To me, it is a high art and an inexact science rolled into one. It is an art because the choices and decisions the translator constantly makes do not follow a single invariable formula leading to readily replicable results; imagination and inventiveness are an inalienable part of the process. It is an inexact science—or an exact art—because there is a clearly defined inventory of translation techniques and pragmatic orientations practitioners of the art consciously or unconsciously recognize and follow.

---

[18] An illustration of degrees of approximation to the original of a complex work of verbal art is provided in Appendix 6, which first defines the characteristics of an ideal translator of Platonov's texts and then gives a comparative analysis of the evolution of a translation by the same team of a brief excerpt from Platonov.

Conclusion

Negotiating Multiculturalism

There are three major ways in which a person or a group can integrate into a culture: assimilation, amalgamation, and accommodation. Assimilation represents the "classical" or oldest and traditional version of becoming a full-fledged member of a different culture. This kind of integration follows the formula A+B+C=A. It means that culture A is the dominant culture, and all the other cultures (B, C and so on) must adapt to or assimilate into the dominant culture by generally giving up their original traditions, values, and language, that is to say, by renouncing their indigenous cultures. Under this system, to become an American, for example, one has to give up everything that is not "American."

Amalgamation follows the formula A+B+C=D, whereby a combination of different cultures creates a new, unique culture. This is the famous "melting pot" theory: everything that is added to the pot melts and fuses together, creating something different each time a new ingredient is added. The best "melting pot" examples come from adopting different cuisines. As for spiritual food, the ingredients are less collectively digestible.

Accommodation is the more recent thinking on cultural identity. The formula is A+B+C=A+B+C. This is also called the "salad bowl" theory, where, as ingredients in a salad, people are thrown or mixed together, contributing on individual bases to the overall appearance and taste. In fact, the expectation is that the more one adds to the salad, the better it tastes. It is this conception—whereby people of different cultures speaking different languages can live together happily—that German Chancellor Angela Merkel expressed her disillusionment with when she addressed the young members of her conservative Christian Democratic Union in Potsdam, near Berlin, on 16 October 2010. In her view, coexistence of self-isolating cultures within one nation state is proving problematic. She has become the first Western world leader to state her position so bluntly. "We kidded ourselves a while. [...] And of course, the approach [to build] a multicultural [society] and to live side by side and to enjoy each other [...] has failed, utterly failed," she said.[1] According to Merkel, one of the key reasons for this failure was the refusal of immigrants to master the German language.

---

[1] Matthew Clark, "Germany's Angela Merkel: Multiculturalism Has 'Utterly Failed,'" *Christian Science Monitor*, 17 October 2010, http://www.csmonitor.com/World/Global-News/2010/1017/Germany-s-Angela-Merkel-Multiculturalism-has-utterly-failed

Obviously, in different interethnic and intercultural situations, all three models operate simultaneously—each up to a point, of course. But the pivotal issue of integration or even just coexistence is still language.[2] Knowing the language and the culture it represents is the crucial condition of societal assimilation, amalgamation, and accommodation, no matter the configuration of their interaction in a specific setting. And yet it is usually the importance of linguistic proficiency, including translation skills, that is generally undervalued in education and international discourse.

In its recent "Statement on Language Learning and United States National-al Policy,"[3] the Modern Language Association (MLA), which is the principal professional association in the United States for scholars of language and literature, came out strongly in support of promoting foreign language and culture education in the USA. The statement says, in part, that "anyone interested in the long-term vitality and security of the United States should recognize that it will be detrimental for Americans to remain overwhelmingly monolingual and ill-informed about other parts of this increasingly interdependent world" [...], that the MLA is "deeply alarmed by the drastic and disproportionate budget cuts in recent years to programs that fund advanced language study" [...], and that "recent research suggests that language learning enhances critical brain functions throughout an individual's life. For all these reasons, the MLA views the study of languages and literatures as central to American education at every level."

It is indeed deplorable and incredible that linguistic ignorance and incompetence are still rampant and lead to superficial, mediocre, and cliché- and oversimplification-driven statements about other cultures. The interethnic tensions throughout the world indicate loudly and clearly that it is only through mastering the "other" language, with all of its political, economic, sociocultural, ethical, and aesthetical "embeddedness," that an immigrant or a cross-cultural mediator (consultant, translator, interpreter, or politician, for that matter) can realistically hope to be accepted and trusted by the "other side" as a reliable partner in any undertaking. The following anecdote of global currency from a very recent past illustrates the point. On 6 March 2009, during an official meeting with the Russian Foreign Minister Sergei Lavrov in

---

[2] Among others, the translation theorist Juliana House has this to say about the role of language in all kinds of interaction: "Language is the prime means of an individual's acquiring knowledge of the world, of transmitting mental representations and making them public and intersubjectively accessible. Language is thus the prime instrument of a 'collective knowledge reservoir' to be passed from generation to generation. But language also acts as a means of categorizing cultural experience, thought and behaviour for its speakers. Language and culture are therefore most intimately (and obviously) interrelated" (House 2002, 95).

[3] For the full text, see http://www.mla.org/ec_us_language_policy?goback=%2Egde_2585509_member_124928204. The statement was issued by the MLA Executive Council on 6 June 2012.

Geneva, the then U.S. Secretary of State Hillary Clinton publicly presented the Russian foreign minister with a symbolic mock remote control with a big red reset button, purportedly to underscore the Obama administration's readiness to press the reset button in the by then somewhat frayed Russian-American relationship. There were two words—one in Russian above the button of the device and the other in English underneath the button. The English word was "Reset," and its translation into Russian read "Peregruzka," which means "overload" or "overcharged." The friendly American gesture was upended by a small amusing "translation malfunction." The translation should have been "perezagruzka," which looks and sounds similar to the erroneous translation. A correspondent for the Russian NTV television channel called it a "symbolic mistake." It was good that the button was on a symbolic device.

Linguistic knowledge is central in cognitive development, too. Recent studies show that "linguistic knowledge is not encapsulated from the rest of cognition, but is part and parcel of it: the structures of language (including both forms and their associated meanings) reflect and shape more general cognitive structures, whether universal or culture-specific, in a dynamic interplay mediated by the *use* of language" (Achard and Kemmer 2004, xviii). Expert translation is the highest manifestation of language use and is the major, though underappreciated, agency of sociocultural change across national borders. To paraphrase Tim Parks, as long as there is expert translation, "the world cannot become the monolithic thing globalization otherwise threatens to make it. Also, as long as there are different languages we will be free to shake off our individual identities, often more a burden than a boast, and reconstruct ourselves in otherness" (247), thus accepting multiculturalism and engaging with it at significantly deeper levels.

Of course, talking about amalgamation and assimilation, even a four-year foreign language course taken from scratch in college is not equivalent to translation expertise and will not secure complete integration into a native speakers' community—much more individual work is needed. But there is a shortcut. One of the underestimated ways of achieving advanced level proficiency in a foreign language and thereby acquiring deeper insights into the mindset of the "Other" is to read complex literature in one's native language, comparing the texts with their translation/s in the relevant foreign language. With multiple translations of major classics and mass fiction prose available today, reading two or three carefully selected translations of a work of verbal art in parallel with its original in the reader's native language would be a huge step toward appropriating the other culture in an authentic, comprehensive way. Even foreignized adaptations of original texts in parallel bilingual readers will go a long way toward enhancing one's proficiency in a foreign language. Both complex literature and simplified texts are the results of translators' work.

Be it globalization or localization, there is no getting away from the pervasiveness of translation: it is necessary to achieve success, lead an esthetically and intellectually more rewarding existence, and sometimes simply to survive. But translations vary according to the linguistic proficiency, cultural outlook, and educational level of the translator operating under complex sociocultural constraints in different places and at different times. Given the multiplicity of translations, how can one make an educated choice of a translation worth reading? To solve this problem, I advocate developing and establishing what Timothy Sergay and I call "translation variance studies,"[4] or comparative translation studies—an interdisciplinary field of study that would involve second language acquisition, lexicology, linguostylistics, lexicography, linguistics, sociolinguistics, cultural studies, comparative literary studies, social psychology, sociology, and history, to name just the main relevant subject areas. Among other things, this book is an attempt to illustrate what comparative multi-textual translation studies, or translation variance studies, can do.

The translator from Spanish into English Edith Grossman points out in her recent book *Why Translation Matters* that "translation may well be an entirely separate genre, independent of poetry, fiction, and drama, and that the next great push in literary studies should probably be to conceptualize and formulate the missing critical vocabulary. That is to say, it is certainly possible that translations may tend to be overlooked or even disparaged by reviewers, critics, and editors because they simply do not know what to make of them, in theory or in actuality" (2010, 47).[5] In discussing the various components or aspects of "the other in translation" in this book, I attempt to provide and clarify some vocabulary and material for just such a "push" in the direction of comparative translation studies.

---

[4] The term "translation variance studies" emerged in the course of numerous discussions that Professor Timothy Sergay (SUNY, Albany) and myself have had in recent years on the subject of multiple translations and pseudo translation reviews. He is as much to be credited or criticized for it as I am.

[5] A "translator user guide" for dummies is offered in Appendix 8 as a first step toward understanding the unique nature of a translator's/interpreter's work.

Appendix 1

Pevear and Volokhonsky's and Briggs's Translations of Platon Karataev's Story

In the two translations below, instances of what students felt to be problem areas are italicized, and selected illustrative examples of translation strategies used are underlined both in the Russian text and its translations and specified by the following abbreviations: neut. (neutralization), dom. (domestication), for. (foreignization), contam. (contamination), and styl. (stylization).

Толстой, Л. Н. *Война и мир*. Собрание сочинений в 20-и томах. Том 7. М.: Государственное издательство художественной литературы, 1963, с. 176–79.	Leo Tolstoy. *War and Peace*. Translated from the Russian by Richard Pevear and Larissa Volokhonsky. New York: Alfred A. Knopf. 2007, pp. 1062–63.	Tolstoy, L. N. *War and Peace. A New Translation by Anthony Briggs*. London: Penguin Books, 2005, pp.1181–82.
[1] Пьер знал эту историю давно, Каратаев раз шесть ему одному рассказывал эту историю, и всегда с особенным, радостным чувством. Но как ни хорошо знал Пьер эту историю, он теперь прислушался к ней, как к чему-то новому, и тот тихий восторг, который, рассказывая, видимо, испытывал Каратаев, сообщился и Пьеру. История эта была о старом купце, благообразно и богобоязненно жившем с семьей и по-	Pierre had long known this story. Karataev had told it to him alone some six times, and always with a special, joyful feeling. But however well Pierre knew this story, he now listened to it as something new, and the quiet rapture that Karataev clearly felt as he told it communicated itself to Pierre. It was a story about an old merchant, who lived a seemly and God-fearing life with his family, and went once with a comrade,	Pierre knew this story well. Karatayev had told it to him half a dozen times before, always with particular pleasure. But even though it was very familiar Pierre listened now as if it was something new, and the gentle sense of rapture that Karatayev was enjoying as he told it communicated itself to Pierre as well. It was the story of an old merchant, a good man who had lived a *Godfearing* life with his

ехавшем однажды с то-варищем, богатым куп-цом, к Макарью.	a rich merchant, to the Makary.[1]	family, and who went off one day to the fair at Makary with a friend of his, a rich merchant.
[2] Остановившись на по-стоялом дворе, оба купца заснули, и на другой день товарищ купца был най-ден зарезанным и ограб-ленным. Окровавленный нож найден был под по-душкой старого купца. Купца судили, наказали кнутом и, выдернув ноз-дри, – как следует по порядку, говорил Кара-таев, – сослали в каторгу.	Having stopped at an inn, the two merchants went to bed, and the next day the comrade was found mur-dered and robbed. The bloody knife was found under the merchant's pil-low. The merchant was tried, punished with the *knout*, and, having had his nostrils slit, *was*—in due order, as Karataev said— *sent to hard labor*.	They had put up at an inn together and gone to bed, and the next morning the rich merchant was dis-covered with his throat cut and his things stolen. A bloodstained knife was found under the old mer-chant's pillow. The merchant was tried and flogged, and had his nos-trils slit—all according to the law, as Karatayev said – and he *was sent to hard labour*.
[3] – И вот, братец ты мой (на этом месте Пьер за-стал рассказ Каратаева), проходит тому делу годов десять или больше того. Живет старичок на ка-торге. Как следовает, по-коряется, худого не дел-ает. Только у бога смерти просит. – Хорошо. И со-берись они, ночным дел-ом, каторжные-то, так же вот как мы с тобой, и старичок с ними. И зашел разговор, кто за что стра-дает, в чем богу виноват. Стали сказывать, тот душу загубил, тот две, тот поджег, тот беглый, так ни за что. Стали старичка	"And so, *brother mine* (contam., styl.)" (Pierre arrived at this point in Karataev's story), "ten years or more go by after this affair. The old man lives at hard labor. Duly sub-mits, does nothing bad. Only asks God for death. Good (for., styl.). And the convicts got together, a nightly thing, like you and me here, and the old man was with them. They *started* talking about who *suffers* for what, and what he's guilty of before God. They *began* telling: this one killed a man, that one killed two, another set a	'So, listen, brother (neut.) …' (It was at this point that Pierre had come in on the story.) 'After this a dozen years or more goes by. The old man is still a convict. Resigned to 'is fate, 'e is, as is only right. Never does nothin' wrong. The only thing 'e prays to God for is death … Right then … (dom., contam.) One night *they be all gathered together, them convicts*, just like *we be 'ere*, and the old man with 'em. And *they starts* talkin' about what *they'm all in for*, what they done wrong in the eyes of God.

---

[1] The Makary: in the early 19th century, the famous trade fair near Nizhnii Novgorod, close to the St. Makary Monastery, hence the name of the fair.

спрашивать: ты за что, мол, дедушка, страдаешь? Я, братцы мои миленькие, говорит, за свои да за людские грехи страдаю. А я ни душ не губил, ни чужого не брал, акромя что нищую братию оделял. Я, братцы мои миленькие, купец; и богатство большое имел. Так и так, говорит. И рассказал им, значит, как все дело было, по порядку. Я, говорит, о себе не тужу. Меня, значит, бог сыскал. Одно, говорит, мне свою старуху и деток жаль. И так-то заплакал старичок. Случись в их компании тот самый человек, значит, что купца убил. Где, говорит, дедушка, было? Когда, в каком месяце? все расспросил. Заболело у него сердце. Подходит таким манером к старичку – хлоп в ноги. За меня ты, говорит, старичок, пропадаешь. Правда истинная; безвинно напрасно, говорит, ребятушки, человек этот мучится. Я, говорит, то самое дело сделал и нож тебе под голова сонному положил. Прости, говорит, дедушка, меня ты ради Христа.

fire, another was a runaway, so he did nothing. They started asking the old man: 'What are you suffering for, grandpa?' 'I, my dear brothers,' he says, 'am suffering for my own and other people's sins. I didn't kill anybody, or take anything that wasn't mine, but even gave to beggars (neut.). I, my dear brothers, was a merchant; I had great wealth.' *Thus and so, he says. That is,* he told them how the whole thing went, in proper order. 'I don't grieve over myself,' he says. 'God, *that is,* has found me. I only pity my old woman and children.' And so the old man wept. In their company there happened to be the very man who had killed the merchant. 'Where did it happen, grandpa?' he says. 'When, in what month?'—he asked everything. His heart *ached* inside him. He *goes* up to the old man and—*plop* at his feet. 'You're perishing because of me, old man. It's the real truth. This man is suffering, *lads* (dom., styl.),' he says, guiltlessly and needlessly. I did that deed,' he says, 'and put the knife under your head while you slept. Forgive me, grandpa,' he says, 'for Christ's sake.'"

Lots of good stories. One of 'em was in for murder, another for two murders, somebody else 'ad set fire to somethin', and there was a wanderin' tramp who never done nothin' wrong. So *they turns* to the old man and they says, "What are you in for, Grandad?" "Me? Payin' for me sins, *I be,* me dear brothers," says 'e, "and everybody else's sins as well. I 'aven't murdered nobody, or *pinched* nothing, just given what I 'ad to the poor (neut., contam.). Used to be a merchant, I did, me dear brothers. I 'ad lots o' money." And 'e tells 'em all. *'Ow* things 'as worked out for 'im, all the details of 'is story bit by bit. "Not bothered about meself," says 'e, "I been picked out by God. Only one thing wrong," says 'e, "I do feel sorry for me old woman, and the kiddies." And 'e sheds a few tears. And it so 'appened in that company was the very man, you know, what 'ad killed the merchant. "Where did all this 'appen, Grandad?" says 'e. "When was it? What month?" Wanted to know all the details. *'Eartbroken* 'e was. Goes up to the old man just like that, 'e does, an' falls down at 'is feet. "You *be*

		in 'ere, old man," says 'e, "for somethin' what I done." 'Tis God's truth. This man *be* innocent. *'E be sufferin'* for nothing, *lads* (dom., styl.)," says *e*. "I done that job," says 'e, "an' put that knife under *yer 'ead* while you was asleep. Forgive me, Grandad. For God's sake, forgive me!" says 'e.'
[4] Каратаев замолчал, радостно улыбаясь, глядя на огонь, и поправил поленья.	Karataev fell silent, smiling joyfully, gazing at the fire, *and he adjusted the logs.*	Katayev paused with a blissful smile on his face and stared into the fire, poking the logs.
[5] Старичок и говорит: бог, мол, тебя простит, а мы все, говорит, богу грешны, я за свои грехи страдаю. Сам заплакал горючьми слезьми. Что же думаешь, <u>соколик</u>, – все светлее и светлее сияя восторженной улыбкой, говорил Каратаев, как будто в том, что он имел теперь рассказать, заключалась главная прелесть и все значение рассказа, – что же думаешь, соколик, объявился этот убийца самый по начальству. Я, говорит, шесть душ загубил (большой злодей был), но всего мне жальче старичка этого. Пускай же он на меня не плачется. Объявился: списали, послали бумагу, как следует. Место дальнее, пока суд да дело, пока все	"And the old man says: 'God will forgive you, and we're all sinful before God, I'm suffering for my own sins.' And he wept bitter tears. And what do you think, *little falcon* (for., styl.)?" Karataev was speaking with a rapturous smile that beamed brighter and brighter, as if what he was about to tell contained the chief delight and the whole meaning of the story, "what do you think, *little falcon*, this same murderer denounced himself to the authorities. 'I killed six men,' he says (he was a great villain), 'but I'm sorriest for this old man. Let him not *lament* on account of me.' He declared it: they wrote it down, duly sent a letter. This was a far-off place, it was a while before	'Then the old man, 'e says, "God will forgive you," says 'e, "but *we'm* all sinners in the eyes of God," says 'e. "I *be sufferin'* for me own sins." And 'e wept bitter tears. Then guess what, <u>*me old darling*</u> (dom., styl.),' said Karatayev, with an ever-broadening beatific smile, as if to indicate that the best bit, the whole point of the story was about to come. 'Guess what, *me old darling*. That murderer went up to them at the top and confessed. "I *seen six men off*," says 'e ('e being a real wrong 'un), "but I'm right sorry for this little old man. *'E* shouldn't *'ave* to suffer 'cos o' me." Went an' confessed, 'e did. 'Twas all wrote down on paper and

бумаги списали как
должно, по начальствам,
значит. До царя доход-
ило. Пока что, пришел
царский *указ*: выпустить
купца, дать ему наград-
дения, сколько там прису-
дили. Пришла бумага,
стали старичка разыски-
вать. Где такой старичок
безвинно напрасно стра-
дал? От царя бумага выш-
ла. Стали искать. – Ниж-
няя челюсть Каратаева
дрогнула. – А его уж бог
простил – помер. Так-то,
соколик, – закончил Кара-
таев и долго, молча улы-
баясь, смотрел перед
собой.

everything got done, *all the
papers filled out as they
ought, to the authorities, that
is*. It went all the way to
the tsar. Time passed, the
tsar's *ukase* came: release
the merchant, give him a
reward, as much as they
decided. Where's that old
man who has suffered
guiltlessly and needlessly?
A paper has come from
the tsar. They started
searching." Karataev's *lower jaw quivered*. "But God
had already forgiven
him—he was dead. There
it is, *little falcon*," Karataev
concluded and for a long
time, smiling silently, he
looked straight in front of
him.

sent off, as is only right.
Bloomin' (dom., styl.)
miles away. Looked at by
all the judges. Then it all
gets wrote down again
right and proper by them
at the top. Know what I
mean? Gets to the Tsar.
Then an order comes
down from the Tsar. Let
the merchant go. Give *'im
'is* compensation, like
what the judges *'as* said.
Piece o' paper arrives.
Everybody sets to (dom.),
looking for the old man.
Where's that little old
man gone what was in-
nocent and shouldn't 'ave
seen all this sufferin'? *'Ere
be* a paper from the Tsar!
Looked everywhere they
did.' Karatayev's jaw
trembled. 'But God 'ad
forgiven 'im. *'E* was dead!
That's *'ow* it *'appened, me
old darling*!' Karatayev
came to the end of the
story, and sat there for
some time staring ahead
with a smile on his face
and nothing more to say.

Appendix 2

Lotovskii's Preface to His Translation (Abridged)

Rita Rait-Kovaleva's excellent Russian translation of J. D. Salinger's […] novel *The Catcher in the Rye* became a cult text for my generation—those whose youth passed during the Soviet 1950–60s. The novel's young protagonist Holden Caulfield's protest against the falsity that surrounded him—a protest that, true enough, didn't often go beyond his inner sense of alienation and a wish not to be involved—resonated with the double standards of existence that prevailed in the Soviet society of the day. […]

Nearly half a century has gone by since the Salinger novel (or rather a novella by Russian standards) was first published in Russian translation. But, judging by the number of its reprints in the USA, Russia, and elsewhere, the demand for it has not abated. My new translation […] has been dictated by the following considerations. (The translator's love of Salinger and his novel is not a cogent enough reason, so we will keep it in parentheses). A close reading of the original shows that the classic translation is not entirely accurate. The inaccuracies were caused by different reasons. These can be grouped under three categories. 1) Censorship (or self-censorship). First of all, the [Russian] title itself "Nad *propast'iu* vo rzhi" is reminiscent of the agitprop cliché *propast' kapitalizma,* meaning "the abyss, or chasm, of capitalism." The original uses the word "cliff," that is to say, "a high very steep face of rock"—not "abyss," "gulf," or "precipice," which (in Russian) would be *propast', bezdna,* or *puchina.* 2) The translator (due to Soviet isolation) just could not know some American *realia* [culture-specific terms] (for example, those relating to sports, jazz, youth slang, etc.). 3) Aesthetic preference. The author of the translation has weeded out of the text all of its "parasitic words" [tediously repeated textual space/time-fillers] and coarse expressions, thus making the narrator sound bland, smooth, and cultured, so to speak, and depriving the text of the "rawness" characteristic of spoken speech in general. Incidentally, Samuil Marshak did exactly the same when he made the coarse language of the Scottish bard Robert Burns—whose concealed quote is used in the title *The Catcher in the Rye*—sound more "genteel." Apart from everything else, as a lady, Rait-Kovaleva tried to avoid racy turns of phrase. Or, perhaps, she was forced to do so in the presence of another redoubtable grande dame by the name of Censorship.

As a result the New York teenager Holden Caulfield, who is the first-person narrator of the story, comes across as an overly genteel and refined individual, due to which the incongruity between his inner nobility and his vulgar way of expressing himself becomes less pronounced. It was this core discrepancy that made me undertake a new version of a translation. I must repeat, though, that the previous translation[1] was executed at a high artistic level and that I am not an adherent of literalist translations insofar as they are damaging to the accuracy and completeness of the translation. To be fair, the work was easier for me than for Rait-Kovaleva in all respects. It was not that I relied heavily on her translation, but it did inspire me.[2]

---

[1] Lotovskii seems to be unaware of Nemtsov's 2008 translation of *The Catcher in the Rye.*

[2] For the full Russian text of Lotovskii's "Translator's Preface," see http://7iskusstv.com/ 2010/ Nomer2/Lotovsky1.php.

Appendix 3
Three Translations of the First Paragraph of *The Catcher in the Rye*

J.D. Salinger (1951) *The Catcher in the Rye*	Рита Райт-Ковалева (1960) *Над пропастью во ржи*	Максим Немцов (2008) *Ловец на хлебном поле*	Яков Лотовский (2010) *Над пропастью во ржи*
If you really want to hear about it, the first thing you'll probably want to know is where I was born, and what my lousy childhood was like, and how my parents were occupied and all before they had me, and all that David Copperfield kind of crap, but I don't feel like going into it, if you want to know the truth. In the first place, that stuff bores me, and in the second place, my parents would have about two hemorrhages apiece if I told anything pretty personal about them. They're quite touchy about anything like that, especially my father. They're nice and all – I'm not saying that – but they're also touchy as hell. Besides, I'm not	Если вам на самом деле хочется услышать эту историю, вы, наверно, прежде всего захотите узнать, где я родился, как провел свое дурацкое детство, что делали мои родители до моего рождения, словом, всю эту дэвид-копперфилдовскую муть. Но, по правде говоря, мне неохота в этом копаться. Во-первых, скучно, а во-вторых, у моих предков, наверно, случилось бы по два инфаркта на брата, если бы я стал болтать про их личные дела. Они этого терпеть не могут. Вообще-то они люди славные, я ничего не говорю, но обидчивые до чертиков.	Если по-честному охота слушать, для начала вам, наверно, подавай, где я родился и что за погань у меня творилась в детстве, чего предки делали и всякоразно, пока не заимели меня, да прочую Дэвид-Копперфилдову херню, только не в жилу мне про все это трындеть, сказать вам правду. Во-первых, достало, во-вторых, предков бы по две кондрашки хватило, если бы я стал про них чего-нибудь личное излагать. Они насчет такого чувствительные, особенно штрик. Не, они нормальные, всяко-разно, я ничего не хочу сказать, но чувствительные, как не знаю что. А кроме того, так я вам и	Если вы и в самом деле непрочь услышать обо всем об этом, вам сперва, наверно, захочется узнать из каких я мест, как прошло мое сопливое детство, род занятий моих родителей и прочую муру в духе Дэвида Копперфильда. Но, честно говоря, неохота в этом ковыряться. Во-первых, скучно, во-вторых, моих предков, наверно, хватила бы инфаркт, если б я стал трепаться про их личные дела. Они у меня жутко осторожные насчет этого, особенно отец. Нет, родители прекрасные и все такое, никто ничего не говорит, но осторожные до предела. Короче, я не

going to tell you my whole goddamn autobiography or anything. I'll just tell you about this madman stuff that happened to me around last Christmas just before I got pretty run-down and had to come out here and take it easy. I mean that's all I told D.B. about, and he's my brother and all. He's in Hollywood. That isn't too far from this crumby place, and he comes over and visits me practically every weekend. He's going to drive me home when I go home next month maybe. He just got a Jaguar. One of those little English jobs that can do around two hundred miles an hour. It cost him damn near four thousand bucks. He's got a lot of dough, now. He didn't use to. He used to be just a regular writer, when he was home. He wrote this terrific book of short stories, The Secret Goldfish, in case you never heard of him. The best one in it was "The Secret Goldfish." It was about this

Да и не собираюсь рассказывать свою автобиографию и всякую такую чушь, просто расскажу ту сумасшедшую историю, которая случилась прошлым Рождеством. А потом я чуть не отдал концы, и меня отправили сюда отдыхать и лечиться. Я и ему – Д.Б. – только про это и рассказывал, а ведь он мне как-никак родной брат. Он живет в Голливуде. Это не очень далеко отсюда, от этого треклятого санатория, он часто ко мне ездит, почти каждую неделю. И домой он меня сам отвезет – может быть, даже в будущем месяце. Купил себе недавно «ягуар». Английская штучка. Может делать двести миль в час. Выложил за нее чуть ли не четыре тысячи. Денег у него теперь куча. Раньше, когда он был дома, он был настоящим писателем. Может, слыхали – это он написал мировую книжку рассказов

выложил всю автобиографию, ага. Я вам только про безумное расскажу, что со мной случилось на прошлое Рождество, перед тем как меня шарахнуло и пришлось расслабляться. То есть, это я и Д.Б. рассказывал, а он мне брательник всяко-разно. Живет в Голливуде. От этих своей недалеко – считал, каждые выходные в гости ко мне приезжает. И домой меня отвезет, когда я, наверно, туда через месяц поеду. Он только что «ягуар» себе прикупил. Английская хрень такая, двести миль в час выжимает. Выкатил за него аж четыре штуки. У него теперь грошей много. А раньше вот не было. Раньше он обычный писатель был, когда жил дома. Сочинил уманную книжку рассказов – «Тайная золотая рыба» называется, если не слыхали про него. Лучший рассказ там – эта «Золотая рыбка» и

собираюсь излагать свою дурацкую автобиографию от и до. Просто хочу рассказать про всю эту катавасию, что случилась со мной под Рождество, когда я чуть не отдал концы – и в результате попал сюда для поправки здоровья. Я уже рассказывал все это Д.Б. Он мне родной брат и т. д. и т. п. Он теперь в Голливуде. Это не очень далеко от этого вшивого места, и он часто навещает меня по выходным. Он и домой увезет меня отсюда, может даже, в следующем месяце. Он купил себе недавно «Ягуар». Английская такая штуковина, дает миль двести в час. Выложил за нее около четырех тысяч баксов. Бабки у него теперь водятся. Не то что раньше. Зато раньше, когда он жил дома, он был настоящим писателем. Он написал классную книжку рассказов «Тайная рыбка», может, кто слышал. Лучший там рассказ так и называется «Тайная

little kid that wouldn't let anybody look at his goldfish because he'd bought it with his own money. It killed me. Now he's out in Hollywood, D.B., being a prostitute. If there's one thing I hate, it's the movies. Don't even mention them to me (pp. 1-2).

«Спрятанная рыбка». Самый лучший рассказ так и называется – «Спрятанная рыбка». Там про одного мальчишку, который никому не позволял смотреть на свою золотую рыбку, потому что купил ее на собственные деньги. С ума сойти, какой рассказ! А теперь мой брат в Голливуде, совсем скурвился. Если я что ненавижу, так это кино. Терпеть не могу (pp. 5-6).

есть. Про пацана, который никому свою золотую рыбку не показывал, потому что он ее на свои деньги купил. Я чуть не сдох. А теперь он в Голливуде, Д.Б. то есть, – собой торгует. Кино это я просто ненавижу – как мало что. Про кино мне лучше и не заикайтесь (pp. 9-10).

рыбка». Там про одного малыша, который никому не давал взглянуть на свою золотую рыбку, потому что купил ее на свои деньги. Обалдеть можно! А теперь Д.Б. в Голливуде. Совсем скурвился. Вот чего я не терплю, так это кинофильмы. Блин, на дух не выношу! (Pp. 2-3)

Appendix 4

Skaz-Forming Linguistic and Stylistic Means in the *Catcher in the Rye* Original and Its Translations

Salinger	Rait-Kovaleva	Nemtsov	Lotovskii
Evaluative-emphatic adjectives:			
If you really like to hear [...] *what my lousy childhood was like* 1	как провел свое дурацкое детство 5	что за погань у меня творилась в детстве 9	как прошло мое сопливое детство 2
I'll just tell you about this madman stuff that happened to me 1	Расскажу ту сумасшедшую историю, которая случилась 5	я вам только про безумное расскажу, что со мной случилось 9	Просто хочу рассказать про всю эту катавасию, что случилась со мной 2
That isn't too far from this crumby place 1	Это не очень далеко отсюда, от этого треклятого санатория 5	От этих своясей недалеко 9	Это не очень далеко от этого вшивого места 2
some *hotshot* guy on a horse 2	этакий *хлюст*, верхом на лошади 6	какой-нибудь *ферт* на лошади 10	*крутой такой* чувак верхом на лошади 3
I was standing [...] right next to this *crazy* cannon 2	я стоял [...] около *дурацкой* пушки, которая там торчит 7	возле этой *долбанутой* пушки, что в Американской революции бабахала всяко-разно 10	рядом с этой *дурацкой* мортирой 3

a *phony* slob 3	трепло несусветное 7	*дутый халдей* 11	*простое фуфло* 4
on top of that *stupid* hill 4	на этой треклятой горке 8	на верхушке этого *дурацкого холма* 12	на верху этого *дурацкого холма* 5
It was that kind of a *crazy* afternoon 5	день был какой-то сумасшедший 10	День вообще долбанутый 13	День был какой-то сумасшедший 6
Slang nouns:			
He's got a lot of *dough* now 1	Денег у него теперь *куча* 6 (The use of the neutral *деньги* for the slang noun *dough* is compensated for by using the slangy *куча* for the neutral *a lot*)	У него теперь *грошей* много 10	*Бабки* у него теперь водятся 2
She probably knew what a phony *slob* he was 3	Наверно, сама знает, что он *трепло несусветное* 7	Наверно, сама знает, что он *дутый халдей* 11	
I kept standing next to that crazy cannon [...], freezing my *ass* off 4	Словом, стоял я у этой дурацкой пушки, чуть *зад* не отморозил 8-9	Ладно, стою рядом с долбанутой пушкой [...], а *жопа* подмерзает 12	
They didn't have too much *dough* 5	Денег у них в обрез 10 (NT – not translated)	*Грошей* у них немного 13	
Idioms (phrases whose meaning does not directly follow from the meanings of their component parts):			

Giving a positive assessment of his brother's story, Holden Caulfield says: "It killed me" 2	*С ума сойти, какой рассказ!* 6	*Я чуть не сдох* 10	*Обалдеть можно!* 3
Strictly for the birds 2	*Вот уж липа!* 6	Это для лохов 10	*Полная туфта!* 3
The game with Saxon Hall was supposed to be *a very big deal* at Pencey 2	Считалось, что для Пэнси этот матч *важней всего на свете* 6	В Пенси играть с Саксом-Холлом – *всегда кипиш* 10	Игра с Сэксом-холлом считалась для Пэнси делом *важнее некуда* 3
(You couldn't see the grandstand) *too hot* 2	Трибун я *как следует разглядеть* не мог 7	Трибуны разглядишь *не сильно* 10	Что на трибунах, *особенно не разглядишь* 3
Talking about his position as the manager of the fencing team, Holden Caulfield says, "Very big deal" 3	*Важная шишка* 7	*Не хрен собачий* 11	*Большой начальник* 4
freezing my ass off 4	*чуть зад не отморозил* 8-9	*а жопа подмерзает* 12	*и чуть жопу не отморозил* 5
and it was *cold as a witch's teat* 4	*холодно, как у ведьмы за пазухой* 8	*колотун, как у ведьмы за пазухой* 12	*холодина, как у ведьмы за пазухой* 5
And all / and stuff (filler words used to complete a sentence in a "lazy" way, implying blasé world-weariness):			

how my parents were occupied *and all* 1	что делали мои родители до моего рождения 5 (NT)	чего предки делали *и всяко-разно* 9	род занятий моих родителей --- --- 2 (NT)
they're nice *and all* 1	*Вообще-то они люди славные* 5	Не, они *нормальные* (italicized in the translation) *всяко-разно* 9	Нет, родители прекрасные *и все такое* 2
and he's my brother *and all* 1	а ведь он мне *как ни как* родной брат 5	а он мне *брательник* (italicized in the translation) *всяко разно* 9	Он мне родной брат *и т. д. и т. п.* 2
And I didn't know anybody there that was splendid and clear-thinking *and all* 2	И ни одного "благородного и смелого" я не встречал 6 (NT)	И никого великолепного или здравомыслящего я там тоже не встречал 10 (NT)	Что-то я там не встречал блестящих и благородных *и т. д. и т. п.* 4
right next to this crazy cannon that was in the Revolutionary war *and all* 2	около дурацкой пушки, которая там торчит, *кажется, с самой* войны за независимость 7	возле этой долбанутой пушки, что в Американской революции бабахала *всяко-разно* 10	рядом с этой дурацкой мортирой, что торчит там со времен войны за Независимость *и т. д. и т. п.* 3
I left all the foils and equipment *and stuff* on the goddamn subway 3	Я забыл рапиры, и костюмы, *и вообще всю эту петрушку* в вагоне метро 8	Я, нафиг, забыл все рапиры *и прочее* в метро 11	Я забыл рапиры, маски *и все причандалы* в этом чертовом метро 4
not applying myself *and all* 4	И вообще не занимался *и все такое* 8	не брался за ум *и всяко-разно* 11	и *вообще все нафиг* забросил 4
it was December *and all* 4	дело было в декабре 8 (NT)	В общем, декабрь *и всяко-разно* 12	дело было в декабре 5 (NT)

my fur-lined gloves right in the pocket *and all* 4	Вместе с теплыми печатками – они там и были, в кармане 8 (NT)	а в кармане были перчатки на меху *и всяко-разно* 12	вместе с меховыми перчатками в кармане 5 (NT)
all those goddamn checkups *and stuff* 5	на проверку и на это дурацкое лечение 10 (NT)	и сюда приперся – все эти анализы сдавать *и прочую херню* 13	и попал сюда на обследование *и все такое прочее* 6
That kind of (to express blasé world-weariness):			
and all that David Copperfield kind of crap 1	всю эту дэвид-копперфилдовскую *муть* 5	да прочую Дэвид-Копперфилдову *херню* 9	и прочую муру в духе Давида Копперфильда 2
that kind of stuff 5	такую штуку 9	такую хренотень 12	такую вещь 5
Clauses of condition and concession (used for emphasis and familiar contact maintenance [phatic function]):			
If you really want to hear about it 1	Если вам на самом деле хочется услышать эту историю 5	Если по-честному охота слушать 9	Если вы и в самом деле непрочь услышать обо всем об этом 2
if you want to know the truth 1	по правде говоря 5	сказать вам правду 9	честно говоря 2
in case you never heard of him 1	может, слыхали 6	Если не слыхали про него 10	может, кто слышал 3
If there's one thing I hate, it's the movies 2	Если я что ненавижу, так это кино 6	Кино это я просто ненавижу – как мало что 10	Вот чего я не терплю, так это кинофильмы 3

if you want to know the truth 5	по правде говоря 9	Если по-честному 12	если уж говорить честно 6
that *stuff* 1	1 (NT)	9 (NT)	2 (NT)
this madman *stuff* 1	Сумасшедшую *историю* 5	*безумное* 9	*катавасию* 2
that kind of *stuff* 5	*штуку* 9	*хренотень* 12	*вещь* 5
This (phatic-familiar):			
this madman stuff 1	*ту* сумасшедшую историю 5	безумное 9 (NT)	*эту* катавасию 2
this terrific book 1	мировую книжку 6 (NT)	уматную книжку 10 (NT)	классную книжку 2 (NT)
It was about *this* little kid 2	про *одного* мальчишку 6	про пацана 10 (NT)	про *одного* малыша 3
this school that's in Agerstown 2	это закрытая средняя школа в Эгерстауне 6 (NT)	Это *такая* школа в Эйджерстауне 10	это частная школа в Эгерстауне 3 (NT)
this crazy cannon 2	дурацкой пушки 7 (NT)	*этой* долбанутой пушки 10	*этой* дурацкой мортирой 3
this fencing meet 3	состязание 7 (NT)	турнир 11 (NT)	на *эту самую* встречу 4
to look at *this* map 3	смотреть на схему 8 (NT)	на карту глядеть 11 (NT)	следить *по этой самой* схеме 4
He wrote me *this* note 3	А он мне прислал записку 8 (NT)	А он мне записку написал 11 (NT)	он прислал мне (NT) записку 4 (NT)
this teacher that taught biology 5	*Наш* учитель биологии 9	*этот* биолог 12	Учитель биологии 5 (NT)
Goddamn / damn			

(as emphasis):			
I'm not going to tell you my whole *goddamn* autobiography 1	Да я и не собираюсь рассказывать свою автобиографию и *всякую такую чушь* 5	так я вам и выложил всю автобиографию, *ага* 9	я не собираюсь излагать свою *дурацкую* автобиографию от и до 2
It cost him *damn* near four thousand bucks 1	Выложил за нее *чуть ли не* четыре тысячи 6 (The *damn* is conveyed by using the more colloquial *выложил* for the neutral *cost* and the more emphatic *чуть ли не* for the neutral *near*)	Выкатил за него *аж* четыре штуки 10 (NT but the *damn* is compensated for by using the more colloquial *выкатил* for the neutral *cost*)	Выложил за нее – около четырех тысяч баксов 2 (NT but the *damn* is compensated for by using the more colloquial *выложил* for the neutral *cost*)
They don't do any *damn* more molding at Pensey 2	*Вот уж липа!* Никого они там не выковывают 6	*Это для лохов. Ни шиша* в Пенси не *лепят* 10 (This is just one example of the numerous instances of Nemtsov's enhancing translations)	*Полная туфта! Ни фига* особенного они не *формируют* 3 (This is just one example of the numerous instances of Lotovsky's enhancing translations)
I was the *goddamn* manager of the fencing team 3	Я капитан этой *вонючей* команды. *Важная шишка* 7	Я, *нафиг,* заведовал фехтовальной командой. *Не хрен собачий* 11	Я был в команде как бы за старшего. *Большой начальник!* 4
on the *goddamn* subway 3	в вагоне метро 8 (NT)	Я, *нафиг,* забыл все рапиры и прочее в метро 11	в этом *чертовом* метро 4

all these *goddamn* checkups and stuff 5	на проверку и на это *дурацкое* лечение 10	все эти анализы сдавать и прочую *херню* 13 (The semi-vulgar slang term *херня* is likely used to compensate for the untranslated *goddamn*)	обследование и все такое прочее 6 (NT)
I *damn* near fell down 5	и я чуть не *грохнулся* 10 (The colloquial *грохнулся* is likely used to compensate for the untranslated *damn*)	и я там чуть не *грохнулся* 13 (The colloquial *грохнулся* is likely used to compensate for the untranslated *damn*)	чуть не *загремел костьми* 6 (The slang phrase *загремел костьми* is likely used to compensate for the untranslated *damn*)
Or anything / something:			
Besides, I'm not going to tell you my whole goddamn autobiography *or anything* 1	Да я и не собираюсь рассказывать свою автобиографию *и всякую такую чушь* 5	А кроме того, так я вам и выложил всю автобиографию, *ага* 9	Короче, я не собираюсь излагать свою автобиографию от и до 2 (NT)
you were supposed to commit suicide *or something* if old Pencey didn't win 2	И, если бы наша школа проиграла, нам всем полагалось *чуть ли не* перевешаться с горя 6–7	и если Пенси не выиграет, прям хоть в петлю 10 (NT)	Если наша школа продует, всем надо повеситься *или типа того* 3
I only had on my reversible and no gloves *or anything* 4	На мне была только куртка – *ни* перчаток, *ни черта* 8	А на мне только двусторонняя куртейка и никаких перчаток, *ничего* 12	На мне только и всего, что куртка – *ни* перчаток, *ни фига* 5
no sun out *or anything* 5	Ни проблеска солнца, *ничего* 10	никакого ни солнца, *ничего* 13	ни проблеска солнца, *ничего* 6

They didn't have a maid *or anything* 5	У них прислуги нет *и вообще никого нет* 10	У них ни горничной не было, *никак* 13	У них нет прислуги *и вообще никого* 6
Emphatic syntactic constructions:			
Where I want to start telling is the day I left Pencey Prep 2	*Лучше всего начну рассказывать* с того дня, как я ушел из Пенси 6	*Я вот откуда начну* – с того дня, как свалил из подготовишки Пенси 10	*Наверно*, начну с того дня, как я ушел из Пэнси 3
What I liked about her, she didn't give a lot of horse manure about what a great guy her father was 3	*Понравилось мне то, что* она тебе не вкручивала, какой у нее замечательный папаша 7	*А мне в ней понравилось, что* она не лепит тебе всякий навоз, мол, какой у нее штрик четкий 11	Мне, например, понравилось, что она не втирает про своего папашу, какая он важная птица 4 (NT)
It has a very good academic rating. *It really does* 4	У них очень высокая академическая успеваемость, *серьезно, очень высокая* 8	Там очень хорошая академическая успеваемость. *Куда деваться* 12	Это у них быстро, ребят вышибают на раз. Чтобы держать высокий рейтинг по успеваемости. Он у них высокий, *что есть, то есть* 5
(The) Hell (as emphasis):			
I was standing way *the hell* up on Thomsen Hill 2	я стоял *черт знает где*, на самой горе Томпсона 7	Стою *аж* на самой вершине Томсен-хилла 10	я стоял наверху холма Томсена 3 (NT)
I was getting *the hell* out 4	я отсюда уезжаю навсегда 9 (NT)	Мне сразу стало ясно, что меня, *нафиг*, тут больше нет 12	и я сразу понял: хорошо, что *уматываю* отсюда навсегда 5 (*The hell* is compensated for by using the slang verb *уматываю* for

			the neutral *getting out*)
It was icy *as hell* 5	Дорога вся обледенела *до черта* 10	А она вся обледенела, *как не знаю что* 13	Все *на фиг* обледенело 6
Old (A noun modifier expressing the speaker's attitude of familiarity to the person or thing concerned):			
old Pencey 2	наша школа 6 (NT)	Пенси 10 (NT)	наша школа 3 (NT)
old Selma Thurmer 3	дочка нашего директора 7 (NT)	*Эта* Селма Тёрмер 11	дочка нашего директора 4 (NT)
old Spencer 3	зайти к *старику* Спенсеру 8	шел попрощаться с *этим* Спенсером 11	зайти к *старику* Спенсеру 4
old Spencer's house 5	добежал до *старика* Спенсера! 10	когда до *этого* Спенсера добрался 13	к дому *старика* Спенсера 6
old Mrs. Spencer 5	*старушка* Спенсер 10	*эта* миссис Спенсер 13	*эта* миссис Спенсер 6
Sort of:			
and we *sort of* struck up a conversation 3	и разговорились 7 (NT)	и мы *чуток даже* потрепались 11	и *вроде как* разговорились 4
but you felt *sort of* sorry for her 3	но ее *почему-то* было жалко 7	но ее *все равно как-то* жалко 11	но есть в ней *что-то* симпатичное 4
I was *sort of* disappearing 5	мне вдруг *показалось*, что я исчез 10	[я] понял, что *как бы* исчезаю 13	мне вдруг *стало казаться*, что я *как бы* исчезаю 6

She was *sort of* deaf 6	Она была *намножко глуховата* 10	Она *как бы глуховата* 13	Она *вроде как немного глуховата* 6–7
I *sort of* brushed my hair back with my hand 6	я *пригладил волосы ладонью* 11 (NT)	я, *с понтом,* волосы пятерней себе пригладил 13	я взъерошил волосы руками 7 (NT)
Boy (for emphasis; followed by a statement or a rhetorical question):			
Boy, I rang that doorbell fast 5	*Ух и* звонил же я в звонок 10	*ух как* я жал на звонок 13	*и сходу* надавил на звонок 6
Boy, did I get in that house fast 6	Я *пулей* влетел к ним в дом 10	*Ух как* я рванул внутрь 13	Я *прямо* влетел к ним в дом 6
Hyperbole (exaggeration for emphasis and for showing off):			
my parents would have about two hemorrhages apiece 1	*у моих предков, наверно, случилось бы по два инфаркта на брата* 5	*предков бы по две кондрашки хватило* 9	*моих предков, наверно, хватил бы инфаркт* 2
if there's one thing I hate, it's the movies 2	*Если я что ненавижу, так это кино* 6	*Кино это я просто ненавижу – как мало что* 10	*Вот чего я не терплю, так это кинофильмы* 3
Don't even mention them to me 2	Терпеть не могу 6	Про кино вы мне лучше и не заикайтесь 10	Блин, на дух не выношу! 3
They advertise in about a thousand magazines 2	Ее [рекламу] печатают чуть ли не в тысяче журналов 6	Они ее [рекламу] в тыще журналов ляпают 10	Они тыщу раз печатали ее [рекламу] в журналах 3

Your were supposed to commit suicide or something if old Pencey didn't win 2	если ба наша школа проиграла, нам всем полагалось чуть ли не перевешаться с горя 6–7	и если Пенси не выиграет, прям хоть в петлю 10	Если наша школа продует, всем надо повеситься или типа того 3
but she wasn't exactly the type that drove you mad with desire 3	но не такая это девчонка, чтоб по ней с ума сходить 7	только по таким, как она, сохнуть как-то не очень 11	но она не из тех, кто может вызвать безумное желание 4

Appendix 5

Applying Theory to Practice: How Do You Translate *Supercalifragilisticexpialidocious* into Russian?

The simple examples examined in the sections devoted to Ermolovich in chapter 7 are all well and good. But how do you go about translating something that seems totally untranslatable? How would you translate, for example, the artificial but widely understood in the English-speaking world word "supercalifragilisticexpialidocious" into Russian? Google Translate has no answer: it translates it as "supercalifragilisticexpialidocious." End of story. But it would have an answer if Professor Ermolovich's translation of this charming jawbreaker of a word "from the inside" of the communicative situation had been fed into it. Obviously, it hasn't been so far. So here is how Professor Ermolovich went about finding a translation solution to this one.

The word *supercalifragilisticexpialidocious* is used many times in the song that Mary Poppins and her friend the chimney-sweep, artist, and singer Bert sing together in the Walt Disney 1964 classic musical "Mary Poppins." The word entered the English language, and many English speakers use it and know its provenance. It basically means "great," "fantastic," "stupendous," "wonderful" or "super-cool" and can be used as a straightforward facetious evaluative statement or a regular exclamation to describe something that surprises and delights you. It is also the word that Mary Poppins suggests you say when you do not know what to say.

Back in 2008, Ermolovich analyzed the quality of the Russian translation of the more difficult parts of the dubbed Russian version of the film (mostly its songs and jokes). Interestingly, the film never became widely known and popular in the Soviet Union or post-Soviet Russia. Ideological considerations aside, Ermolovich implies that part of the reason was its less than enchanting translation as compared to the original charming text. Among other translation problems that were not resolved satisfactorily, Ermolovich singles out the transliteration of *supercalifragilisticexpialidocious* as "superkalifradzhilistikekspialidoshes." To any Russian this sounds like your typical "barbarism"—a crude foreignization of a translation. Ermolovich defines four problems that the translator failed to resolve: (1) the word in Russian is not grammatically marked—it is not clear what part of speech it is supposed to represent (it is an adjective in English); (2) its ecstatically positive evaluative connotation is lost; (3) although the transliteration is as long as the original word, morphologically, it does not contain the transparent highly bookish or scientific-sounding morphemes; and, finally, (4) it sounds extraordinary not owing to a highly imaginative use of the Russian language but because of its total foreignness (Ermolovich 2008). The identification of the problems of the translation determined Ermolovich's search for a solution in Russian—a word that would be (1) grammatically recognizable, (2) have a positive evaluative connotation, (3) be long and bookish, and (4) sound extraordinary in Russian in a recognizably Russian way. He came up with "superarkhiekstraul'tramegagrandiozno," which almost completely fulfills all the requirements for a translation approximation that he set himself. A stroke of genius, if you ask me.

Since 2008, Ermolovich's translation of *supercalifragilisticexpialidocious* as "superarkhiekstraul'tramegagrandiozno" has been picked up by the Russian Wikipedia (http://ru.wikipedia.org), used in a translation of the NASA astronomer Jack Lissauer's press conference on Russian television,[1] and even used in a modified form in the Russian translation of the American singer Fergie's song "Labels or Love" from the *Sex and the City* television series:

When I walk out the store, store	Когда выхожу из магазина, магазина,
I guess I'm <u>supercalifragi-sexy</u>...	Я думаю, я <u>суперархиэкстраультрасексуальна</u>.
	(Ermolovich 2011a, 44).[2]

---

[1] Lissauer: "There is only one word that I can think of that adequately describes the new finding we are announcing today: the Kepler 11 system of six transiting planets is supercalifragilisticexpialidocious!" Translation: "Есть только одно слово, которым можно в полной мере описать открытие, обнародованное сегодня, – суперархиэкстраультрамегаграндиозно" (Ermolovich 2011a, 44).

[2] See the song lyrics and their Russian translation at the website lyrsense.com, accessed 21 August 2013, http://soundtrack.lyrsense.com/index.php?q=sex_and_the_city/labels_or_love.

Appendix 6

Translating Platonov

In his 2010 interview for SRAS (the School of Russian and Asian Studies), Robert Chandler, the famous British Russian-to-English translator who, in the space of the preceding 15 years, had twice spearheaded a team-translation of Soviet author Andrei Platonov's exceptionally complex and imaginative novel *The Foundation Pit*, gives the following extended description of what it takes to operate as an effective translator of linguistically and culturally intricate fiction prose—in this case by Platonov:

> The ideal translator of Platonov would be bilingual and have an encyclopedic knowledge of Soviet life. He would be able to detect buried allusions not only to the classics of Russian and European literature, but also to speeches of Stalin, to articles by such varied figures as Bertrand Russell and Anatolii Lunacharskii (the first Bolshevik Commissar for Enlightenment), to copies of *Pravda* from the 1930s and to long-forgotten works of Soviet literature. He would be familiar with Soviet-speak, with the rituals and language of Russian Orthodoxy, with everyday details of Russian peasant life, with the terminology of mechanical and electrical engineering, and with the digging of wells and the operation of steam locomotives. This imaginary translator would also be a gifted and subtle punster. Most important of all, his ear for English speech patterns would be so fine that he could maintain the illusion of a speaking voice, or voices, even while the narrator or the individual characters are using extraordinary language or expressing extraordinary thoughts. Much has been written about Platonov's creativity and language; not enough has been written about the subtlety with which—even in narrative—he reproduces the music of speech, its shifts of intonation and rhythm. If Platonov's command of tone and idiom were less than perfect, his infringements of linguistic norms would by now seem self-conscious and dated. In short, Platonov is a poet, and almost every line of his finest work poses problems for a translator. A perfect translation, like the original, would sound not only extraordinary and shocking, but also—in some indefinable way—right and natural. And so ... I realized long ago that the only way to go about the task of translating Platonov was to find collaborators. One indication of how deeply many Russian writers and

critics admire Platonov is the extent of their generosity to the translators; I now have a large list of people I can turn to for help. Above all, I have the good fortune to have as my closest collaborators my wife, who shares my love of Platonov, and the brilliant American scholar Olga Meerson. Olga was brought up in the Soviet Union, she knows a great deal about Russian Orthodoxy, she has written a brilliant book about Platonov and she has the sensitive ear of someone who once trained as a professional violinist. She has deepened our understanding of almost every sentence of *Soul* and *The Foundation Pit*. Our new translation[1] is, by the way, an entirely new translation—not merely a revision of the translation we did for Harvill in 1994.[2] There are passages in the first translation that I still like, but at the time we were working in the dark, with little contact with Russian scholars. The new translation, on the other hand, is—I believe—the product of at least some degree of understanding. No other work of literature, by the way, means so much to me that I have wanted to translate it twice! (Chandler 2010)

Perhaps an even more decisive step toward conveying Platonov's unique authorial style was made by Chandler and his team of collaborators (Elizabeth Chandler, Nadia Bourova, Angela Livingstone, Olga Meerson, and Eric Naiman) in their most recent retranslation of Platonov's *Happy Moscow* (Platonov 2012). Chandler and his team did the first translation of the story in 2001 (Platonov 2001). This time round, they expanded the circle of collaborators by including Olga Meerson. In the introduction to the 2012 retranslation, Chandler writes: "All of us found ourselves apologizing for ways in which we had inadvertently toned down his [Platonov's] starkness; all of us wanted to revise our translations, to reproduce more faithfully details of syntax or vocabulary choices that we had previously thought unimportant or even failed to notice."[3]

To illustrate the operative complexities Chandler refers to in his interview, here is a comparative glimpse of the very beginning of Platonov's

---

[1] Andrey Platonov, *The Foundation Pit*, trans. Robert Chandler, Elizabeth Chandler, and Olga Meerson (New York: New York Review Books, 2009).

[2] Andrey Platonov, *The Foundation Pit*, trans. Robert Chandler and Geoffrey Smith (London: The Harvill Press, 1996).

[3] Liesl Schillinger, "Soviet Dreams," review of *Happy Moscow*, by Andrey Platonov, *New York Times*, 28 December 2012, Sunday Book Review, http://www.nytimes.com/2012/12/30/books/review/happy-moscow-by-andrey-platonov.html?nl=books&emc=edit_bk_20121228.

novella (*povest'*) *The Foundation Pit*,[4] followed by the two variant translations by Chandler and his collaborators:

В день тридцатилетия личной жизни Вощеву дали расчет с небольшого механического завода, где он добывал средства для своего существования. В увольнительном документе ему написали, что он устраняется с производства вследствие роста слабосильности в нем и задумчивости среди общего темпа труда. Вощев взял на квартире вещи в мешок и вышел наружу, чтобы на воздухе лучше понять свое будущее. Но воздух был пуст, неподвижные деревья бережно держали жару в листьях, и скучно лежала пыль на безлюдной дороге — в природе было тихое[5] [такое] положение. Вощев не знал, куда его влечет, и облокотился в конце города на низкую ограду одной усадьбы, в которой приучали бессемейных детей к труду и пользе. Дальше город прекращался — там была лишь пивная для отходников и низкооплачиваемых категорий, стоявшая, как учреждение, без всякого двора, а за пивной возвышался глиняный бугор, и старое дерево росло на нем, одно среди светлой погоды. Вощев добрел до пивной и вошел туда на искренние человеческие голоса. Здесь были невыдержанные люди, предававшиеся забвению своего несчастья, и Вощеву стало глуше и легче среди них. (Platonov 2000, 21)

The Foundation Pit. Translated by Robert Chandler and Geoffrey Smith (1996).

On the thirtieth anniversary of the beginning of his private life, Voshchev was sacked from the small machine factory where he had until then got the means for his subsistence. His dismissal notice stated that he was being removed from production on account of a situation of

The Foundation Pit. Translated by Robert Chandler, Elizabeth Chandler, and Olga Meerson (2009).

On the day of the thirtieth anniversary of his private life, Voshchev was made redundant from the small machine factory where he obtained the means for his own existence. His dismissal notice stated that he was being removed from production on account of weakening strength in him

---

[4] Andrei Platonov, *Kotlovan. Tekst, materialy tvorcheskoi istorii* (St. Petersburg: Nauka, 2000). See also *Internet biblioteka Alekseia Komarova*, Andrey Platonov, *Kotlovan* (Minsk: Mastatskaia literatura, 1990), accessed 6 August 2012, http://ilibrary.ru/text/1010/p.1/index.html.

[5] The "definitive edition published by Pushkin House in Moscow"—this is what the blurb of the 2009 version of the translation says—has the word "tikhoe," whereas the edition that Chandler and Smith used for their 1996 translation must have had the word "takoe," hence the difference in the translation of this part of the text: "such was the situation in nature" (1996) and "the situation in nature was quiet."

ongoing personal weakness and thought-fulness amid the general tempo of labour.

and thoughtfulness amid the general tempo of labor.

Voshchev went to his room, put his things into a bag and then went back outside so as to get a better understanding of his future in the fresh air. But the air was empty, the motionless trees were carefully hoarding the heat in their leaves, and the dust lay dully on the deserted road—such was the situation in nature. Voshchev had no idea where to head for, and at the end of the town he leant his elbows on the low fence of a home where children with no family were taught to work and be useful. After that the town petered out; the only remaining building was a pub for migrants and low-paid categories that had no yard and looked more like some administrative building, with a clay mound behind it and an old tree that grew on its own there in the middle of the bright weather. Voshchev made his way to the pub and went inside, drawn by the sound of warm human voices. The people there were rowdily devoted to drowning their sorrows, and among them Voshchev felt more cut off and at ease. (1)

In his lodgings Voshchev took his things into a bag; he then went outside so as better to understand his future out in the air. But the air was empty, motionless trees were carefully holding the heat in their leaves, and dust lay boringly on the deserted road—the situation in nature was quiet. Voshchev did not know where he felt drawn, and at the end of the town le leaned his elbows on the low fence of a large house where children with no family were being habituated to labor and use. After that the town stopped; there was only a beer room for workers from villages and low-paid categories. Like some official business or other, this stood without any yard, and behind it rose a clay mound, and an old tree grew on its own amid bright weather. Voshchev made his way to the beer room and went inside, towards sincere human voices. Here were untempered people, abandoned to the oblivion of unhappi-ness, and among them Voshchev felt more cut off and at ease. (1)

Whereas in the first version the translators try to make things "clearer" for the reader by interpreting the "sense" of what is being said and using more nat-urally collocating vocabulary, in the second version, they are trying to pre-serve Platonov's defamiliarizing, bordering on a "foul," so to speak, use of language. For example, in the second version, we have "In his lodgings Voshchev *took his things into a bag; he then went outside [...]"; whereas in the first variant, this was translated in a more "normative" way as "Voshchev went to his room, put his things into a bag and then went back outside [...]." The change was likely made to signal the basically incorrect use of the Russian verb brat' (vziat') instead of klast' (polozhit') in Platonov's "Voshchev *vzial na kvartire veshchi *v meshok i vyshel naruzhu [...]." Strictly speaking, you cannot vziat' veshchi v meshok. Another example of the same nature is Platonov's dal'she gorod prekrashchalsia. In the normal run of things, a town cannot "prekrashchat'sia," as in "to stop," unless its usual activities are meant to have come to a stop. Is this what Platonov meant? Or is it a hint at the un-educated use of Russian in Voshchev's free indirect interior monologue? It is hard to say. In any case, the translators change the neutralizing, "smoothing-over" "the town petered out" in their first version to the somewhat jarring "the town stopped" in the second.

Let us consider a complete sentence (the second sentence of the second paragraph in the passage under discussion): "No vozdukh byl pust, nepo-dvizhnye derev'ia berezhno derzhali zharu v list'iakh, i skuchno lezhala pyl' na bezliudnoi doroge—v prirode bylo takoe polozhenie." The more smoothly metaphorical *were hoarding* of the first translation (in "motionless trees were carefully hoarding the heat in their leaves") is replaced, in the second, with a simpler, more down-to-earth metaphor—*were holding*. This creates a more direct—less abstract and more "visual"—image of the tree leaves holding the heat like a heavy ("oppressive") object, careful not to drop it. "Hoarding the heat" was a "more literary" paraphrase. In another place in the same sentence, the slightly more literalist first-version translation "the dust lay dully on the deserted road" is replaced, in the second version, with "dust lay boringly on the deserted road." In this case, "boringly" is somewhat more "literalist" than "dully," which makes the phrase "dust lay boringly on the deserted road" intrude on the reader's consciousness to a greater extent, in my perception, than does the more "easy" collocation "the dust lay dully on the deserted road." The translators seem to have thought their first-version translation too much of a smooth alliterative clause to be fitting for Platonov's somewhat disjointed style of narration and so felt it necessary to create a starker metaphor.

Some of the changes aimed at a greater approximation to Paltonov's style seem to be debatable. Thus "obtained the means for his own existence" of the second translation is hardly an improvement, in this respect, over "got the means for his subsistence" (see the first sentence of the passage above). In the second sentence of the first paragraph, the second version has "on account of weakening strength in him and thoughtfulness amid the general tempo of labor." To me this reads more fluidly than the "on account of a situation of on-going personal weakness and thoughtfulness amid the general tempo of labour" of the first version. I would say that the first-version variant of this part of the sentence is more indicative of the numerous wordy, awkward collocations spread around the Platonov text.

The translators' "retouching" of imagery is done alongside some re-tweaking of the functional style (register) of the first translation to bring it more in line with the Russian original. For example, the Russian *dali raschet* was first translated as "was sacked," but then, most likely realizing that "was sacked" belongs to the colloquial register while *dali raschet* is neutral bordering on bookish, the translators changed the translation to "was made redundant."

An interesting change can be traced in the use of the definite and "zero" articles. In the first translation, the definite article "the" is used before "motionless trees," "dust," and "bright weather." The absence of the definite article, i.e. the use of a "zero article," in the second translation makes the text more "abstract" and creates a greater sense of general alienation between the protagonist and the surrounding physical world—the sense of a greater indifference of the world toward Voshchev.

Finally, the second translation is done in American English, so "labour" is respelled as "labor," "leant" is replaced with "leaned," and "pub" becomes "beer room." Thus, in the second version, the translators are making a conscious effort to get across Platonov's defamiliarizing—in the sense of "borderline-correct,"—at times tautological, and graphically metaphorical style without half-explaining the metaphors or "normalizing" the language. On the whole, looking at the entire text, I would say that both translations mutually complement each other because I can see some advantages and disadvantages in conveying linguistic detail, imagery, and associations in either of them. But the main aim of the retranslation seems to have been achieved: in the retranslation, we get a better sense of Platonov's unique authorial style.

Appendix 7

Translation Think Tanks, Anti-Prizes, and Competitions

Think Tanks

Who are the current translation theory and practice thinkers that define the conceptual apparatus and standards of translation practices in Russia today—in 2013? I would identify several such centers of thought or think tanks. One group of translation experts that has assumed the role of standard setters and quality controllers in the field of Russian translation studies (it has consolidated itself over the last nine years—since the beginning of the publication of the translators' journal *Mosty* in 2004) is based in the Department of English Language Translation of the Moscow State Linguistic University (MSLU), formerly the Moscow State Maurice Thorez Institute of Foreign Languages—popularly known in Russia as *MGPIIYa imeni Morisa Toreza* or just *Moris Torez*. The group, which I refer to as the *Mosty* or *Torezovtsy Group*, is spearheaded by Professor Dmitrii Ivanovich Ermolovich, Professor Viktor Konstantinovich Lanchikov, and Professor Dmitrii Mikhailovich Buzadzhi, Chair of the MSLU Department of English Language Translation. As members of the editorial board of *Mosty* and prolific writers on translation, they are the key figures that define the translation scene in Russia today. There are some other—lesser—individual and collective blog-driven centers of translation thought, too, but this trio is the most visible through their publications and blogs. Buzadzhi, Lanchikov, and Ermolovich are famous practicing translators, lexicographers, translation theorists, and teachers of translation who have revived and are carrying on the traditions of the Russian-Soviet school of translation that was deinstitutionalized during perestroika and the "wild 1990s" period. Their work is focused on asserting translation studies as a unique field of expertise requiring years of deliberate improvement of one's translation skills, which is empirically confirmed by the findings of the emergent science of expertise studies (see, first and foremost, Shreve and Angelone 2010). As the contents of the *Mosty* journal show, Lanchikov, Buzadzhi, and Ermolovich can always be counted on to be the first to provide in-depth analyses of the translation quality of book and film translations as well as making theoretical statements on various translation issues. They are what I would call the "quality controllers" of translation products, whom I privately refer to as the "brain, honor, and conscience"[1] of Russian translation studies. I use the phrase in a very positive, friendly and respectful sense.

Besides the *Mosty* journal, the latest translation studies materials and discussions can be found on the http://www.thinkaloud.ru/scienceak.html site, whose name, "Think Aloud," is a reference to the "think-aloud protocol" research method in translation expertise studies whereby the translator makes a taped running commentary on the operations s/he carrying out while translating a text. This is the site set up by the MSLU professors, including Lanchikov and Buzadzhi. (Ermolovich runs a separate site—http://yermolovich.ru/). Alongside the *Mosty* journal, the *Torezovtsy*'s Thinkaloud site spearheads the still somewhat disjointed but more democratic and perhaps more efficient than in Soviet times—unrestricted by location or any official imprimatur—effort of reinstitutionalizing literary translation as a high art. As I mentioned earlier, its previously Soviet state-run infrastructure disintegrated in the late 1980s–early 1990s. Here is part of the description of the site by its creators:

Welcome to Think Aloud!

The name "Think Aloud" refers to the method of analyzing the translation process in which a translator comments on his actions as he works. Our site enables translators and other people facilitating interlingual communication to "think aloud" for the benefit of their colleagues and those sharing their interests and concerns.

As you can see from the section names on this website (academic works, popular articles on translation, graduation papers, reviews, translations, creative works), we are interested in a wide range of translation-related materials. The selection criteria we use are very simple: to be posted on our website, a material must be useful, original and respectful towards readers and opponents.

This site was created by translators educated at the Moscow State Linguistic University (the Maurice Thorez Institute of Foreign Languages) and those who endorse its views on translation. This is naturally reflected in our postings. Our resource, however, is open to people with other translation backgrounds if they have something interesting to share.

We started the site because we were dissatisfied with the current state of affairs. At the moment, online translation-related materials in Russian and of reasonable quality (apart from classical translation studies) are few and randomly placed, whereas many interesting

---

[1] The phrase comes from the famous comment by V. I. Lenin on the quality of the Communist Party—"The Party is the mind, honor and conscience of our era." The part "the mind/brain, honor, and conscience" has entered everyday language as a so-called "winged phrase."

articles, clever observations and brilliant translations are available only to a handful of insiders (http://www.thinkaloud.ru/).

There are also some other centers of expert translation thought in Russia today, notably, the Union of Translators of Russia (http://www.translators-union.ru/), the *Inostrannaia Literatura* (Foreign Literature) journal (http://magazines.russ.ru/inostran/), the Bakanov School of Translation (http://www.bakanov.org/)—it seems to be doing the bulk of literary translations today (on average 120 books a year, mostly translations from English), the Lingvo Association of Lexicographers (http://www.lingvoda.ru/), the Community of Creative Translators (http://inojazychniki.livejournal.com/)—and also individual (unaffiliated) translators and popular translation commentators like Leonid Volodarskii (http://www.lvolodarsky.ru/) and Dmitrii Puchkov (Goblin) (http://oper.ru/), currently the most popular Russian voiceover translator of films, and some others.

To reiterate, all of the above-enumerated online centers of translation thought advocate literary translation as highly erudite expertise in opposition to semi-professionalism and dilettantism, amateurishness, and downright hackwork. They are the de-facto quality controllers of translation products. Of course, given the output of translated fiction prose alone, these people would not be able to cope with evaluating such vast masses of material. Nor do they set such a goal for themselves. But they do their share. Fortunately, there are other "mechanisms" that work to ensure that the translations that come out are of decent quality.

Translation Anti-Prizes

An important translation quality watchdog in Russia since 2001 has been the biweekly *Knizhnoe obozrenie* (Book Review)—the literary ratings and fiction prose and poetry reviewing body of the Russian Federal Press and Mass Communications Agency. The 24-page biweekly newspaper has been published since 1966. In 2001 *Knizhnoe obozrenie* and the Russian General Directorate for International Book Fairs established four annual prizes: for the worst fiction prose translation, the worst copyediting, the worst proof corrections—which they called "Abzats"—and for "complete violation of norms of book publishing" (http://www.livelib.ru/magazine/post/3047), which they called "Polnyi abzats" (*total abzats*). They also instituted a special anti-prize called "Pochetnaia bezgramota" (honorable illiteracy commendation), awarded for "exceptionally cynical crimes against Russian verbal art" (http://www.livelib.ru/magazine/post/3047).

The "normal" meaning of *abzats* is "paragraph." But in Russian slang it is used as an echoic euphemism for the vulgar Russian slang term *pizdéts*—an interjection meaning that something is terminally "fucked up" (yes, with the exact same level of vulgarity). The euphemistic names of the anti-prizes

"Abzats" and "Polnyi abzats" can be translated politely as "Epic Failure" and "Beyond Epic Failure," respectively.[2] "Prize-winners" are determined by a special panel of expert judges on the basis of reader opinions sent to *Knizhnoe obozrenie*. At the time of this writing (July 2013), the chairperson of this panel of judges was Aleksandr Mikhailovich Nabokov, the editor-in-chief of *Knizhnoe obozrenie*.

The cast-in-bronze "Abzats" anti-prize was designed by the sculptor Vladimir Trulov. It represents a pen that is broken in two places and looks like the letter Z (besides being similar to a copyeditor's symbol suggesting a new paragraph). The Z stands on a crumpled sheet of paper.[3] The deeper-layer sociocultural significance of the sculpture is that the shape of the letter Z looks similar to the numeral "2," which is a Russian failing grade—like an *F*— on the five-point grading scale generally used at Russian educational institutions. It is also reminiscent of a swan's neck—a broken one in this case. The word *swan* (*lebed'* in Russian) is sometimes used by parents and students to refer to the failing grade "2." Thus, one might hear: "Swans are swimming all over your daily school record book" (*U tebia v dnevnike odni lebedi plavaiut*), meaning your daily school report is full of *F*s.

In 2012 the "Polnyi Abzats" prize was awarded to *Vy ne gadzhet: Manifest* (*You Are Not a Gadget: A Manifesto* [New York: Vintage Books, 2012]) by Jaron Lanier, translated into Russian by M. Kononenko (Moscow: Astrel, Corpus, 2012). The "Abzats" prize for the worst translation went to the Russian translation of Maurice Georges Dantec's *Comme le fantome d'un jazzman dans la station Mir en deroute* (*Prizrak dzhazmena na padaiushchei stantsii "Mir"* [A Jazzman's Ghost on the Falling Space Station "Peace"]), translated by A. Dadykin (Moscow: Ripol Klassik, 2011).

The "Polnyi Abzats" prize for 2013 was awarded to Tatiana Sibileva's translations of Tom Garrett's *Led Zeppelin* and Mary Clayton's *Elvis* (Moscow: Astrel', 2013).[4] The worst translation "Abzats" prize for 2013 went to the translator Irina Evsa for her translations of *The Divine Comedy*, *Faustus*, and other classical works.[5]

At the awards ceremony in March of 2012, the chairperson of the panel of expert judges, *Knizhnoe obozrenie* Editor-in-Chief Aleksandr Nabokov had a lot of harsh things to say about the reasons for the anti-prizes that were being awarded. In particular, talking about the book *You Are Not a Gadget*, he first

---

[2] *Polnyi pizdets* is a very common interjection, and the reader will recall that Puchkov-Goblin's "funny translations" studio is called "Polnyi Pe," which is *Polnyi pizdets!* (See chap. 2.)

[3] See the website of *LiveLib* magazine, http://www.livelib.ru/magazine/post/3047.

[4] Roman Kholodov, "Antipremiii goda vruchili avtoram samykh plokhikh perevodov literaturnykh proizvedenii," *Uchitel'skaia gazeta*, 13 March 2013, http://ug.ru/news/7214.

[5] *Wikipedia*, "Abzats (Premiia)," http://ru.wikipedia.org/wiki/%D0%90%D0%B1-%D0%B7%D0%B0%D1%86_(%D0%BF%D1%80%D0%B5%D0%BC%D0%B8%D1%8F)

made a pun on the transliteration of the English word gadget" as "gadzhet,"[6] which sounds in Russian similar to "he/she defecates," and in the end characterized the translation as "one big viscous nightmare" (*odin bol'shoi viazkii koshmar*; Vovk 2012). *Knizhnoe obozrenie* takes translation evaluation very seriously. I must say, though, that in cases like these I usually get a sneaking feeling that in criticizing cultural products Russian intellectuals tend to go overboard and, as a rule, walk a very thin line between being boorishly rude and professionally abrasive. A bit of American political correctness would not hurt here.

Translation Competitions

Another means of translation quality control are various "best translation" national and international competitions. Each year the national guild of translators called "Masters of Literary Translation," sponsored by the Boris Yeltsin Foundation and the *Inostrannaia Literatura* literary journal, awards its "Masters" prizes—what it likes to call the translation equivalents of Oscars— in three nominations: prose fiction, poetry, and children's literature.[7] In 2010, in the category "Best Fiction Prose/Literary Translation," the first prize was awarded to Aleksandr Bogdanovskii's translation of José Saramago's novel *Todos los Nombres* (All the Names); in the category of "Best Poetry Translation," the first prize was won by Marina Boroditskaia for her translation of a collection of 17th-century English poetry called in Russian *Angliiskie poety-kavalery semnadtsatogo veka* (2008);[8] and the first prize in the category "Children's Literature" was shared by Liubov' Gorlina and Natalia Shakhovskaia for their translations, respectively, of the Norwegian novel by Jon Evo, *Sola er en Feit Gud* (1999), (*The Sun is a Tough God*) and of the French novel by Marie-Aude Murail *Oh, Boy!*

   Perhaps the most wide-ranging prose and poetry translation competition, called "Muzyka perevoda" (The Music of Translation) is run annually by *Knizhnoe obozrenie* via the Internet. In an editorial entitled "The Triumph of Translators" in its first issue of 2011, *Knizhnoe obozrenie* reported that in 2010 1,108 translations of prose and poetry were submitted by professionals and

---

[6] The word *gadzhet* sounds somewhat similar to the adjective *gadkii/gadok* (vile, gross) and the noun *gadost'* (vileness, dirt) and especially similar to the verb *gadit'* (to defecate)—*gadit* (he/she) defecates—3rd person singular, present tense).

[7] See the editorial "Oskar dlia masterov," *Knizhnoe Obozrenie*, no. 1 (2299) (12–23 January 2011): 2, http://www.knigoboz.ru/uploads/mod_issue/KO-1_2011_view.pdf.

[8] "Zhurnal'nyi zal: *Angliiskie poety-kavalery semnadtsatogo veka* i 'Kratkie zhizneopisaniia' Dzhona Obri," trans. Marina Boroditskaia, *Inostrannaia literatura*, no. 3 (2008), http://magazines.russ.ru/inostran/2008/3/bo5.html.

amateurs from 92 cities in Russia and 26 countries.[9] (*Knizhnoe Obozrenie* 2011b). Eight main winners were determined by a *Kniznoe Obozrenie* panel of judges, selected among translation experts, and by about 40,000 members of the general public who graded the translations and voted online. Eleven more translators received special prizes from the outside sponsors of the competition. In the category "Prose Translation" the first prize was won by Natal'ia Budina for her translation of the American author Natalie Babbitt's story "Ashes" in her collection of stories *The Devil's Storybook* (1974).[10]

---

[9] See the editorial "Triumf perevodchikov," *Knizhnoe Obozrenie*, no. 1 (2299) (12–23 January 2011): 2, http://www.knigoboz.ru/uploads/mod_issue/KO- 1_2011_view.pdf.

[10] A detailed account of the winners in different nominations in 2012 can be found in the article "Muzyka perevoda IV. Novosti konkursa. Pobediteli konkursa 2012," at the site Muzyka perevoda (http://konkurs.itrex.ru/).

Appendix 8

A Translator User's Guide

In 2008 a "Translator User Guide" was posted on a previously little known site, Inojazychniki.[1] The "guide" consisted of a series of humorous instructions on how to use translators and interpreters. Very soon it went viral across the translators' community. The instructions are tongue-in-cheek and facetious in form but dead serious in essence. They are the interior monologue of a seasoned translator/interpreter—something like the things translators would like to tell people they are working for but probably won't because they don't want to sour the relationship. The "user guide" is a must-know for anyone who resorts for the first time to the help of translators and interpreters—a kind of "translator user guide for dummies." The instructions are in Russian and given in random order. Here I offer my translation of the majority of them in a slightly regrouped order:

1. Give me the context first.
2. Give me the context, dumbass.
3. I don't know off the top of my head how to translate this word. Give me the context.
4. No, these are not hieroglyphics, these are just meaningless squiggles that the manufacturer slapped onto the t-shirt so that some sucker like you would buy it.
5. If I work in an A–B mode, it means that I translate from language A into language B. This doesn't mean that I can translate in the opposite direction. Nor does it mean that I'm fluent in writing and speaking in language A.
6. If I do written translating in an A–B mode, that doesn't automatically mean that I will just as easily be able to do simultaneous interpretation on the subject of plumbing accessories contraband.
7. There is no such unit of text-size measurement as "one A4 sheet." The unit of text measurement is 1,800 print characters. Write this down somewhere. Also, there is no such unit of text measurement as "there's not much there."

---

[1] "Aveleen" to LiveJournal, 22 May 2008, accessed 15 August 2013, http://aveleen.livejournal.com/1718710.html

8. If I said I would do the text by 6 p.m. tomorrow, don't think that this deadline will remain unchanged if in the course of my work you keep giving me additional "there's-not-much-there" texts for translation.

9. If I interpret (do oral translating), I charge for my time—not for the number of words I say. If in the course of your negotiations I was silent for two hours because your clients happened to know your language themselves, you will still have to pay me for two hours of my work.

10. If you have hired me to do consecutive interpreting, make damn pauses in which I could translate.

11. O.K. Now that you know about having to make pauses for me to translate in, please, don't make them after every couple of words.

12. Don't expect me to give you a one-word translation of the word *uzh* or the word *poka* out of context.

13. I only translated a text dealing with an aortal valve transplantation operation. Don't ask me how exactly it is performed and what the possible consequences are […].

14. Spaces between words also count as print characters. If you don't want to pay for them, insert them yourself […]. Digits [number symbols] count as characters, too […].

15. Expect me to ask to be paid for my translation even if it's just two lines and even if you're my mom-dad-husband-brother-guru. It may happen that I won't charge you anything. In this I'm guided by some mystical principles known only to me.

16. Don't ask a native speaker for the correct translation. It will most likely be useless because s/he will turn out to be illiterate and sure as hell clueless about the principles of translation.

17. Knowing two languages does not mean being able to translate between them.

18. Don't ask the first native speaker you run into to check over my translation.

19. How do I know if I will be able to do the translation? Show me the text first.

20. Machine translation is a vice.

21. Don't send me somebody else's translation for me "to check over just in case." I will most likely have to expend a lot of nervous energy to retranslate the potboiler completely. And you will most likely have to pay me as well.

22. If the original was 2,000 characters long and the translation turned out to be 3,000 characters long, stop yelling that I have purposely lengthened the translation. Languages differ. Your grievance is misguided.

23. There is a chance that a translator will turn a mediocre text in language A into a daisy in language B, but the chance is slim.
24. A translation of a poem is not necessarily a poem.
25. Don't ask me if the translation is correct without providing the original.
26. Nah, consecutive interpreting is not the same as simultaneous interpreting.
27. Don't make sharp noises and stop telling jokes while I'm interpreting and you sit next to me. I'm in a parallel reality and would prefer to stay there until the end of the paragraph.
28. No, there will be no discounts. No, there will be no discounts in the case of a "wholesale" translation either. If you don't stop pestering me, I will raise my fees.
29. If you want me to translate a turbo-vacuum pump assembly instruction manual, make sure you don't skip pages 4 through 9 on the simple grounds that "there are just pictures there."
30. During negotiations don't add "Translate for him" to every phrase you say. This is exactly what I'm doing here.
31. Don't try to make my interpreting easier for me by speaking in a strange accent or interspersing what you say with words from a third language.
32. If I translated your joke and your interlocutor is just smiling politely, don't glower at me. Different cultures have different kinds of humor. It's not my fault.

IMHO: Written in a translator's blood.

Bibliography

Abeliuk, Evgeniia, and Konstantin Polivanov. 2009a. *Istoriia russkoi literatury XX veka: Kniga pervaia. Nachalo XX veka.* Moscow: Novoe literaturnoe obozrenie.

―――. 2009b. *Istoriia russkoi literatury XX veka: Kniga vtoraia. Posle revoliutsii.* Moscow: Novoe literaturnoe obozrenie.

Achard, Michel, and Suzanne Kemmer, eds. 2004. *Language, Culture and Mind.* Stanford, CA: CSLI Publications.

Adams, Douglas. 1979–92. *The Hitchhiker's Guide to the Galaxy.* London: Pan Books.

Afanas'ev, Aleksandr. 2010. *Narodnye russkie skazki.* Moscow: Eksmo.

Aleksandrova, O. V., and T. V. Nazarova, eds. 1988. *Metody lingvisticheskikh issledovanii.* Moscow: Moskovskii gosudarstvennyi universitet im. M. V. Lomonosova.

Anderman, Gunilla, and Margaret Rogers. 2003. *Translation Today: Trends and Perspectives.* Clevedon, UK: Multilingual Matters.

Andrews, Edna, and Elena A. Maksimova. 2010. *Russian Translation: Theory and Practice.* London: Routledge.

Baer, Brian James. 2006. "Literary Translation and the Construction of a Soviet Intelligentsia." *The Massachusetts Review* 47 (3): 537–60.

―――, ed. 2009. *Translation and Interpreting Studies* 4 (2). [Journal of the American Translation and Interpreting Studies Association]

―――, ed. 2011. *Contexts, Subtexts and Pretexts: Literary Translation in Eastern Europe and Russia.* Amsterdam: John Benjamins Publishing Company.

Baker, Mona. 1996. "Corpus-Based Translation Studies: The Challenges that Lie Ahead." In *Terminology, LSP and Translation: Studies in Language Engineering in Honour of Juan C. Sager,* edited by Harold L. Somers, 175–86. Amsterdam: John Benjamins Publishing Company.

―――, ed. (1998) 2005. *Routledge Encyclopedia of Translation Studies.* London: Routledge.

Bakhtin, Mikhail. 1981. *The Dialogic Imagination.* Edited by Michael Holquist. Translated by Caryl Emerson and Holquist. Austin: University of Texas Press.

―――. 2000. "Problemy tvorchestva Dostoevskogo." In *Sobranie sochinenii,* vol. 2, *Problemy tvorchestva Dostoevskogo. Stat'i o L. Tolstom. Zapisi kursa lektsii po istorii russkoi literatury,* 11–174. Moscow: Russkie slovari.

Ball, Alan M. 2003. *Imagining America: Influence and Images in Twentieth-Century Russia*. Lanham, MD: Rowman & Littlefield.

Balslev, Anindita Niyogi. (1991) 1999. *Cultural Otherness: Correspondence with Richard Rorty*. 2nd ed. Atlanta: Scholars Press.

Barbaresi, Lavinia Merlini. 2002. "Text Linguistics and Literary Translation." In Riccardi, *Translation Studies*, 120–32.

Barkhudarov, L. S. 1975. *Iazyk i perevod: Voprosy obshchei i chastnoi teorii perevoda*. Moscow: Mezhdunarodnye otnosheniia.

Barnes, Julian. 2011. *The Sense of an Ending*. New York: Alfred A. Knopf.

Batuman, Elif. 2010. *The Possessed: Adventures with Russian Books and the People Who Read Them*. New York: Farrar, Straus and Giroux.

Baudelaire, Charles. 1923. *Tableaux Parisiens*. Heidelberg: Verlag von Richard Wiedbach.

Beaugrande, Alain de, and Wolfgang Ulrich Dressler. 1981. *Introduction to Text Linguistics*. London: Longman.

Bednarek, Monika, and J. R. Martin, eds. 2011. *New Discourse on Language: Functional Perspectives on Multimodality, Identity, and Affiliation*. London: Continuum International.

Bellos, David. 2011. *Is That a Fish in Your Ear? Translation and the Meaning of Everything*. New York: Faber and Faber.

Benjamin, Walter. 1968. "The Task of the Translator." In *Illuminations*, edited by Hannah Arendt, 69–82. New York: Schocken Books.

Berdy, Michele A. 2010. *The Russian Word's Worth: A Humorous and Informative Guide to Russian Language, Culture, and Translation*. Moscow: Glas.

Berdy, Michele, D. M. Buzadzhi, D. I. Ermolovich, M. A. Zagot, V. K. Lanchikov, and P. R. Palazhchenko. 2010. "Kinoperevod: Malo chto ot Boga, mnogo chego ot Goblina. 'Kruglyi stol' v redaktsii 'Mostov.'" *LiveInternet.ru*, 5 April. Accessed 16 August 2013, http://www.liveinternet.ru/users/japonica/post124063834.

Berdy, Michele, and Viktor Lanchikov. 2006. "Uspekh i uspeshnost': Russkaia klassika v perevodakh R. Pevear i L. Volokhonsky." *Mosty: Zhurnal perevodchikov*, no. 1 (9): 18–31.

Berezowski, Leszek. 1997. *Dialect in Translation*. Wrocław: Wydawnictwo Uniwersytetu Wrocławskiego.

Berlin, Brent, and Paul Kay. 1969. *Basic Color Terms: Their Universality and Evolution*. Berkeley: University of California Press.

Berlin, Isaiah. 1997. "The Pursuit of the Ideal." In *The Proper Study of Mankind: An Anthology of Essays*, edited by Henry Hardy and Roger Hausheer, 1–16. New York: Farrar, Straus and Giroux.

Berman, Antoine. 1992. *The Experience of the Foreign: Culture and Translation in Romantic Germany*. Translated by S. Heyvaert. Albany: State University of New York Press. [Originally published in French in 1984]

Black, Shameem. 2010. *Fiction Across Borders: Imagining the Lives of Others in Late Twentieth-Century Novels*. New York: Columbia University Press.

Bloom, Harold. 1973. *The Anxiety of Influence: A Theory of Poetry.* New York: Oxford University Press.

———. 1994. *The Western Canon: The Books and School of the Ages.* New York: Riverhead Books.

Boghossian, Paul A. 2006. *Fear of Knowledge: Against Relativism and Constructivism.* Oxford: Clarendon Press/Oxford University Press.

Bondarev, Nikita. 2008. "Zakon mozaiki protiv zakona Moiseia: Otvet na stat'iu 'Anatomiia poshlosti.'" *Russkii mir,* 11 April. http://www.russkiymir. ru/russkiymir/ru/publications/articles/article0072.html.

Bourdieu, Pierre. 1984. *Distinction: A Social Critique of the Judgement of Taste.* Translated by Richard Nice. London: Routledge. [French original completed in 1979]

Boyd, Richard. 1979. "Metaphor and Theory Change: What is a Metaphor For?" In *Metaphor and Thought,* 2nd ed., edited by Andrew Ortony, 481–532. Cambridge: Cambridge University Press.

Breeze, Ruth. 2011. "Critical Discourse Analysis and Its Critics." *Pragmatics* 21 (4): 423–525.

Breus, E. V. 2007. *Kurs perevoda s angliiskogo iazyka na russkii: Uchebnoe posobie.* Moscow: R. Valent.

Brown, Deming. 1962. *Soviet Attitudes toward American Writing.* Princeton, NJ: Princeton University Press.

Burak, A. L. 2010. *Translating Culture-1: Words./Perevod i mezhkul'turnaia kommunikatsiia-1: Slova.* Moscow: R. Valent.

———. 2011. "Some Like it Hot—Goblin-Style: 'Ozhivliazh' in Russian Film Translations." *Russian Language Journal* 61: 5–31.

———. (2006) 2013. *Translating Culture-2: Sentence and Paragraph Semantics./Perevod i mezhkul'turnaia kommunikatsiia-2: Semantika predlozheniia i abzatsa.* Moscow: R. Valent.

Burak, A. L., and Timothy Sergay. 2011. "Translations, Retranslations, and Multiple Translations: A Case for Translation Variance Studies." *Russian Language Journal* 61: 3–4.

Burkhardt, Armin, ed. 1990. *Speech Acts, Meaning and Intentions: Critical Approaches to the Philosophy of John R. Searle.* Berlin: Walter de Gruyter.

Buzadzhi, D. M. 2011a. "Zakalka perevodom: Ob ideologicheskoi storone perevodcheskoi praktiki i prepodavaniia perevoda." *Mosty: Zhurnal perevodchikov,* no. 1 (29): 55–66.

———. 2011b. "K voprosu ob opredelenii poniatiia 'perevod.'" *Mosty: Zhurnal perevodchikov,* no. 2 (30): 44–55.

Chandler, Robert. 2010a. "A Passion for Collaboration." *The New York Review of Books,* 13 May, 69.

———. 2010b. "Translation as a Career and a Love: Interview with Robert Chandler." By Josh Wilson. Accessed 10 October 2010, www.sras.org/robert_ chandler_on_translation_as_a_career.

Chelnokov, Aleksei. 2013. *"Bogoroditsa, progoni!" Kto zakazal "naezd" na tserkov'?* Moscow: Iauza-Press.

Chertanov, Maksim. 2010. *Zhizn' zamechatel'nykh liudei: Kheminguei.* Moscow: Molodaia gvardiia.

Chouliaraki, Lilie, and Norman Fairclough. 2000. *Discourse in Late Modernity.* Edinburgh: Edinburgh University Press.

Chudakov, A. P., and M. O. Chudakova. *Kratkaia literaturnaia entsiklopediia.* Edited by A. A. Surkov. Vol. 6. Moscow: Sovetskaia entsiklopediia, 1971.

Chukovskii, Kornei. 1966. *Vysokoe iskusstvo.* In *Kornei Chukovskii: Sobranie sochinenii v shesti tomakh,* 3: 237–833. Moscow: Khudozhestvennaia literatura.

———. 1984. *A High Art.* Translated and edited by Lauren G. Leighton. Knoxville: University of Tennessee Press.

Cronin, Michael. 2009. *Translation Goes to the Movies.* New York: Routledge.

Cunningham, Michael. 2010. "Found in Translation." *The New York Times,* 2 October. Accessed 7 October 2010, www.nytimes.com/2010/10/03/opinion/03cunningham.html?_r=1&scp=3&sq=michael%20cunningham&st=c-s-e.

Davis, Wayne. 2013. "Implicature." In *Stanford Encyclopedia of Philosophy,* edited by Edward N. Zalta. Spring 2013 edition. Stanford, CA: Stanford University. http://plato.stanford.edu/archives/ spr2013/entries/implicature/.

Deleuze, Gilles. (1968) 1994. *Difference and Repetition.* Translated by Paul Patten. New York: Columbia University Press.

Deleuze, Gilles, and Félix Guattari. (1991) 1994. *What is Philosophy?* Translated by Hugh Tomlinson and Graham Burchell. New York: Columbia University Press.

Denzin, N. K., and Y. S. Lincoln, eds. 1994. *Handbook of Qualitative Research.* Thousand Oaks, CA: Sage Publications.

Derrida, Jacques. (1967) 1980. *Writing and Difference.* Translated by Alan Bass. Chicago: University of Chicago Press.

———. (1976) 1998. *Of Grammatology.* Translated by Gayatri Chakravorty Spivak. Baltimore: Johns Hopkins University Press.

———. 1979. "Living on /Border Lines." In *Deconstruction and Criticism,* translated by J. Hulbert, edited by Harold Bloom et al., 75–176. New York: Seabury Press.

———. 1982. *Margins of Philosophy.* Translated by Alan Bass. Chicago: University of Chicago Press.

———. 1983. *Dissemination.* Translated by Barbara Johnson. Chicago: University of Chicago Press.

———. 1985a. "Des Tours de Babel." In *Difference in Translation,* translated and edited by J. Graham, 165–248. Ithaca, NY: Cornell UniversityPress, 1985.

———. 1985b. *The Ear of the Other: Texts and Discussions with Jacques Derrida. Otobiography, Transference, Translation.* Translated by Peggy Kamuf. English edition edited by Christie McDonald. French edition edited by

Claude Levesque and Christie McDonald. Lincoln: University of Nebraska Press.

Diamond, Bruce J., and Gregory M. Shreve. 2010. "Neural and Psychological Correlates of Translation and Interpreting in the Bilingual Brain: Recent Perspectives." In *Translation and Cognition*, edited by Shreve and Erik Angelone, 289–321. Amsterdam: John Benjamins.

Dimitrov, Vladimir, and Bob Hodge. 2002. *Social Fuzziology: Study of Fuzziness of Social Complexity*. New York: Physica-Verlag.

Dovlatov, Sergei. 1980. *Solo na undervude*. Paris: Tret'ia volna.

Dudek, Sarah. 2003. "Walter Benjamin and the Religion of Translation." *Cipher Journal*. Accessed 14 August 2013, http://www.cipherjournal.com/html/dudek_benjamin.html.

Dyson, Freeman. 2012. "Science on the Rampage." *The New York Review of Books*, 5 April 2012, 38–39.

Eco, Umberto. 2001. *Experiences in Translation*. Translated by Alastair McEwen. Toronto: University of Toronto Press.

Egorushkin, Konstantin. "Russian as a Foreign Language: Otvet na stat'iu 'Zakon mozaiki…'" *Russkii mir*, 21 April 2008. Accessed 14 August 2013, http://www.russkiymir.ru/russkiymir/ru/publications/articles/article0074.html.

Eikhenbaum, B. M. 1969. "Kak sdelana 'Shinel'' Gogolia." In *O proze: Sbornik statei*, 306–26. Leningrad: Khudozhestvennaia literatura.

Emerson, Caryl. 1983. "Translating Bakhtin: Does His Theory of Discourse Contain a Theory of Translation?" *Revue de l'Université d'Ottawa* 53 (1): 23–33.

———. 1994. "Perevodimost'." *Slavic and East European Journal* 38 (1): 84–89.

———. 1997. *The First Hundred Years of Mikhail Bakhtin*. Princeton, NJ: Princeton University Press.

———. 2008. *The Cambridge Introduction to Russian Literature*. Cambridge: Cambridge University Press.

Engels, F. (1877–78) 1976. *Anti-Düring*. Peking: Foreign Languages Press.

Ermolovich, D. I., and T. M. Krasavina. 2008. "Chto mozhno sdelat' iz konfetki." *Mosty: Zhurnal perevodchikov*, no. 3 (19): 60–70. Available on D. I. Ermolovicha's personal web site, http://yermolovich.ru/index/0-46.

———. 2009. "O 'Longmane' bednom zamolvite slovo." *Mosty: Zhurnal perevodchikov*, no. 2 (22): 46–57. Available on D. I. Ermolovicha's personal web site, http://yermolovich.ru/index/0-69.

———. 2011a. "Kritika na sluzhbe praktiki." *Mosty: Zhurnal perevodchikov*, no. 1 (29): 43–44.

———. 2011b. "Slepaia vavilonskaia rybka." *Mosty: Zhurnal perevodchikov*, no. 2 (30): 56–71. Available on D. I. Ermolovicha's personal web site, http://yermolovich.ru/Yermolovich_Most2-30-2011.pdf.

Fairclough, Norman. 1989. *Language and Power*. London: Longman.

———. 1995. *Critical Discourse Analysis: The Critical Study of Language*. London: Longman.

Fairclough, Norman. 2003. *Analysing Discourse: Textual Analysis for Social Research*. London: Routledge.

———. 2006. *Language and Globalization*. London: Routledge.

Fisher, Anne. 2010. "Translation and Interpreting as Professions: Interview with Anne Fisher." By Josh Wilson. *School of Russian and Asian Studies* newsletter, 30 September. www.sras.org/anne_fisher_translation_interpreting.

Foster, Thomas C. 2003. *How to Read Literature Like a Professor: A Lively and Entertaining Guide to Reading Between the Lines*. New York: Harper.

———. 2008. *How to Read Novels Like a Professor*. New York: Harper.

Foucault, Michel. 1972. *The Archeology of Knowledge and the Discourse on Language*. Translated by A. M. Sheridan Smith. New York: Pantheon Books.

———. 1980. *Power/Knowledge: Selected Interviews and Other Writings, 1972–1977*. Edited by Colin Gordon. New York: Pantheon Books.

Friedberg, Maurice. 1977. *A Decade of Euphoria: Western Literature in Post-Stalin Russia, 1954–1964*. Bloomington: Indiana University Press.

———. 1997. *Literary Translation in Russia: A Cultural History*. University Park: Pennsylvania State University Press.

Fuller, Alexandra. 2012. "Hemingway's Fiery Rival. (War reporter Martha Gellhorn finally gets her due)." *Newsweek*, 21 May, 46–47.

Gal', Nora. 2003. *Slovo zhivoe i mertvoe*. Moscow: Sofia.

Gandel'sman, Vladimir. 2008. "Gluboko vdokhnut'." *Vozdukh* (Moscow), no. 1. http://www.litkarta.ru/projects/vozdukh/issues/2008-1/interview/.

Garbovskii, N. K. 2004. *Teoriia perevoda*. Moscow: Izdatel'stvo Moskovskogo gosudarstvennogo universiteta.

Gasparov, M. L. (1971) 1988. "Briusov i bukvalizm." In *Poetika perevoda: Sbornik statei*, edited by S. Goncharenko, 29–62. Moscow: Raduga.

———. 2000. *Zapisi i vypiski*. Moscow: Novoe literaturnoe obozrenie.

Ginzburg, Lidiia. 2002. *Zapisnye knizhki: Vospominaniia. Esse*. St. Petersburg: Iskusstvo-SPB.

Golyshev, Viktor. 2001. "Parshivuiu knigu khorosho perevesti nel'zia." *Russkii zhurnal*, 14 May, old.russ.ru/krug/20010628-kal-pr.html.

———. 2010. "Vstrecha s perevodchikom Viktorom Golyshevym (chast' 1)." By Elena Kalashnikova. YouTube video, 9:58, taped 12 May 2010. Posted by "Andrey Neonov," 23 May 2010. http://www.youtube.com/watch?v=ETqLKJF1PNM.

Grewendorf, Günter, and Georg Meggle, eds. 2002. *Speech Acts, Mind, and Social Reality: Discussions with John R. Searle*. Dordrecht: Kluwer Academic Publishers.

Gribanov, B. 1970. *Kheminguei: Zhizn' zamechatel'nykh liudei*. Moscow: Molodaia gvardiia.

Grice, H. P. 1957. "Meaning." *Philosophical Review*, no. 66: 377–88.

———. 1975. "Logic and Conversation." In *Syntax and Semantics*, vol. 3, *Speech Acts*, edited by P. Cole and J. Morgan, 41–58. New York: Academic Press.

Gromov, Andrei. 2008. "Anatomiia poshlosti." *Russkii mir*, 8 April. http://www. russkiymir.ru/russkiymir/ru/publications/articles/article0064.html.

Grossman, Edith. 2010. *Why Translation Matters*. New Haven: Yale University Press.

Gunn, Giles. 1979. *The Interpretation of Otherness*. New York: Oxford University Press.

Gutt, Ernst-August. 1998. "Pragmatic Aspects of Translation: Some Relevance-Theory Observations." In Hickey, *The Pragmatics of Translation*, 41–53.

Halliday, M. A. K. 1973. *Explorations in the Functions of Language*. London: Edward Arnold.

———. 2003. *On Language and Linguistics*. New York: Continuum.

Hatim, Basil, and Jeremy Munday. 2004. *Translation: An Advanced Resource Book*. London: Routledge.

Hemingway, Ernest. (1926) 2006. *The Sun Also Rises*. New York: Scribner.

———. (1929) 1932. *A Farewell to Arms*. New York: The Modern Library.

Hendrickson, Paul. 2011. *Hemingway's Boat: Everything He Loved in Life, and Lost, 1934–1961*. New York: Knopf.

Hermans, Theo. 1996. "The Translator's Voice in Translated Narrative." *Target* 8 (1): 23–48.

———, ed. 2006. *Translating Others*. 2 vols. Manchester, UK: St. Jerome Publishing.

———, ed. 2007. *The Conference of the Tongues*. Manchester, UK: St. Jerome Publishing.

Hervey, G. J. Sándor. 1998. "Speech Acts and Illocutionary Function in Translation Methodology." In Hickey, *The Pragmatics of Translation*, 10–24.

Hickey, Leo, ed. 1998. *The Pragmatics of Translation*. Clevedon: Multilingual Matters.

House, Juliane. (1971) 1981. *A Model for Translation Quality Assessment*. Tübingen: Narr.

———. 1997. *Translation Quality Assessment: A Model Revisited*. Tübingen: Narr.

———. 1998. "Politeness in Translation." In Hickey, *The Pragmatics of Translation*, 54–71.

———. 2002. "Universality Versus Culture Specificity in Translation." In Riccardi, *Translation Studies*, 92–110.

Hymes, Dell. 1974. "Speech Act/Communicative Act: Components and Functions." In *Foundations of Sociolinguistics: An Ethnographic Approach*. Philadelphia: University of Pennsylvania Press. http://www.utexas.edu/courses/stross/ant307_files/components.htm.

Ilf, Ilya, and Evgeny Petrov. 2009a. *The Little Golden Calf*. Translated by Anne O. Fisher. Montpelier, VT: Russian Life Books.

———. 2009b. *The Golden Calf*. Translated by Konstantin Gurevich and Helen Anderson. Rochester, NY: Open Letter.

Ilf, Ilya, and Evgeny Petrov. 2011. *The Twelve Chairs*. Translated by Anne O. Fisher. Evanston, IL: Northwestern University Press.

Jääskeläinen, Riitta. 2010. "Are All Professionals Experts? Definitions of Expertise and Reinterpretation of Research Evidence in Process Studies." In *Translation and Cognition*, edited by Gregory M. Shreve and Erik Angelone, 213–37. Amsterdam: John Benjamins.

Jakobson, R. (1959) 1971. "On Linguistic Aspects of Translation." In *Selected Writings II: Word and Language*, 260–66. The Hague: Mouton.

———. 1975. "Strukturalizm: 'za' i 'protiv'." Translated from the English by I. A. Mel'chuk. In *Strukturalizm "za" i "protiv": Sbornik statei*, edited by E. Ia. Basin and M. Ia. Poliakov, 193–230. Moscow: Progress. This volume is also available online, accessed 15 August 2013, www.philology.ru/linguistics1/jakobson-75.htm.

———. 1987. "Linguistics and Poetics." In *Selected Writings*, vol. 3, *Poetry of Grammar and Grammar of Poetry*, edited by K. Pomorska and S. Rudy, 18–51. The Hague: Mouton.

Kalashnikova, Elena. 2008. *Po-russki s liubov'iu: Besedy s perevodchikami*. Moscow: Novoe Literaturnoe Obozrenie.

Kashkin, I. A. 1966. *Ernest Kheminguei*. Moscow: Khudozhestvennaia literatura.

———. 1977. *Dlia chitatelia-sovremennika: Stat'i i issledovaniia*. Moscow: Sovetskii pisatel'.

Kelly, Nataly, and Jost Zetzsche. 2012. *Föund in TṙansĿatión: How Language Shapes Our Lives and Transforms the World*. New York: Perigee.

Kheminguei, Ernest. 1959. *Izbrannye proizvedeniia (komplekt iz dvukh knig)*. Moscow: Gosudarstvennoe izdatel'stvo khudozhestvennoi literatury.

———. 1981. *Sobranie sochinenii v chetyrekh tomakh*. Edited by B. Gribanova, M. Lorie, and A. Startseva. Moscow: Khudozhestvennaia literatura.

———. 2010a. *Sobranie sochinenii v 7 tomakh*. Moscow: AST Publishers.

———. 2010b. *Fiesta (I voskhodit solntse)*. Moscow: AST Publishers.

———. 2010c. *A Farewell to Arms*. Moscow: AST Publishers.

Kodzasov, S. V. 2009. *Issledovaniia v oblasti russkoi prosodii*. Moscow: Iazyki slavianskikh kul'tur.

Koren, Leonard. 2010. *Which "Aesthetics" Do You Mean? Ten Definitions*. Point Reyes, CA: Imperfect Publishing.

Kukharenko, V. A., N. K. Riabtseva, and A. D. Shveitser, eds. 1988. *Perevod i interpretatsiia teksta. (Sbornik nauchnykh trudov)*. Moscow: Nauka.

Lanchikov, V. K. 2002. "Istoricheskaia stilizatsiia v sinkhronicheskom khudozhestvennom perevode." *Perevod i diskurs: Vestnik MGLU*, no. 463: 115–22.

———. 2009. "Razvitie khudozhestvennogo perevoda v Rossii kak evoliutsiia funktsional'noi ustanovki." *Vestnik Nizhegorodskogo gosudarstvennogo lingvisticheskogo universiteta im. N. A. Dobroliubova*, no. 4: 163–72. Available at "Thinkaloud," http://www.thinkaloud.ru/sciencelr.html.

Lanchikov, V. K. 2011a. "Perevod 'tam i togda.' Ob odnoi perevodcheskoi mistifikatsii." *Mosty: Zhurnal perevodchikov*, no. 1 (29): 37–42.

———. 2011b. "Topografiia poiska: Standartizatsiia v iazyke khudozhestvennykh perevodov i ee preodolenie." *Mosty: Zhurnal perevodchikov*, no. 2 (30): 30–38. (For the second part of this article, see http://www.thinkaloud. ru/feature/lan-topo.pdf.)

Lanchikov, V. K., and E. N. Meshalkina. 2008. "Kitaitsy na maskarade, ili Khudlo ot Nastika." *Mosty: Zhurnal perevodchikov*, no. 3 (19): 12–23.

Lecercle, Jean-Jacques. 1990. *The Violence of Language*. London: Routledge.

———. 1999. *Interpretation as Pragmatics: Language, Discourse, Society*. New York: St. Martin's Press.

Leech, Geoffrey. 1983. *Principles of Pragmatics*. London: Longman.

Leighton, Lauren G. 1991. *Two Worlds, One Art: Literary Translation in Russia and America*. DeKalb: Northern Illinois University Press.

———, trans. and ed. 1984. *The Art of Translation: Kornei Chukovsky's High Art*. Knoxville: University of Tennessee Press.

Lermontov, M. Iu. 1840. *Geroi nashego vremeni*. http://www.klassika.ru/read. html?proza/lermontov/geroi.txt.

———. 2001. *A Hero of Our Time*. Translated by Paul Foote. London: Penguin Books.

———. 2004. *A Hero of Our Time*. Translated by Marian Schwartz. New York: Modern Library Paperback Edition.

———. 2009a. *A Hero of Our Time*. Translated by Natasha Randall. London: Penguin Books.

———. (1958) 2009b. *A Hero of Our Time*. Translated by Vladimir Nabokov and Dmitri Nabokov. Boston: Overlook TP.

Levesque, Claude, and Christie McDonald, eds. 1982. *L'oreille de l'autre*. Montreal: Vlb Editeur.

Levinas, Emmanuel. 1972. *Humanism of the Other*. Translated from the French by Nidra Poller. Urbana: University of Illinois Press.

Lodge, David. 1992. *The Art of Fiction*. London: Penguin Books.

Mackey, Louis H., and John R. Searle. 1984. "An Exchange on Deconstruction by Louis H. Mackey, reply by John R. Searle." *The New York Review of Books* 31 (1) (2 February). http://www.nybooks.com/issues/1984/feb/02/.

Makarov, M. L. 2003. *Osnovy teorii diskursa*. Moscow: Gnozis.

Malmkjær, Kirsten. 1998. "Cooperation and Literary Translation." In Hickey, *The Pragmatics of Translation*, 25–40.

Marcus, Paul. 2008. *Being for the Other: Emmanuel Levinas, Ethical Living and Psychoanalysis*. Milwaukee: Marquette University Press.

Marshak, Samuil. [1930s?]. *Rasskaz o neizvestnom geroe*. Moscow: Khudozhestvennaia literatura. Available at the web site Biblioteka poezii, accessed 16 August 2013, http://marshak.ouc.ru/rasskaz-o-neizvestnom-geroe.htm.

Marusenkov, Maksim Petrovich. 2010. "Absurdistskie tendentsii v tvorchestve V. G Sorokina." Avtoreferat dissertatsii na soiskanie uchenoi stepeni kandidata filologicheskikh nauk, Moskovskii gosudarstvennyi universitet, http://www.philol.msu.ru/~ref/avtoreferat2010/marusenkov.pdf.

May, Rachel. 1994. *The Translator in the Text: On Reading Russian Literature in English.* Evanston, IL: Northwestern University Press.

McGinn, Colin. 2010. "Is Just Thinking Enough?" Review of *Making the Social World: The Structure of Human Civilization*, by John R. Searle. *The New York Review of Books* 57 (1) (11 November): 58–60. http://www.nybooks.com/issues/2010/nov/11/.

Merton, Robert K. 1957. *Social Theory and Social Structure.* Rev. ed. London: The Free Press of Glencoe.

————. 1964. *Theory and Social Structure.* New York: The Free Press.

————. 1979. *Qualitative and Quantitative Social Research: Papers in Honor of Paul Lazarsfeld.* New York: Free Press.

Mikhailin, V. Iu. 2002. "Perevedi menia cherez made in: Neskol'ko zamechanii o khudozhestvennom perevode i o poiskakh kanonov." *Novoe literaturnoe obozrenie*, no. 53. Available online on the Web site of *Russkii zhurnal*, http:// magazines.russ.ru/nlo/2002/53/mihail.html#top.

Miles, M. B., and A. M. Huberman. 1994. *Qualitative Data Analysis.* 2nd ed. Thousand Oaks, CA: Sage Publications.

Miller, James. 2011. *Examined Lives: From Socrates to Nietzsche.* New York: Farrar, Straus and Giroux.

Milton, John, and Paul Bandia, eds. 2009. *Agency in Translation.* Amsterdam: John Benjamins.

Morson, Gary Saul. 2010. "The Pevearsion of Russian Literature." *Commentary Online.* July/August.http://www.commentarymagazine.com/viewarticle.cfm/the-pevearsion-of-russian-literature-15468.

Munday, Jeremy. 2001. *Introducing Translation Studies: Theories and Applications.* London: Routledge.

Naficy, Hamid, and Teshome H. Gabriel, eds. 1993. *Otherness and the Media: The Ethnography of the Imagined and the Imaged.* Longhorn, PA: Harwood Academic Publishers.

Neary, Lynn. 2007. "'War and Peace' Sparks Literary Skirmish." *National Public Radio*, 22 October 22. http: //www.npr.org/templates/story/story.php?storyId=15524432.

Nesmelova, Ol'ga. 2006. "Evolutsiia 'russkogo' vospriiatiia tvorchestva E. Khemingueia." http://www.nbuv.gov.ua/portal/Soc_Gum/Alsvu/2006_3/11.htm

Nesterov, Anton. 2002. "'Perevod' ili 'mother tongue'?" *Novoe literaturnoe obozrenie*, no. 53: 314–18.

Norton, David. 2011. *The King James Bible: A Short History from Tyndale to Today.* Cambridge: Cambridge University Press.

Ortega y Gasset, José. (1930) 1994. *The Revolt of the Masses.* New York: W. W. Norton & Company.

Parfenov, Leonid. 2009a. *Namedni: Nasha era. 1961–1970.* Moscow: KoLibri.

————. 2009b. *Namedni: Nasha era. 1971–1980.* Moscow: KoLibri.

Parks, Tim. 2007. *Translating Style: A Literary Approach to Translation, a Translation Approach to Literature.* 2nd ed. Kinderhood, NY: St. Jerome Publishing.

—. 2012. "Mysteries of the Meta-Task." In *The Iowa Review.* http://iowareview.uiowa.edu/?q=page/mysteries_of_the_metatask.

Parsons, Talcott. 1967. *Sociological Theory and Modern Society.* New York: The Free Press.

Paul, Gill. 2009. *Translation in Practice.* Champaign, IL: Dalkey Archive Press.

Penrose, Roger. 1996. *Shadows of the Mind: A Search for the Missing Science of Consciousness.* Oxford: Oxford University Press.

Platonov, A. 1991. "Schastlivaia Moskva." *Novyi Mir,* no. 9: 9–58.

—. 1996. *The Foundation Pit.* Translated by Robert Chandler and Geoffrey Smith. London: The Harvill Press.

—. 2000. *Kotlovan. Tekst, materialy tvorcheskoi istorii.* St. Petersburg: Nauka.

—. 2001. *Happy Moscow.* Translated by Robert and Elizabeth Chandler with Angela Livingstone, Nadia Bourova and Eric Naiman. London: Harvill.

—. 2009. *The Foundation Pit.* Translated by Robert and Elizabeth Chandler and Olga Meerson. New York: New York Review Books.

—. 2012. *Happy Moscow.* Translated by Robert and Elizabeth Chandler with Nadia Bourova, Angela Livingstone, Olga Meerson, and Eric Naiman. New York: New York Review Books.

Polonsky, Rachel. 2012. "Violent, Ecstatic Russians." *The New York Review of Books.* 22 March, 28–30.

Postrel, Steven R., and Edward Feser. 2000. "Reality Principles: An Interview with John R. Searle." *Reason Magazine.* February, 1–6. http://reason.com/archives/2000/02/01/reality-principles-an-intervie.

Puchkov, D. Iu. 2009a. Interview on Radio Hit, 11 October. Accessed 17 August 2013, http://oper.ru/video/view.php?t=175.

—. 2009b. Interview on Radio Zenit, 27 October. Accessed 17 August 2013, http://oper.ru/video/view.php?t=177.

—. 2010a. Interview on Radio Maiak, 5 March. Accessed 17 August 2013, http://oper.ru/video/view. php?t=206.

—. 2010b. Interview on Radio Zenit, 3 September. Accessed 17 August 2013, http://oper.ru/video/view.php?t=240.

—. 2010c. "Voprosy i otvety dlia *Sostav.ru,*" 2 November. Accessed 17 August 2013, www.oper.ru/torture/read.php?t=1045689369.

—. 2011. Interview on Radio Baltika, 25 April. Accessed 17 August 2013. www.oper.ru/video/view.php?t=307.

—. 2012. Interview on Radio Maiak, 15 March. Accessed 17 August 2012, www.oper.ru/video/view.php?t=382.

—. 2013. Interview on Ekho Moskvy radio, 31 January. Accessed 17 August 2013, www.oper.ru/video/view.php?t=481.

Punch, Keith F. 1998. *Introduction to Social Research: Quantitative and Qualitative Approaches*. London: Sage Publications.

Pushkin, A. S. 1961. *The Captain's Daughter and Other Stories*. Translated by Natalie Duddington. London: Dutton.

Pushkin, Aleksandr. 1975. *Eugene Onegin: A Novel in Verse*. Translated by Vladimir Nabokov. Vol. 1, *Introduction and Translation*; vol. 2, *Commentary and Index*. Princeton, NJ: Princeton University Press.

Ragin, C. C. 1987. *The Comparative Method: Moving Beyond Qualitative and Quantitative Strategies*. Berkeley: University of California Press.

Rahimi, Forough, and Mohammad Javad Riasati. 2011. "Critical Discourse Analysis: Scrutinizing Ideologically-Driven Discourses." *International Journal of Humanities and Social Science* 1 (16) (November): 107–12.

Riccardi, Alessandra, ed. 2002. *Translation Studies: Perspectives on an Emerging Discipline*. Cambridge: Cambridge University Press.

Richmond, Yale. 2011. "The Kitchen Debate." In *The Best of "Russian Life: Fine Readings from Two Decades*. Vol. 1, *History and Culture*, edited by Paul E. Richardson, 433–40. Montpelier, VT: Russian Life Books.

Ricoer, Paul. 2006. *On Translation: Thinking in Action*. Translated by Eileen Brennan. London: Routledge.

Rust, Joshua. 2009. *John Searle: Contemporary American Thinkers*. Bodmin, UK: Continuum.

Rybkin, Pavel. 2003. "Perevodnye kartinki." *Bol'shoi gorod*, 22 November, 1. http://www.bg.ru/article/3158/.

Rylkova, Galina. 2007. *The Archeology of Anxiety: The Russian Silver Age and Its Legacy*. Pittsburgh: University of Pittsburgh Press.

Said, Edward W. 1979. *Orientalism*. New York: Vintage Books.

————. 1994. *Culture and Imperialism*. New York: Vintage Books.

Salindzher, Dzh. D. [J. D. Salinger]. 1991. *The Catcher in the Rye*. New York: Little, Brown and Company.

————. 1998. *Lovets na kraiu rzhanogo polia detstva. Deviat' rasskazov*. Translated by S. Makhov. Moscow: AIaKS.

————. 2008. *Lovets na khlebnom pole*. In *Sobranie sochinenii*, translated by Maksim Nemtsov, 5–206. Moscow: Eksmo.

————. 2010a. *Nad propast'iu vo rzhi*. Translated by Rita Rait-Kovaleva. Moscow: Eksmo.

————. 2010b. *Nad propast'iu vo rzhi*. Translated by Iakov Lotovskii. *Zhurnal Sem' iskusstv*, no. 2 (3) (February). http://7iskusstv.com/2010/Nomer4Lotovsky1.php.

————. 2010c. *Nad propast'iu vo rzhi*. Translated by Iakov Lotovskii. *Zhurnal Sem' iskusstv*, no. 4 (5) (April). http://7iskusstv.com/2010/Nomer4Lotovsky1.php.

Salter, James. 2011. "The Finest Life You Ever Saw." *The New York Review of Books* 58 (15) (13 October): 4–8.

Savory, Theodore. 1959. *The Art of Translation*. London: Jonathan Cape.

Scarpa, Federica. 2002. "Close and Closer Apart? Specialized Translation in a Cognitive Perspective." In Riccardi, *Translation Studies*, 133–49.

Schiffrin, Deborah, Deborah Tannen, and Heidi E. Hamilton, eds. 2003. *The Handbook of Discourse Analysis*. Blackwell Handbooks in Linguistics. Malden, MA: Wiley-Blackwell.

Schillinger, Liesl. 2012. "Soviet Dreams: 'Happy Moscow,' by Andrey Platonov." *The New York Times Sunday Book Review*, 28 December, http://www.nytimes.com/2012/12/30/books/review/happy-moscow-by-andrey platonov.html?nl=books&emc=edit_bk_20121228.

Schopenhauer, Arthur. 1970. *Essays and Aphorisms*. Selected and translated with an introduction by R. J. Hollingdale. London: Penguin Books.

Sdobnikov, V. V., and O. V. Petrova. 2006. *Teoriia perevoda*. Moscow: AST-Vostok-Zapad.

Searle, John R. 1969. *Speech Acts*. Cambridge: Cambridge University Press.

———. 1983a. *Intentionality*. Cambridge: Cambridge University Press.

———. 1983b. "The Word Turned Upside Down." *The New York Review of Books* 30 (16) (27 October). http://www.nybooks.com/articles/archives/1983/oct/27/the-word-turned-upside-down/.

———. 1984. "An Exchange on Deconstruction" (reply to Louis H. Mackey). *The New York Review of Books* 31 (1) (2 February). http://www.nybooks.com/articles/archives/1984/feb/02/an-exchange-on-deconstruction/?page=3.

———. 1993. "Rationality and Realism: What Is at Stake?" *Daedalus* 122 (4) (Fall 1993): 55–84.

———. 1998. *Mind, Language, and Society: Philosophy in the Real World*. New York: Basic Books.

———. 2001. *Rationality in Action*. Cambridge, MA: MIT Press.

———. 2004. "Toward a Unified Theory of Reality." *Harvard Review of Philosophy*, no. 12: 93–135.

———. 2005. *Mind: A Brief Introduction*. Fundamentals of Philosophy. Oxford: Oxford University Press.

———. 2008. *Philosophy in a New Century: Selected Essays*. Cambridge: Cambridge University Press.

———. 2009. "Why Should You Believe It?" *The New York Review of Books* 56 (14) (24 September): 88–92.

———. 2010. *Making the Social World: The Structure of Human Civilization*. Oxford: Oxford University Press.

Sendich, Munir. 1999. *English Counter Russian: Essays on Criticism of Literary Translation in America*. New York: Peter Lang Publishing.

Sergay, Timothy. 2011. "New but Hardly Improved: Are Multiple Retranslations of Classics the Best Cultural Use to Make of Translation Talent?" *Russian Language Journal* 61: 33–50.

Shlapentokh, Vladimir. 1984. *Love, Marriage, and Friendship in the Soviet Union: Ideals and Practices*. New York: Praeger Publishers.

Shlapentokh, Vladimir. 2004. *An Autobiographical Narration of the Role of Fear and Friendship in the Soviet Union*. Lewiston, ME: Edwin Mellen Press.

———. 2007. In collaboration with Joshua Woods. *Contemporary Russia as a Feudal Society: A New Perspective on the Post-Soviet Era*. New York: Palgrave Macmillan.

Shmid, V. [Wolf Schmid]. 2003. *Narratologia*. Moscow: Iazyki slavianskoi kul'tury. http://www.gumer.info/bibliotek_Buks/Literat/shmid/index.php.

Shreve, Gregory. 2002. "Knowing Translation: Cognitive and Experiential Aspects of Translation Expertise from the Perspective of Expertise Studies." In Riccardi, *Translation Studies*, 150–71.

———. 2006. "The Deliberate Practice: Translation and Expertise." *Journal of Translation Studies* 9 (1): 27–42.

Shreve, Gregory M., and Erik Angelone. 2010. "Translation and Cognition: Recent Developments." In Shreve and Angelone, *Translation and Cognition*, 1–13. Amsterdam: John Benjamins.

———, eds. 2010. *Translation and Cognition*. Amsterdam: John Benjamins.

Slovonovo: Slovar' sovremennoi leksiki, zhargona i slenga. www.slovonovo.ru.

Solodub, Iu. P., F. B. Al'brekht, and A. Iu. Kuznetsov. 2005. *Teoriia i praktika khudozhestvennogo perevoda*. Moscow: Akademiia.

Sorokin, Vladimir. 1992. "Liubov'." In *Pervyi subbotnik. Sbornik rasskazov*. Moscow: Russlit. The beginning and end of the story can be found on Sorokin's web site, accessed 18 August 2013, http://www.srkn.ru/texts/persub_part18.shtml.

———. 2002. *Led*. Moscow: Ad Marginem. http://www.srkn.ru/texts/led_part01.shtml.

———. 2004. *Put' bro*. http://www.srkn.ru/texts/bro_part01.shtml.

———. 2005. *23000*. http://www.srkn.ru/texts/23000_part08.html.

———. 2011a. *Day of the Oprichnik*. Translated by Jamey Gambrell. New York: Farrar, Straus and Giroux.

———. 2011b. *Den' oprichnika*. Moscow: AST/ASTREL'.

Spanier, Sandra, and Robert W. Trogdon, eds. 2011. *The Letters of Ernest Hemingway*. Vol. 1, *1907–1922*. Cambridge: Cambridge University Press.

Sperber, Dan, and Deirdre Wilson. 1995. *Relevance: Communication and Cognition*. 2nd ed. Malden, MA: Blackwell Publishing.

Steiner, George. 1998. *After Babel: Aspects of Language and Translation*. 3rd ed. Oxford: Oxford University Press.

Stephens, Mitchell. 1994. "Jacques Derrida and Deconstruction." *The New York Times Magazine*, 23 January. http://www.nyu.edu/classes/stephens/Jacques%20Derrida%20-%20NYT%20-%20page.htm.

Strelkova, Natalia. 2012. *Russian-English Translation: Tactics and Techniques for the Translator*. New York: Hippocrene Books.

Strukov, Vlad. 2011. "Translated by Goblin: Global Challenge and Local Response in Post-Soviet Translations of Hollywood Films." In *Contexts,*

Subtexts and Pretexts: Literary Translation in Eastern Europe and Russia, edited by Brian James Baer, 235–48. Amsterdam: John Benjamins.

Sturge, Kate. 2007. *Representing Others: Translation, Ethnography and the Museum.* Edited by Theo Hermans. Manchester, UK: St. Jerome Publishing.

Theunissen, Michael. 1984. *The Other: Studies in the Social Ontology of Husserl, Heidegger, Sartre, and Buber.* Translated by Christopher Macann with an introduction by Fred R. Dallmayr. Cambridge, MA: The MIT Press.

Thirlwell, Adam. 2010. "The Poet's Head on a Platter." *The New York Review of Books* 57 (8) (13 May): 48–51. http://www.nybooks.com/articles/archives/2010/may/13/poets-head-platter/?page=1.

Tolstoy, L. N. 1899. *What is Art?* Translated by Aylmer Maude. London: W. Scott. http://babel.hathitrust.org/cgi/pt?view=image;size=100;id=mdp.39015007053500;page=root;seq=11;num=v.

―――――. 1951. *Polnoe sobranie sochinenii. Seria pervaia. Proizvedeniia.* Moscow: Gosudarstvennoe izdatel'stvo khudozhestvennoi literatury.

―――――. 1963. *Sobranie sochinenii v 20-i tomakh.* Vols. 4–7. Moscow: Gosudarstvennoe izdatel'stvo khudozhestvennoi literatury.

―――――. 2005. *War and Peace.* Translated by Anthony Briggs. London: Penguin Books.

―――――. *War and Peace.* 2007. Translated by Richard Pevear and Larissa Volokhonsky. New York: Alfred A. Knopf.

―――――. 2007. *War and Peace: Original Version.* Translated by Andrew Bromfield. New York: Ecco.

Toury, Gideon. 1995. *Descriptive Translation Studies and Beyond.* Amsterdam: John Benjamins.

Tymoczko, Maria, and Edwin Gentzler, eds. 2002. *Translation and Power.* Amherst: University of Massachusetts Press.

Tynianov, Iu. 1967. *Arkhaisty i novatory.* Munich: Wilhem Verlag.

Tyulenev, Sergei. 2001. *Applying Luhmann to Translation Studies: Translation in Society.* London: Routledge.

Ubin, I. I. 2004. "Nemelkie 'melochi' v zhizni perevodchika." *Mosty: Zhurnal perevodchikov*, no. 3: 42–47.

Usova, Galina. 2003. *I Bairona v soavtory voz'mu: Kniga o Tat'iane Grigor'evne Gnedich.* St. Petersburg: DEAN.

Vail', Petr, and Aleksandr Genis. (1988) 1998. *60-e: Mir sovetskogo cheloveka.* 2nd ed. Moscow: Novoe literaturnoe obozrenie.

Van Dijk, Teun A. 1997. *Discourse as Structure and Process of Discourse Studies: A Multidisciplinary Introduction.* Vol. 1. London: Sage Publications.

―――――. 2001. "Critical Discourse Studies: A Sociocognitive Approach." In *Methods of Critical Discourse Analysis*, 2nd ed., edited by R. Wodak and M. Meyer, 62–86. London: Sage Publications.

Van Dijk, Teun A., ed. 1985. *Handbook of Discourse Analysis*. Vol. 1, *Disciplines and Discourse*; vol. 2, *Dimensions of Discourse*; vol. 3, *Discourse and Dialogue*. London: Academic Press.

Venuti, Lawrence. 1998. *The Scandals of Translation*. London: Routledge.

—————. 2011. "Towards a Translation Culture." *The Iowa Review*, 21 September. http://iowareview.uiowa.edu/page/towards_a_translation_culture.

—————, ed. 1995. *The Translator's Invisibility: A History of Translation*. London: Routledge.

—————, ed. 2000. *The Translation Studies Reader*. London: Routledge.

Vinogradov, V. V. (1926) 1980. "Problema skaza v stilistike." In *Izbrannye trudy. O iazyke khudozhestvennoi prozy*, 42–55. Moscow: Nauka.

Vlakhov, S. I., and S. P. Florin. 2006. *Neperevodimoe v perevode*. 3rd ed. Moscow: R. Valent.

Vicari, Giuseppe. 2008. *Beyond Conceptual Dualism: Ontology of Consciousness, Mental Causation, and Holism in John R. Searle's Philosophy of Mind*. Amsterdam: Rodopi.

Volkov, Solomon. 2008. *Istoriia russkoi kul'tury XX veka: Ot L'va Tolstogo do Aleksandra Solzhenitsyna*. Moscow: EKSMO.

Volodarskii, Leonid. 2011a. "Vashi voprosy." Accessed 27 January 2011, http://volodarskiy.ru/section/questions/?sid.

—————. 2011b. "Televizor b'et v golovu: Interv'iu dlia 'Literaturnoi gazety.'" http://widescreen.boxmail.biz/cgi-bin/guide.pl?action=article&id_razdel=43644&id_article=61731.

Vonnegut, Kurt. 1975. *Zavtrak dlia chempionov. Roman*. Translated by R. Rait-Kovaleva. *Inostrannaia literatura*, nos. 1–2.

Vovk, Svetlana. 2012. "Antipremiia 'Polnyi Abzats' dostalas' knige *Vy ne gadzhet. Manifest.*" *RIA Novosti*. Moscow, 14 March. http://www.ria.ru/culture/20120314/594706947.html.

Wodak, Ruth, and Michael Meyer, eds. 2012. *Methods of Critical Discourse Analysis*. 2nd ed. Los Angeles: Sage Publications.

Wood, James. 2010. "In a Spa Town." Review of *A Hero of Our Time* by Mikhail Lermontov, translated by Natasha Randall. *The London Review of Books* 32 (3) (11 February): 19–21.

—————. 2008a. Interview on *Marketplace of Ideas*, 16 September. http://colinmarshall.libsyn.com/index.php?post_id=380948.

—————. 2008b. *How Fiction Works*. New York: Farrar, Straus and Giroux.

Wood, Michael. 2008. "Crabby, Prickly, Bitter, Harsh." *London Review of Books* 30 (10) (22 May): 11–12.

Index